The

EVERYTHING Cat Book 2nd Edition

Dear Reader,

Taking care of a cat, or any companion animal, is a big responsibility. The purpose of this book is to help prepare and educate you for that task. Cats are not disposable creatures to be tossed out when you tire of them. They are intelligent animals that need and deserve our care to survive in a modern, industrialized world that grows more alien to natural wildlife everyday.

After a lifetime of living with cats, I'm convinced they experience feelings and emotions somewhat similar to ours. They develop loving attachments to their human companions, and they experience anxiety when separated from them for too long. I have even known of ailing cats that waited to die until their beloved caretakers returned home to hold them one last time. If you've never been loved by a cat before, you're in for a potentially positive, life-changing growth experience when you acquire your first feline companion. But there's a lot within these pages you need to know to help ensure that your relationship starts off right and evolves smoothly. Learning to live and communicate effectively with a different species that doesn't share our language can be fraught with many pitfalls. I hope this book will help you avoid most of them and enjoy your experience as a cat owner.

Best of luck,

Karen Leigh Davis

The EVERYTHING® Series

Editorial

Publishing Director	Gary M. Krebs
Director of Product Development	Paula Munier
Associate Managing Editor	Laura M. Daly
Associate Copy Chief	Brett Palana-Shanahan
Acquisitions Editor	Kate Burgo
Development Editor	Katie McDonough
Associate Production Editor	Casey Ebert

Production

Director of Manufacturing	Susan Beale
Associate Director of Production	Michelle Roy Kelly
Cover Design	Paul Beatrice Matt LeBlanc Erick DaCosta
Design and Layout	Heather Barrett Brewster Brownville Colleen Cunningham Jennifer Oliveira
Series Cover Artist	Barry Littmann

THE EVERYTHING® CAT BOOK

2nd Edition

All you need to know about
caring for your favorite feline friends

Karen Leigh Davis

Adams Media
Avon, Massachusetts

An Everything® Series Book.
Everything® and everything.com® are registered trademarks of F+W Publications, Inc.

Published by Adams Media, an F+W Publications Company
57 Littlefield Street, Avon, MA 02322 U.S.A.
www.adamsmedia.com

ISBN 10: 1-59337-577-8
ISBN 13: 978-1-59337-577-5
Printed in the United States of America.

J I H G F E D C B A

Library of Congress Cataloging-in-Publication Data
Davis, Karen Leigh
The everything cat book / Karen Leigh Davis. -- 2nd ed.
p. cm.
Includes index.
ISBN 1-59337-577-8
1. Cats. I. Title.

SF447.D37 2006
636.8--dc22
2006015951

Contents

Top Ten Fun and Fascinating Feline Tidbits / x

Introduction / xi

1 Understanding Cats / 1

The Long Process of Domestication **2** • The Cat's Primary Senses **5** • Sleeping and Hunting Habits **9** • How Cats Communicate **11** • Intelligence **14** • How Cats Learn **15** • Magnificent Cousins **16**

2 All about Breeds / 19

Cat Breeds Overview **20** • Coat-Length Genetics **24** • Shorthaired Cats **25** • Longhaired Cats **28** • Short-Tailed Cats **31** • Cats with Unusual Coats **32** • Wild-Looking Spotted Cats **33** • Cats with Other Striking Features **34** • Cats of Many Colors **35**

3 Choosing a Cat Companion / 39

The Finer Points of Felines **40** • Important Considerations **41** • Mixed Breed or Purebred? **44** • One Cat or Two? **46** • Male or Female? **47** • Considering an Adult Cat over a Kitten **49** • The Indoor Versus Outdoor Debate **50** • Pet Identification **53**

4 The Right Cat for You / 55

Taking in a Stray Cat **56** • Adopting from a Shelter **59** • Choosing a Healthy Cat or Kitten **60** • Finding Kittens Through the Classifieds **61** • Hallmarks of a Good Breeder **63** • Finding a Good Breeder **65** • Visiting the Breeder **67** • Buying from a Pet Shop **71**

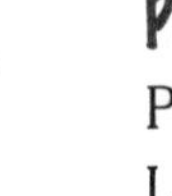

Preparing for Kitty's Arrival / 73

Pet-Supply Shopping List **74** • Pet Carrier **74** • Cat Food and Dishes **75** • Litter and a Litter Box **77** • Scratching Post **78** • Cat Beds and Perches **79** • Toys **80** • Grooming Supplies **81** • Harness and Leash **83**

A Cat-Safe Home / 85

A Safe, Clean Environment **86** • Cat-Proofing the Indoors **86** • Chemical Hazards **89** • Household Appliances **90** • Toxic Plants **91** • Dangers in the Yard **93** • Holiday Hazards **95**

Kitty Comes Home / 97

Special Arrangements for the First Few Days **98** • Family Introductions **100** • Setting a Basic Routine **104** • Providing a Stable Environment **105** • When Things Don't Work Out **106**

Feline Feeding Basics / 109

Commercial Cat Foods **110** • What to Look for on a Label **111** • Life Stage Feeding **112** • Feeding Strategies **114** • Nutritional Problems **116** • Don't Forget Water **119**

Dealing with Eating Problems / 121

Obesity **122** • Putting a Cat on a Weight-Loss Diet **123** • Preventing Obesity **124** • Keeping Your Cat Active **125** • Leash Training **126** • Dealing with Finicky Eaters **128** • Treats **129** • Feeding in the Multi-Cat Household **130**

Feline Dental Care / 133

The Cat's Teeth **134** • Common Feline Dental Problems **134** • Signs of Dental Problems **137** • Care of Teeth and Gums **138** • Professional Cleaning **141** • Diet and Dental Health **141** • Prevention is the Best Medicine **142**

11 **Grooming Cats / 145**

Shedding **146** • Getting Your Cat Used to Grooming **148** • Trimming Nails **150** • Bathing Your Cat **151** • Grooming the Older Cat **153** • Removing Mats **153** • Cleaning Ears **154**

12 **Cat Health Care Basics / 157**

The Physical Feline **158** • What to Look for in a Veterinarian **163** • Finding a Good Veterinarian **165** • Annual Checkups **164** • Signs of Illness **169** • Medicating Cats **171** • Health Care for the Aging Cat **172** • Euthanasia **173**

13 **Common Illnesses / 177**

Feline Diseases **178** • Other Common Conditions **185** • Cancer **188** • Feline Lower Urinary Tract Disease (FLUTD) **189** • Kidney Dysfunction **189** • Diabetes **191** • Thyroid Disease **192** • Common Conditions in Older Cats **193**

14 **First Aid and Emergency Care / 197**

First Aid and Vital Signs **198** • Injuries **199** • Animal Attacks **204** • Burns **205** • Cardiopulmonary Resuscitation (CPR) **206** • Poisoning **207** • Choking **208** • Hypo- and Hyperthermia **208** • Seizures **211**

15 **Parasites of the Cat / 213**

Parasitic Infections **214** • Fleas **215** • Ticks **217** • Ear Mites **217** • Other External Parasites **218** • Internal Parasites **219** • Parasites Associated with Flies **221** • Heartworms **222** • Protozoan Parasites **223**

16 **Cat-Training Basics / 225**

Scratching Behavior **226** • Litter Box Behavior **230** • Territorial Marking **233** • Plant-Eating Behavior **238** • Jumping Behavior **239** • Teaching Name Recognition **240** • Crate Training **241** • Socialization **241**

Understanding Territorial and Aggressive Behavior / 245

Marking Behaviors **246** • Aggression and Temperament **247** • Fear Aggression **248** • Territorial Aggression **248** • Maternal and Paternal Aggression **250** • Play Aggression **251** • Competitive Aggression **252** • Redirected Aggression **254**

Feline Reproduction / 259

Spaying and Neutering **260** • Reproductive Cycles and Mating **261** • Pregnancy and Gestation **263** • Preparing for Birth **263** • Delivery **264** • Caring for the Mother and Kittens after Delivery **266** • Kitten Development **267** • Good Nurturing Means Good Cats **270**

Breeding Purebreds / 273

Cat Shows **274** • Basic Feline Genetics **275** • Creating Breeding Stock **277** • Arranging a Mating **279** • Selling Kittens **280** • Letting the Kittens Go **283**

Showing Cats / 285

When Did Cat Shows Begin? **286** • Why Do People Show Cats? **287** • Cat-Show Classes **288** • Entering a Cat Show **290** • Preparations for the Show **291** • Rehearsing for the Big Day **293** • Arriving at the Show **294** • After the Show **295**

Appendix A: Books and Magazines / 297

Appendix B: Associations, Organizations, and Breed Registries / 299

Index / 301

Dedication

To Snooky, Jagger, Orphan, Hoot, Cinder, Brandon, and Samantha, who all helped me become a better, more knowledgeable cat person. I honor your memory by loving and caring for the cats that share this time of my life, and by helping other people learn to love, appreciate, and care for their pets the way I loved you.

Top Ten Fun and Fascinating Feline Tidbits

1. The ancient Egyptian sun god Ra took the form of a cat in order to fight the forces of evil.
2. A Chinese myth says the cat originated from a cross between a lion and a monkey. From the lion came courage, dignity, grace, and strength, and from the monkey came curiosity, playfulness, and a mischievous nature.
3. Ernest Hemingway, Mark Twain, Henry David Thoreau, Frederic Chopin, Emily Brontë, Leonardo da Vinci, Claude Monet, and Teddy Roosevelt all loved cats and preferred their company to that of dogs.
4. Japanese mythology tells of evil changeling cats that would murder princesses and assume their forms in order to cast evil spells on the princes of the realm.
5. The ruling class of ancient Egypt believed that cats held great power with the gods, and looked to certain feline movements and behaviors as predictions of the future.
6. The average cat has five toes on the front feet and four on the hind feet, but an inherited trait known as polydactyly can cause a cat to have extra toes on the front feet.
7. Cats rarely get carsick. The same inner ear structure that gives the cat its uncanny sense of balance also safeguards it from getting motion sickness.
8. White cats have a much higher chance of having some level of genetically linked hearing deficiency than do cats of different colors.
9. According to legend, the Manx cat, a tailless breed, dawdled as it went up the ramp of Noah's ark. An impatient Noah slammed the door on the cat's tail, cutting it off short.
10. According to legend, kinked tails, a genetic abnormality sometimes seen in the Siamese and other Asian breeds, are said to have originated with the royal Siam princesses, who removed their rings before bathing and placed them on the tails of their royal Siamese cats for safekeeping.

Introduction

The cat. An animal of endless subtlety, elegance, and grace. Discriminating yet tender, stylish yet capable, the cat has fascinated and beguiled humans for thousands of years. Unlike the faithful, dutiful dog, whose motivations are plain for all to see, the cat has never been that easy to typecast. An independent, elusive, mysterious, refined, and unpredictable animal, the feline seems to pride itself on being capable of stepping back into its wild ways at a moment's notice.

Revered by the ancient Egyptians, feared and maligned by zealots during Europe's Middle Ages, respected and valued as a competent mouser and ratter, and treasured as a sublime companion by scores of different cultures throughout history, the cat has been and continues to be a provocative and absorbing subject of interest for many, including artists, doctors, psychologists, writers, scientists, philosophers, and everyday people like you and me.

But what are these quiet creatures really like? Why are they so fastidiously clean? What enables them to be such fantastic athletes? Why are they such efficient hunters? How do they perceive their world? Can they see and hear things that humans cannot? And why have they been so misunderstood by mankind at times? You'll find the answers to these questions and much more contained here.

If you've never had a cat before, you'll also learn all about acquiring and owning one. Anyone who has ever lived with a cat knows that "ownership" is arranged according to the cat's terms and not yours. Part of the charm of having a cat companion is being able to understand and share in the life of an animal that clearly appreciates the creature comforts of a warm, loving home, yet forever maintains a close kinship with all things wild and untamed.

Within these pages, you will find information on a wide range of topics about cats, including history, anatomy, psychology, common illnesses, health and dental care, breed differences, proper diet, breeding, and showing, as well as why it's so important to spay or neuter your cat if you're not intent on becoming a professional breeder.

Please remember that the health information in this book is designed for your reference only, and cannot substitute for professional advice from a veterinarian. Medical advances occur steadily, treatment protocols change, new vaccines are developed, and new diseases are discovered and conquered. As a pet owner, it is your responsibility to keep up with the changes that can impact your cat's health and well-being. Ongoing pet-owner education is important. Let this book be part of your cat-education foundation. Whether you are considering acquiring a cat, or you already have one and wish to know as much as possible about it, this book is an ideal reference for you. It isn't called *The Everything® Cat Book* for nothing!

So get started! Read and learn as much as you can about cats. Always remember, however, that your veterinarian is your best ally in this effort. Visit your vet on a regular basis and ask questions. This book and other fine references on the market similar to it can help arm you with enough basic knowledge to know what questions to ask. There's even a reading list in the back of this book for your easy reference. It's all up to you to become the best pet owner you can possibly be. Your cat deserves nothing less.

1 Understanding Cats

Wild cats have been around for perhaps millions of years, certainly longer than mankind. The prehistoric saber-toothed tiger was surely capable of taking down a woolly mammoth, just as lions and tigers today can kill large prey. Feline fossils dating back to the Pliocene age, approximately twelve to two and a half million years ago, show many similarities to modern-day cats. Today's domestic cats still stalk, leap, hunt, reproduce, and raise young in much the same way they did at the dawn of human civilization, with an ease and skill never lost through thousands of years of domestication.

The Long Process of Domestication

Domestication created far fewer anatomical and behavioral changes in cats than in animals such as the dog or horse. Perhaps this is because the cat has been domesticated for a far shorter period of time than the dog and other animals. All cats belong to the family Felidae, whose members have whiskers, eyes with slit irises, and retractable or semi-retractable claws, and who hunt prey and eat a meat-based diet.

Cats and humans did not begin their relationship until humans as a society discovered the benefits of practicing agriculture. Mesopotamian and Egyptian cultures became so proficient at farming that they were able to amass surpluses of grain to be stored and used during times of emergency, or simply to be traded to others for a profit. For the first time, this grain surplus allowed communities to compile great wealth, and with it power. But with progress came problems. Rodents regularly raided the grain storage areas, depleting the grain and helping to spread a host of dangerous diseases throughout the human population.

At about this time, ancient cultures began relying on cats to help reduce or eliminate these pests. Here, then, was the likely genesis of the so-called "domestication" of the cat, nature's most efficient rodent controller.

Wildcats

The African wildcat was fairly common to the North African area in ancient times; it was this species that in all likelihood the Mesopotamians and Egyptians first called upon for help with the rodent problem. A bit larger than today's house cat, these animals took to domestication fairly well, and served to drastically reduce the vermin population in and around the granaries and living areas. A feline of similar size also existed in Europe. This ancient European wildcat, probably comparable to today's *Felis sylvestris*, was shyer and more fierce than its African cousin, and did not take to domestication all that well. The Asian or Pallas's cat, *Felis manul*, may have possibly been domesticated by the ancient Chinese, and probably contributed genetically to the numerous longhaired Asian cat breeds we see today.

When Cats Were Gods

To the Egyptian farmers, the job of guarding the grain was so important that cats rose from being mere ratters to revered creatures, seemingly identified with Bastet (also called Bast), the Egyptian goddess of fertility and maternity who had the head of a cat. The population valued cats so strongly that the spread of cats outside of Egypt was severely restricted for many centuries. And in fact, for a time in history, the penalty for killing a cat was death.

E-ssential

Thousands of unearthed cat mummies found by archeologists suggest that the Egyptians believed cats could enter the afterlife with people. X-rays of the mummies, however, reveal that some are skeletons of young cats with broken necks. So, it is not entirely clear whether the cats were sent to the afterlife with their deceased humans or used in ritual sacrifice. Regardless of the reason, it is evident that the Egyptians considered the cat's presence and role in the afterlife important.

It was not until Roman, Babylonian, and Phoenician sailors began transporting them to other areas of the known world that cats became popular in different regions and India, even making it as far East as Japan, where they still remain a much admired creature.

Once the African wildcat made its way to Europe and Asia, it no doubt interbred with the European wildcat and the Asian wildcat to produce different physical and behavioral qualities. Today's domestic kitty is most likely descended from these animals. Over the ensuing years, the cat has undergone some genetic manipulation, resulting in numerous cat breeds of varying shapes, sizes, weights, and colors. However, selective breeding of cats has not yet yielded the extreme variations in sizes and shapes that dog breeding has produced.

When Cats Were Witches

Toward the end of the Roman era and leading into the Middle Ages, cats slowly began to fall into disfavor, probably due to certain sects of religious zealots who believed there was a connection between felines and witchcraft. As the idea that cats were servants of witches and the devil became an all-too-prevalent European belief, religious leaders and commoners alike encouraged the elimination of cats. Cats were burned, sacrificed, tortured, and hunted by pet dogs, which by this time had become humanity's most favored domestic animal.

This undeserved malice toward cats ultimately proved to be a grave misjudgment, however, as the Black Death swept across Europe in the fourteenth century in rodent populations that ran unchecked. Spread by fleas riding on the backs of infected rats, the plague was responsible for killing millions of people, and there weren't enough cats around to dispatch the main culprits. Virtually one-third of the European population succumbed to the dreaded illness. Fortunately, misguided religious prejudices against the cat were not strong enough to outweigh the value of an animal that could eliminate a flea-infested rat that otherwise could mean sure death.

Cats as Companions

By the seventeenth century, the cat was fully back in favor, partly because of a growing artistic respect for feline grace and beauty and partly due to a new appreciation of the animal's cleanliness—a condition that became more respected by the population as new discoveries were made about germs and the way disease spreads. Aristocrats and artists enjoyed taking cats as their pampered pets, and began to selectively breed them for certain traits, including coat length, color, and overall size.

Cats were brought to the Americas by Spanish, French, and English sailors and settlers, again primarily as a safeguard against shipboard grain-thieving rodents. Although not as widely persecuted as in medieval Europe, the cat did suffer somewhat in New England during the brief but dramatic witch-trial period. Fortunately, that era faded quickly, and today the cat outnumbers the dog as the most popular companion animal in the United States.

The Cat's Primary Senses

Cats have five primary senses. Understanding how those senses function, and how cats use them, is crucial to understanding how cats perceive their world.

Vision

Of the five senses, perhaps the most extraordinary is the cat's eyesight, superbly equipped for nighttime hunting. One distinctive feature of the cat's eye is a reflective surface behind the retina known as the tapetum lucidum, the real secret to why cats can see so well in near darkness. This mirror-like apparatus reflects back onto the retina any light not absorbed the first time around, causing the cat's eyes to glow eerily in the dark. This single physical trait, which no doubt seemed otherwordly to an illiterate population, probably accounts for why the cat has been viewed with such awe and mystery throughout the ages. The tapetum lucidum allows cats to use much more of the available light than humans can. They cannot see in total darkness, but they can get around just fine in what to human eyes is pitch black. A clock-radio display or even the clock on a microwave oven or VCR provides your cat with enough light to move through your dark house at night.

Do cats see in color?

More than thirty years ago, scientists proved through careful experimentation that cats can, in fact, see some colors. However, the scientists also concluded that color response in cats is not a necessary ability and not part of their normal behavior. Cats seem to be able to distinguish reds and blues, but have a harder time with greens, shades of white, and yellows.

Although cats see better at night than humans do, they do not see quite as sharply as people do. Humans have an indented area in the center of our retina called the fovea, which has a higher concentration of cones than the rest of the retinal surface. This allows humans (and other animals active primarily by day) to more accurately gauge the position of a stationary object. Cats do not see individual items as sharply, but they detect even the slightest movement much better than we do. This is why their normal prey—mice and other rodents—evolved the strategy of freezing motionless to avoid detection. Cats have superior peripheral (side) vision as well.

Cats also tend to be farsighted and cannot focus well on objects closer than twenty-five to thirty inches away. This suits a predator that needs to spot its prey from great distances, and not right under its nose. The feline eye sacrifices up-close visual acuity in order to excel at spotting crafty prey on the run.

Protecting the outer surfaces of the cat's eyes are the upper and lower eyelids, and between them (at the inner corner near the bridge of the nose) is the nictitating membrane, sometimes called the "third eyelid." This lid automatically closes from the lower inside edge of the eye to the upper outside, affording an additional level of protection for the cat's most valuable sense.

Hearing

Cats have evolved excellent hearing, a result of the need to detect the almost ultrasonic sounds of the small rodents that typically become their dinners in the wild. Cats can hear sounds nearly two octaves higher than those humans are capable of perceiving. This is significantly higher than even the dog's hearing abilities.

The cat's external ear, or pinna, can be moved independently through an arc of about 180 degrees. This gives cats the ability to pinpoint the origin of a sound with great accuracy. The appearance of the pinna can vary somewhat according to species and breed. Those originating from warmer climates tend to have larger ears that radiate heat well and detect prey that may be far across an arid desert plain. Those breeds originally from colder climates normally have smaller ears, a feature that helps minimize the loss of body heat.

The cat's ears do more than just gather and interpret sounds. The vestibular apparatus, located in the inner ear, is responsible for the cat's balance and spatial orientation. Combined with the cat's athletic prowess, this structure gives the cat its well-known righting reflex, allowing the animal to turn in mid air while falling and, in most cases, land on all four feet. However, cats do not always escape injury from falls. On the contrary, veterinarians treat enough trauma from such mishaps to dub the condition "high-rise syndrome."

Smell

The feline sense of smell is the first sense newborn kittens use. Blind for the first two weeks of life, kittens can nevertheless unerringly find their mother's nipple through smell alone. Each kitten tends to go to one particular nipple, at least during the early part of the nursing process, suggesting that its sense of smell is discriminating enough to distinguish one nipple from another.

Although cats do have much better scenting ability than humans, they do not rely on smell as a primary method for locating prey, preferring instead to use their superior vision and hearing. The sense of smell in cats seems to be most important for locating other cats either for mating or territorial concerns.

Cats, and many other mammals, have an extra scenting device called the vomeronasal (or Jacobson's) organ, located just above the hard palate in the mouth. This small cylindrical organ is thought to be involved in the scenting and analysis of sex-related smells, particularly by males scenting out females in heat (estrus). A curious practice shared by many mammals, the flehmen response involves pumping odor molecules up into the vomeronasal organ by rapidly panting through the mouth. While flehming, the cat curls back its upper lip and bars the teeth in a wide sneer. The presence of a female cat's urine typically initiates this peculiar-looking response in an intact tom (male) cat.

Taste

The cat's tongue is covered with small, backward-facing, hook-like structures called papillae, which the cat uses to remove material from the bones of a kill as well as for grooming itself. All cat lovers have probably felt the papillae's raspiness when licked by a kitty. The papillae along the front, back, and sides of the tongue contain the cat's taste buds, which, according to research, can detect salty, acidic, and bitter tastes, but not sweetness, a sensation that only animals that tend to eat sugar-laden carbohydrates seem to possess. Pure carnivores like the cat do not need to sample sweets, unlike their sugar-craving human companions.

Touch

The cat's sense of touch conveys much information about its world, from how bird feathers feel in its mouth to the comfort of a warm bed at night. The cat's skin is peppered with many touch receptors. Perhaps this is why most cats love to be pet, and why some cats can be overstimulated by too much petting. Even the lightest tap will evoke a response, often an automatic arching of the back, followed by a rubbing action against your leg or hand, your cat's way of saying, "Yeah, that's the spot. More of that please."

Cats are fast. Just watch how quickly they can swat at a toy or an unfortunate mouse. A result of the evolution of lots of fast-twitch muscle fibers, cats can move not only quickly, but also silently and deftly. They also can move with deliberate slowness, especially when stalking prey.

The whiskers (or vibrissae) are located on the muzzle, elbows, and eyebrows of the cat. Emerging from nerve bundles directly routed to the brain, the whiskers can transmit pertinent information about the cat's immediate environment. As they are able to pivot at the skin's surface, the cat can move them around voluntarily when necessary. For example, a cat that is holding a mouse or bird in its mouth will almost always have its whiskers pointing down and forward, in direct contact with the unfortunate victim. By doing so, the cat can tell if the prey is still alive and possibly getting ready to bite or struggle for freedom.

Because whiskers impart information about all aspects of the cat's environment, they should never be trimmed. It has been said that cats use their whiskers to gauge whether a narrow crawlway is wide enough for them to slip through. Perhaps the most unique attribute of whiskers is their ability to sense minute changes in air currents around the cat. Solid objects such as a table or desk create subtle disturbances in the surrounding air that the feline's whiskers detect. This allows the cat to maneuver over and around objects even in near darkness.

Sleeping and Hunting Habits

Cats sleep a lot, usually about fourteen to eighteen hours a day, broken down into many small catnaps rather than one long sleep period. No one knows for sure why cats sleep so much, although it may be related to the intense activity level required for hunting prey during the waking hours. Kittens, especially, go wild for hours and then zonk out for two-thirds of the day. The development of portions of the kitten's brain is also known to occur only during sleep. Whatever the reason, understanding your cat's psyche means respecting its need to sleep undisturbed for somewhat lengthy periods, so make sure your kitty has a nice warm, comfy bed all its own in a quiet, out-of-the-way location.

Of course, your cat will probably be wide awake at three o'clock in the morning, pawing and meowing at you, wondering why you won't get up and play. This is because cats are, by nature, nocturnal, creatures that hunt primarily at night. Fortunately, they do have the ability to adjust their schedules to ours.

E-ssential

If your cat gets up too early and prowls during the night, engage in some interactive playtime before bedtime. This will help your cat expend some of that excess energy before turning in. Many cats sleep peacefully all night on their owner's bed and faithfully awaken their owners in the morning, when it's time to be fed.

Domestic cats have a hunting style that most closely reflects the leopard's and wildcat's stalking and climbing habits. When stalking, the cat crouches and creeps forward silently, with pupils wide and eyes fixed intently on its prey. Muscles tensed for instant action, tail twitching in anticipation, the cat prepares to pounce, wriggling its rear, then springing with claws extended. The front paws strike with deadly accuracy, pinioning the prey, and one well-placed death bite quickly ends the struggle.

Other cats' hunting habits vary widely, from the cheetah's full-bore speed on the open plains to the tree-friendly forays of the ocelot. The fishing cat is unique in that it prefers to hunt in the water, using its webbed feet and compact, strong body to swim after its prey. In general, most domestic cats seem to loathe water, and avoid it at all costs.

Predation is what many people like least about cats. Even worse for some owners are those occasions when their outdoor cat drags home a dead bird or mouse and deposits the corpse on their doorstep. This instinctive behavior demonstrates that the cat counts you in as part of its family. That's because mother cats teach their kittens how to recognize and hunt prey by bringing dead or stunned animals to the nest for them to play with. For the rest of their lives, the kittens' play behavior is a rerun of what they learn in the nest and serves as practice to keep their skills honed.

So, the next time your cat delivers an offering to your doorstep, don't take offense and punish it for behaving like a normal, efficient predator. Your cat is just being a cat. To prevent predation, simply keep your cat indoors and let it prey on stuffed catnip mice instead.

How Cats Communicate

To truly understand your cat, you need to know how it communicates. Cats express their feelings, intentions, desires, and attitudes through a complex mix of posturing, vocal, and marking behaviors. The sounds they make, the body postures they assume, and the places they mark with scent all play a role in telling the world just how they feel and what they want.

Body Language

Body language plays a significant role in cat-to-cat communications, and certainly in cat-to-human communications as well. So, as an owner, you need to understand how to interpret what your cat is trying to tell you. The following list tells you what your cat is communicating to you with each of its body parts.

- **Tail:** A straight-up tail with a bit of movement to it usually denotes an alert, contented attitude; this is a cat that is ready to be friendly, yet is actively curious about its environment. If the cat is lying down and has a relaxed tail, then it is in an easygoing mood. If the tail lowers itself slightly and begins to lash back and forth, it usually means worry or anger is building. A downward arched tail is a distinct warning. The tail of an angry or frightened cat will also bristle.
- **Ears:** When a cat's ears are held in an erect, slightly outward position, the cat is usually in a happy, curious mood. When the openings of the ears are rotated forward, it means that the cat is on the alert about something, perhaps a mouse rustling in the grass. If the ears face backward, it normally denotes worry; this cat is on the defensive. If the ears are erect with the openings facing backward, it usually means it's ready to fight. Finally, if the ears are plastered flat against the cat's head, it means the cat is frightened and probably ready to defend itself or run away.
- **Whiskers:** If the whiskers are spread out and pointing forward, the cat is alert and ready for action. If bunched together and out to the sides the cat is most likely relaxed and open to companionship. If

they're plastered to the sides of the cat's face, the cat is surely scared and ready to run or defend itself.

- **Eyes:** If your feline stares intently at someone or something, it usually means it is either very interested or somewhat threatened. A prolonged stare means, "Watch out." If a staring cat begins to blink or avert its eyes, it is generally signaling submission. A cat that is relaxed and calm usually has its eyelids slightly lowered, whereas, a fearful cat's eyes will be wide open with pupils dilated, even though the available light might not warrant it.
- **Posture:** If the cat's whole back is arched and all its hair is bristling, you know it is scared and ready to rumble. Cats that rub their bodies against you are normally happy and content. If a cat flops over on its back, it can mean that it is being playful and happy and wants a tummy rub, a posture that often demonstrates great trust. However, if this same cat has its four paws brandished stiffly in the air, it may mean for you to stay away. This is a classic posture that cats assume when escape from a predator is impossible and a "fight it out" mentality is engaged.
- **Kneading:** A cat that rubs its body against you or kneads its paws into you is not only being affectionate, but also somewhat possessive of you. The latter action is a behavior left over from kittenhood when the little ones kneaded at their mother's teats to stimulate milk production. Your cat's gently touching you with its paw also denotes affection, but a swat with that same paw is telling you to back off.
- **Facial expressions:** The cat's face, though not nearly as expressive as a dog's, nonetheless communicates emotion. A constantly flicking tongue denotes worry, whereas, an open-mouthed pant can mean exhaustion, sickness, or fear. If a male cat has a strange sneering look on its face while panting (the flehmen response), it may mean that it is scenting a female in heat or some other unusual odor.

Experts tend to believe that cats see their human caretakers as parents or siblings rather than "owners" because most cats never truly "grow up" while in the animal/human relationship. Rather, they tend to retain certain kittenish qualities throughout adulthood, as evidenced by behaviors such as kneading with their paws (which kittens do to stimulate milk flow from its mother's teats), and purring when we stroke them (a behavior also seen during nursing and when kittens are groomed by their mothers or siblings).

Vocal Communication

Although vocalization is generally considered the least important of the three modes of feline communication, cats convey a good amount of information to others, especially their human companions, through audible signals. Some breeds (the Siamese, for example) are notably more vocal than others. All, however, exhibit the standard cat sounds at one time or another. The famous "meow" usually means that the cat wants something, is confused, or else is mildly miffed about some situation and wants you to do something about it. The chirps and soft grunts cats sometimes make usually mean, "Welcome home. I'm glad to see you." Mother cats have a soft, soothing chirp they use when calling to their young ones, and sometimes they use this special sound around their human companions as well.

Growling, hissing, crying, and snarling obviously mean that the cat is really ticked off, scared, or angry. Give it some space when you hear these sounds! The wailing cry of the female in heat is a sound no one forgets or appreciates too much, especially at three in the morning. The most widely recognized cat sound of all, the purr, is generally assumed to denote contentment, but may at times mean the cat is worried or perhaps trying to calm itself when stressed, as when a cat purrs in the veterinarian's waiting room.

Intelligence

Intelligence per se is not an easy term to define. What criteria should be used to determine the domestic cat's intelligence? For example, if trainability is used as a barometer for intelligence, then the dog would certainly be considered smarter than the cat. That's not to say that cats can't be trained. They certainly can. There just has to be a reward or something worthwhile in it for them, whereas dogs do tricks merely to please their handlers.

E-ssential

Cats are not pack animals that follow a leader like dogs; instead, they adhere to a fluid hierarchy that can change over time. More often than not, the top cat in a household is a female. In a multiple-cat household, it's easy to tell which cat runs the show—the top cat always occupies the choicest, highest napping places. Intact animals will outrank altered animals, so in the interest of keeping the peace, it's best to have all cats in a household spayed or neutered.

Problem solving is probably a better indicator of intelligence, and cats are pretty good problem-solvers. They understand spatial problems better than dogs, owing to their ability to live in a more three-dimensional environment (dogs can't jump to the top of the fridge too readily). Cats do quite well in maze experiments, and they seem to retain knowledge for a very long time. For instance, if someone strikes a cat, the cat may never trust that person again, retaining the memory of the abuse seemingly forever. Perhaps memory is another measure of intelligence.

The ability to adapt and flourish in different environments is possibly another indicator of intellect. If this is true, then the domestic cat must have quite a head on its shoulders. Living and prospering in nearly every country in the world, cats can not only endure extremes of climate but can seemingly switch from domesticity to feral living at the flip of a switch. Certainly, cats can survive without human mastery, falling back on hunting instincts that have never really been abandoned during all the years of feline domesticity.

How Cats Learn

To better understand your cat's psyche, it is helpful to first understand just how a cat learns about its world. Learned behavior adds to instinctive behavior to widen the cat's repertoire of possible responses, thereby improving its chances for survival.

Observation and Imitation

Cats are quite good at learning specific behaviors by watching other cats, particularly their mothers. After watching its mother stalk and catch a mouse, for example, a kitten or young cat will mimic that behavior and eventually master it. Much scientific testing has been done on how well cats actually learn through observation. For example, one experiment done in the late 1960s at New York Medical College tested three groups of kittens and their ability to learn a behavior simply by watching it being performed by another cat. The scientists wanted the kittens to learn to press a bar in order to get a food reward. One group of six kittens was placed next to the apparatus and given no help at all; they never did figure out what to do. The second group got to repeatedly watch an unrelated adult cat learn to perform the task; these kittens learned to do it in eighteen days. The third group got to watch their own mothers perform. These kittens mastered the task in only five days!

Learning by observation works best in kittens and young cats. Older cats can learn as well, but may take appreciably longer.

Trial and Error

All animals, including humans and cats, can learn by accident, or trial and error. For example, if a human baby cries, he quickly learns that he will get his parents' attention. Likewise, a kitten quickly learns that it can't get to an abandoned tuna sandwich on the kitchen counter by jumping straight up from the kitchen floor, but that if it uses a chair as a transitional step, it can easily get up to the counter and into a whole mess of trouble. Similarly, the cat that accidentally opens a cupboard quickly learns that there is a mother lode of food just waiting inside. This cat will not soon forget how to open cupboards.

Conditioned Response

Two types of conditioning can affect the behavior of cats. In the first, classical conditioning, a cat learns on a subliminal level to perform a certain behavior when given a certain stimulus. For example, classical conditioning is at work when a cat learns to come to the kitchen when it hears the sound of the can opener.

In operant conditioning, the cat learns to repeat a certain behavior that is followed by some sort of reward (usually food), or conversely learns to avoid a behavior that is reliably followed by some unpleasant consequence. This is the main technique used to train cats to perform tricks and to stop undesirable behaviors, such as eating houseplants or scratching furniture. Good behaviors are reinforced, whereas, unwanted behaviors are either replaced with more desirable ones or averted by an unpleasant (though harmless) consequence each time the cat performs the act. An example of positive reinforcement is rewarding the cat with a bit of tuna for sitting in front of you. An example of negative reinforcement (or aversion) is spraying the cat with a water pistol whenever it attempts to chew on a houseplant.

Magnificent Cousins

Although this book is about domesticated cats, it would be remiss not to mention their grand feline relatives, the big cats, especially since domestic cats share many behaviors of their wild cousins. Both physically and socially, your house cat is quite similar to the wild cats.

All cats have the same basic anatomy, although size varies tremendously from species to species (though not as much from breed to breed). The domestic cat is at the lower end of the size scale, with only a dozen or so wild cats being as small or smaller.

Domestic cats seem to have proportionally smaller adrenal glands than do their wild cousins. Perhaps this enhanced their ability to be tamed, for the adrenals produce chemicals that cause an animal to invoke its "fight or flight" survival response.

Larger cats, owing to a variation in skull structure, can roar. Lions, tigers, leopards, and jaguars, because of the enhanced flexibility of the bones connecting the larynx to the skull, can really shake the roof off, so to speak, whereas, our smaller feline companions merely meow.

The domestic cat, in addition to having a smaller body than most of its wild cousins, also has a proportionally smaller brain. Perhaps this is the "devolutionary" result of not really having to think on her feet as much and not being as constantly challenged with life-and-death decisions as in the wild. Necessity really is the mother of invention and intelligence, it would seem.

E-Fact

The domestic cat has a fairly long tail in comparison to its wild brethren. Bobcats and lynxes have conspicuously short tails. Only cats such as the margay and ocelot have proportionally longer tails than the house cat, probably evolved as a result of living in trees. They both use their long tails to aid in balance, and, in the case of the ocelot, for actually grabbing branches for support, much as a monkey would do.

All cats have the same basic reflex and sense capabilities, although some species, such as the serval, have better hearing than others due to larger outer ears. The serval's neck and legs are also proportionately longer than those of all other cats, allowing it to raise its sensitive ears above the savannah grasses it inhabits.

The domestic cat's coat varies quite a bit in comparison to other cat species', owing in large part to selective breeding of desired coat traits. A Persian, for example, has a much longer coat than an Abyssinian. This wide variation of coat length and patterning is not seen in other cat species. A lion is a lion is a lion. Coat differences among the wild species reflect their differing environments. The snow leopard and North American lynx both have thick, insulating coats to conserve body heat in an alpine habitat, whereas, the cheetah and sand cat have short coats to deal with hot environs. Coat thickness and patterning vary widely from species to species, because desert, jungle, savannah, and alpine habitats each call for specific coat densities and "camouflage patterns." The domestic cat's coat density and patternings reflect the genes of their wild beginnings, but basically now rest in the hands of breeders' selection, not natural selection.

2 All about Breeds

Chances are, a specific color or type of cat strikes your fancy most. Perhaps you prefer the fluffy, longhaired Persians or the exotic coloring of the elegant Siamese. The term "cat fancy" refers to people who breed and show cats as a hobby or business. They admire their chosen breed or breeds so much that they dedicate significant time and resources to improving or promoting that breed. This chapter will tell you the basics you need to know about the vast array of cat breeds and where to look for more information.

Cat Breeds Overview

Of the forty or so cat breeds currently recognized by the numerous national and international cat registering associations in existence today, the following rank includes the ten most popular breeds, based on the Cat Fanciers' Association (CFA) registration totals for 2005:

- Persian/Himalayan
- Maine Coon
- Exotic
- Siamese
- Abyssinian
- Ragdoll
- Birman
- Oriental
- American Shorthair
- Tonkinese

What Is a Purebred?

Purebred cats have a pedigree—what most people refer to as "papers"—that traces their lineage back several generations and provides proof of ancestry. Because of their common genetic background, paired members within the same breed, for the most part, produce relatively uniform offspring with predictable traits, such as color, coat type, body conformation, size, and temperament. This is called breeding true.

There are some breeds that do not always breed true. Sometimes, nature arranges this for a good reason. For example, the stub-tailed Manx cat actually has a mutant, lethal gene that kills kittens that inherit a copy of it from both parents. These kittens die before birth, which makes Manx litters small and breeding the Manx extraordinarily challenging and difficult. Kittens that inherit the Manx gene from only one parent have a better chance of surviving to adulthood. Some kittens in a Manx litter may not inherit this gene at all and will have normal tails. Those that do inherit the gene may have one of several different tail lengths, ranging from rumpy, to stumpy, to long.

What is a "breed"?

Cats classified as a particular breed share a common, verifiable ancestry and possess predictable traits, such as coat length and color, eye color, body build, and temperament. The random-bred mutts of the feline world, often called mixed-breeds or moggies (a British term), have an unknown or unverifiable ancestry. While these cats make just as fine a companion as a purebred, what their offspring will grow up to look like is usually a wait-and-see proposition.

Predictable Traits

The nice thing about acquiring a purebred kitten is that you know what it's going to look like when it grows up, whether it's going to have long or short hair, and so forth. Even better, you can predict behavioral attributes to a certain extent. Some breeds are more active and high-energy than others, and researching the characteristics can help you choose a breed that's more to your liking. For example, the Siamese and its related breeds, such as the Balinese, the Oriental Shorthair, and the Colorpoint Shorthair are all very vocal, active, and energetic. If you prefer a quieter cat with a more mellow, laid-back personality, consider a Persian, an Exotic, a British or American Shorthair, or a Maine Coon.

Breed Standard

Owners and breeders of purebreds must register their cats with a cat registering association before they can exhibit them at cat shows and win ribbons and awards. Of the numerous cat registries in North America (see Appendix B), the largest is the Cat Fanciers' Association, which maintains stud books, verifies pedigrees, and sanctions cat shows and clubs. All of the associations perform similar functions, but each sets its own rules for registering and showing cats and accepting new breeds.

At a cat show, purebreds are judged according to a breed standard, which is a written guideline describing the color, conformation, and other characteristics that an ideal representative of the breed should possess. The breed standards are updated periodically. The standards can also vary from one cat association to another, as do sometimes the policies and politics surrounding a particular breed.

For example, most registries recognize the lovely longhaired Himalayan (created from a Persian/Siamese cross) as a separate breed from the Persian. The CFA, however, considers Himalayans a colorpoint version of the Persian, referring to them as the Pointed Pattern Persian. This means that Himalayan owners can register and show their cats as Persians in one association and as Himalayans in another.

E-Fact

Not all Himalayan cats are born with the pointed pattern typical of Siamese coloring. Some carry the colorpoint gene but they may be solid colors and look more like the Persian cats that contributed to the development of their breed. These non-pointed pattern cats are called colorpoint carriers because they can produce kittens with colorpoints. Although useful for breeding, the rules about showing these cats vary widely among the cat registering associations.

The CFA does not recognize any other colors for the Siamese, aside from four basic colors—seal point, chocolate point, blue point, and lilac point. Siamese cats dressed in any other colors, such as the exotic lynx point, are called Colorpoint Shorthairs in the CFA, but are seen as part of the Siamese breed in many other associations.

By now, it should be clear that the cat fancy can be a complicated consortium to figure out. But the beauty of a system that offers so much variety is that there's something in it somewhere to suit just about everybody's fancy, no matter how involved you care to become in the breeding, showing, or simply the enjoyment of cats.

How Are New Breeds Developed?

The rather complex and lengthy process of developing new breeds, or new varieties and colors of existing ones, goes on all the time. Some breeds originate from spontaneous genetic mutations. Characteristics created by mutant genes include the folded ears of the Scottish Fold, the curled-back ears of the American Curl, the stumpy tail of the Manx, the hairless coat of the Sphynx, the wavy hair of the Rex breeds, the curly ringlets of the LaPerm, and the short legs of the Munchkin.

Spontaneous Mutations

Mutations occur naturally when genes alter themselves for whatever reason. Sometimes, a mutation is simply nature's attempt at self-improvement, a way to make an animal better suited to its environment. Under random-bred conditions, most mutations would likely disappear, unless natural selection favored them. Longhaired varieties probably came about in cold climates in this way. However, selective breeding has preserved those mentioned for us to see in the established or experimental breeds we know today.

Most other breeds are created by crossbreeding established breeds with each other to achieve a desired result. The Himalayan is a good example of a breed created by crossing a Siamese with a Persian to achieve a longhaired cat with the exotic colorpoint markings of the Siamese. Another example is the Exotic Shorthair, which is a cross between the Persian and the American Shorthair. The Exotic retained the Persian's quiet, docile nature and cherubic facial features, but without the long, thick coat that requires daily grooming. For this reason, the Exotic, with its low-maintenance, plush, short coat, is sometimes referred to as the lazy man's Persian.

Native Lands

Many breeds, such as the Siamese (Siam), the Persian (Persia), the Turkish Angora and the Turkish Van (Turkey), originated in a particular country. But others, like the Somali, have no real association with the part of the world for which they are named. The Somali was named after Somalia because that nation neighbors the land that was known as Abyssinia (now Ethiopia) long ago. The naming was symbolic because the Somali and the Abyssinian are sister breeds. The Somali is actually a longhaired

Abyssinian. Breeders set out to develop the separate breed after longhaired kittens kept cropping up in their Abyssinian litters. They wanted a way to place value on the kittens and show them, rather than having to cull them from their breeding programs.

Achieving Breed Recognition

Regardless of origin, achieving full recognition for a new breed typically takes years. First, the promoters of a new breed must start by applying to the various cat associations for permission to register their progeny. If accepted for registration, then a certain number of the cats have to be registered before they are eligible to be shown. Even then, the newcomers can only be shown in non-competitive, non-championship classes for a period of time. These are the classes for miscellaneous or experimental breeds and colors. Some associations call them Any Other Variety (AOV) or New Breeds and Colors (NBC) classes.

As long as a new breed holds what's called provisional status in this way, the cats are judged according to a provisional breed standard. The final step to full recognition is reaching championship status, in which the cats become eligible to compete for points and awards in regular and championship classes.

Coat-Length Genetics

Shorthaired cats are more common throughout the world than longhairs because of the genetics that control coat length. The gene that produces a short coat is dominant, while the gene for a long coat is always recessive. When a dominant gene is present, it will mask or suppress the qualities of a recessive gene that may also be present. So there only has to be one dominant gene present for the trait to show, although the recessive gene can lie hidden unexpressed, waiting to surface in future litters. These basic genetic principles apply to any breed.

A cat that carries both the dominant and the recessive gene is capable of producing either short- or longhaired offspring, if paired with a mate carrying like genes. Such cats are said to be genetically heterozygous for that trait. Cats that have two recessive genes for long hair or two dominant genes for short hair are said to be homozygous for that trait.

E-ssential

For a recessive trait, such as long hair, to show, a kitten must inherit two recessive genes for the trait—one from each parent. To have short hair, a kitten needs only one dominant gene from one parent for the trait to show. Obviously, the odds are better for the latter to occur a lot more often that the first scenario.

The lovely longhaired Persians, for example, are homozygous. To have long hair, they must possess two recessive genes for the trait. When Persians are bred to other longhairs, they always produce longhaired offspring. Exotic Shorthair litters, on the other hand, can have a longhair crop up from time to time. This is because the breed was initially created by a Persian and American Shorthair cross, resulting in a mix of dominant and recessive genes. Two Exotics can potentially produce a longhaired kitten if both are heterozygous, or carrying a recessive gene for the longhaired trait.

Shorthaired Cats

Because the gene that governs short coat length is dominant over the one for long hair, shorthaired cats are more numerous around the world. What follows is an overview of the shorthaired breeds.

Abyssinian

This native of ancient Abyssinia is noted for its agouti-colored or "ticked" coat. The Abyssinian's distinctive coloring results from a combination of lighter and darker colors on each hair shaft, giving the coat a "salt-and-pepper" effect.

American Shorthair

Formerly known as the Domestic Shorthair, this breed resembles the common random-bred shorthair more than any other and is often confused as such. However, the difference is that breeders have developed this all-American cat to breed true, which means each cat's progeny possesses a predictable type, temperament, and coat length.

Bombay

Named for Bombay, India, land of the black leopard, this handsome cat has the conformation of the Burmese, but it comes only in jet black with striking gold- or copper-colored eyes.

British Shorthair

Like the American Shorthair, Great Britain's native shorthair was a common street cat until breeders began refining it for predictable characteristics. The cat is usually blue (gray) in color, but other colors are accepted.

Burmese

This Burma native is noted for its glossy brown, plush coat. Legend has it that these cats were once worshiped in Burmese temples.

Chartreux

An elegant beauty hailing from France, the Chartreux is a blue-gray-colored cat with silver-tipped hairs. Its rounded facial features give the cat a pleasant "smiling" appearance, and cats that appear to frown are disqualified in the breed standard.

Colorpoint Shorthair

This breed is virtually the same as the Siamese, except it comes in non-traditional colors (such as red, cream, lynx, and tortoiseshell point) not accepted by the general Siamese breed standard. To show these "off-color" cats, they are registered as a separate breed in some associations and called Colorpoint Shorthairs.

What is a hybrid breed?

A hybrid breed does not arise spontaneously in nature, but rather is man-made through selective breeding of cats with certain characteristics, aimed at achieving a specific result. For example, the Ragdoll cat, with its long coat and exotic coloring is a hybrid, thought to have been developed by crossbreeding Persian, Birman, and Burmese cats, although its exact origins are unknown.

European Burmese

This breed is similar to the Burmese, but with more colors accepted.

Exotic

Also called the Exotic Shorthair, this cat is a shorthaired version of the Persian, with all of the Persian's loveable, laid-back personality traits, but without the daily grooming commitment that a longhaired cat demands.

Havana Brown

This cat with a distinctive solid brown coat and green eyes hails from the same part of the world as the Siamese, Thailand (Siam), and shares some of the same ancient history among the native people there.

Korat

This cat is another Thailand native coveted for its silvery-blue short coat. It was highly prized in ancient times as a good-luck charm among the native people there.

Oriental

Similar to the Siamese, the Oriental comes in many more colors and also in short and long coats.

Russian Blue

A blue cat with green eyes, the Russian Blue is thought to have originated in Russia, where the cold climate fostered the cat's dense, double coat.

Siamese

Named for its native Siam, this popular breed is noted for its exotic darker colorpoint markings on the face, legs, and tail against a lighter body color. Legend has it that these cats were once considered sacred in their native land.

Singapura

This agouti-colored cat, native to the Asian island of Singapore, is probably the smallest of all cat breeds.

Snowshoe

A shorthaired cat with colorpoints and white feet, both the Siamese and the American Shorthair breeds were used to create the Snowshoe. The pointed pattern combined with white boots and mittens, and a white inverted "V" facial marking, makes an attractive cat.

Tonkinese

This breed is basically a cross between a Siamese and a Burmese.

Longhaired Cats

Longhaired cats require a daily grooming commitment on the owner's part in order to prevent the coat from matting. If you are neither able nor willing to spend the necessary time caring for a longhaired cat's coat, then consider one of the shorthair breeds instead. What follows is an overview of the longhaired breeds.

Balinese

This cat looks like a Siamese in body type and coloring but has long hair.

Birman

Known as the Sacred Cat of Burma, this longhaired beauty has a colorpoint coat set off by four white paws.

Chantilly/ Tiffany

An elegant longhair, this breed is primarily a rich chocolate-brown color.

Cymric

This cat is a longhaired version of the tailless Manx.

Himalayan

Named for its Himalayan pattern or colorpoint coloring, this breed was developed from crosses between the Persian and the Siamese. The Himalayan possesses the flat-faced, rounded features of the Persian, as well as its easygoing disposition.

Javanese

This breed is a longhaired version of the Colorpoint Shorthair.

Maine Coon

This American breed noted for its shaggy coat is one of the largest cat breeds.

Nebelung

This relatively new breed is a blue beauty with a silky, silver-tipped coat.

Norwegian Forest Cat

This Norway native is prized for its extremely dense double coat and its large size.

Persian

This popular and classy beauty with its round head, large round eyes, and flat facial features is noted for its docile, laid-back personality and loving disposition.

Ragdoll

This breed has Siamese-type colorpoints set off by white paws and blue eyes.

RagaMuffin

The breed is the same as a Ragdoll, except it comes in more colors, not accepted under the original Ragdoll standard.

Siberian

This Russian longhair is probably the largest of all cat breeds.

Somali

The Somali is a longhaired version of the Abyssinian.

Turkish Angora

This longhaired, predominantly white cat is much revered in Turkey, where it is considered a national treasure and a symbol of purity. Although most Angoras are pure white, other colors are accepted in today's breed standard.

Turkish Van

A close cousin of the Turkish Angora, this longhaired white cat is distinctive because of color patches restricted to the head and tail areas, known as the "van" pattern. The Turkish people consider Angoras and Vans to be the same cat, but they are recognized as separate breeds in the United States.

E-Fact

In Turkey, odd-eyed (one blue eye, one amber eye) white Angoras are especially prized and considered to be "touched by Allah." This belief may stem from a story about Muhammad, founder of the Islamic faith, who supposedly admired cats and once treasured a lovely odd-eyed, white, longhaired cat.

York Chocolate

As its name implies, the York Chocolate is a chocolate-colored cat with a medium-length coat.

Short-Tailed Cats

Some breeds arise out of physical characteristics other than coat length, body type, or coloring. The tailless breeds, for example, resulted primarily from a genetic mutation, which breeders then selectively bred to maintain. The following is an overview of the short-tailed breeds.

American Bobtail

As the name implies, this cat has a naturally occurring short, stubby tail. It comes in short and longhaired varieties and numerous colors. Although its true origins are unknown, some speculate that the breed may have sprung from a bobcat/domestic cat hybrid.

Japanese Bobtail

Another short-tailed cat, this breed is native to the Far East and comes with long or short hair. Calico (mostly white with patches of red and black) bobtails are considered good luck in their native land. The gene that creates the bobtail feature is unrelated to the lethal Manx gene and isn't associated with genetic flaws.

Manx

The best known short-tailed breed of cat hails from the Isle of Man in the Irish Sea, hence its name. It is relatively rare and challenging to breed, due to the lethal nature of the mutant gene that creates the tailless feature in this breed.

Pixie-Bob

This breed is another short-tailed cat that looks like a little bobcat.

Cats with Unusual Coats

If you think cats come only in short or long hair, think again. Selective breeding has created a variety of coat types to suit almost anybody's fancy.

American Wirehair

This breed is basically a domestic shorthair with a wiry coat, which arose in the general cat population as a spontaneous genetic mutation.

Cornish Rex

An English breed distinguished by short, soft, wavy fur, the Cornish Rex is similar to its close cousin, the Devon Rex.

Devon Rex

Hailing from Devon, England, this cat has a wavy coat with curly whiskers. The gene that governs the curly coat is recessive, which means a kitten must inherit a copy from each parent to sport the unusual coat type.

LaPerm

This is a relatively new and unusual breed sporting a curly coat with ringlets of hair.

Selkirk Rex

Another Rex-type curly-coated English breed, this one comes in short- and longhaired varieties.

Sphynx

Perhaps one of the most unusual breeds of all, this hairless cat was created by a spontaneous genetic mutation. The gene is recessive, which means a kitten must receive a copy from each parent in order to be hairless. Some kittens in a Sphynx litter possess more hair than others.

Wild-Looking Spotted Cats

Humankind's fascination with the big, brilliantly marked cats like the leopard probably supplied the driving force behind the selective breeding of domestic spotted cats. The spotted coat in cats is actually a derivation of the typical tabby coloring in which the bars and stripes are broken into smaller segments that look like spots.

Bengal

The exotic Bengal is a hybrid domestic–wild cat cross with leopard-like spots. The breed was spawned by an accidental mating between a domestic cat and a wild Asian leopard cat. Because of its wild blood, the breed is not accepted in all associations.

California Spangled

This spotted-coat cat looks wild but has no wild blood in it. It was deliberately developed through a series of domestic crossbreedings and is still relatively rare worldwide.

Egyptian Mau

This striking breed is a naturally spotted tabby that likely existed in ancient Egypt and was highly prized for its superior hunting prowess. The name "Mau" comes from the Egyptian word for "cat."

Ocicat

This domestic cat with leopard-like spots resembles an ocelot and was developed through deliberate crossbreedings of Abyssinians and Siamese.

Cats with Other Striking Features

Although genetic mutations account for a few strikingly different breeds of cats, the physical variations among cats are not yet as extreme as they are among dogs, which have been selectively bred for a much longer period of time. But who knows what may happen in time.

American Curl

No, this cat doesn't have curly hair, but its ears curl backward as result of a genetic mutation.

Munchkin

This controversial breed has short, stubby legs and a long body slung low to the ground, similar to the dachshund dog breed. It comes in short- and longhaired varieties. While dogs come in many shapes and sizes, domestic cats had all been pretty much the same as far as basic build, at least until the Munchkin came along. Most cat associations have been slow or downright reluctant to accept this breed because of its radically different skeletal structure, which is viewed by some as a deformity.

Scottish Fold

Instead of curling backward, these cats' ears fold forward. The breed originated in a Scotland barnyard but didn't gain popularity until it came to America.

The Scottish Fold's endearing, lop-eared look is due to a genetic mutation that affects the ear cartilage. The gene is also associated with some other skeletal abnormalities that can crop up unless careful breeding practices are observed. This is definitely a breed you want to research first and buy from only the most reputable and well recommended of breeders. All Scottish Folds are born with straight ears that begin to droop at about three weeks of age, if they are going to be folded.

You can find more details about the history and characteristics of each breed simply by visiting the Web sites of the various North American cat registering associations listed in the reference section of this book. Certain breeds are recognized by some associations, but not all. Others are listed under provisional, miscellaneous, or experimental status, because they have not been in existence long enough to become well established or recognized. Recognized simply means that the breed has fulfilled a particular cat registry's criteria for breed establishment, and that it can be shown for points and awards in cat shows sponsored by that organization.

Cats of Many Colors

Cats come in nearly countless colors and patterns. For registration and show purposes, colors are grouped by division as solid (or self) colors, silvers, shadeds, smokes, colorpoints, tabbies, particolors, and bi-colors.

Although many purebreds are bred specifically for their coat or coloring, they are all genetically tabbies. When we hear the term "tabby", most of us think of the familiar stripes and bars on a cat's coat, tail, and legs, and the pronounced "M" on the forehead. The tabby is not a specific breed, but a basic coloring pattern that occurs in purebred and random-bred cats.

The tabby pattern has three distinct variations, all of which give the cat excellent camouflage against tall foliage. The classic or blotched tabby has wide stripes, swirls, patches, or blotches. The mackerel tabby has thin stripes running down its sides from the backbone. The stripes' vertical pattern and placement resembles fish ribs. Finally, there's the spotted tabby with stripes that are broken up so that they look like spots.

The most common colors are the gray tabby, which has black stripes against a silvery gray background; the brown tabby, which has black markings on a reddish-brown background; and the red tabby, which has burnt orange stripes against a lighter yellowish background. Some people refer to the latter as a ginger or yellow tabby, but the correct name for the color, as concerns the cat fancy, is red.

Some tabbies have no stripes at all. The arrangement of genes that influence coat color and pattern can mask or suppress the distinctive tabby markings. If the genes completely mask the bars and stripes, the cat will be a solid color, but underneath, it is a tabby all the same.

Now take a look at some of these other colorings and patterns.

Agouti Coloring

The Abyssinian and Somali sport what's called the agouti pattern in their distinctive reddish-brown coats ticked with bands of darker color. Instead of solid stripes, the hairs have alternating light- and dark-colored bands on each shaft, giving the coat a delicately flecked or ticked appearance. This same pattern occurs in some other species, such as squirrels and groundhogs, and like the bolder tabby stripes, provides good camouflage.

The Dilutes

A dilute color is a paler version of the darker, denser colors, such as black and red. The dilute of black is, of course, slate gray, which cat people refer to as blue. The dilute of red is a lovely pale shade called cream. Recessive genes produce the dilute colors, whereas, dominant genes are responsible for their deeper, darker counterparts. Generally speaking, a cat must inherit two recessive genes, one from each parent, before it will be a dilute color, such as blue or cream, or in some cases a pleasing mixture of the two, called a blue-cream. But only one dominant gene is necessary for blacks and reds, although the cat can carry a hidden recessive gene, which may show up in later litters.

White Spotting and Tuxedos

The random and unique arrangement of genes can produce many beautiful color combinations in cats. When a common genetic occurrence, called the white spotting factor, randomly applies splashes of white to the face, neck, belly, and paws of a black cat, the result is the very elegant and popular tuxedo cat, named such because it looks all dressed up in black and white, complete with gloves and boots, and sometimes a white mustache. When this same pattern occurs against the dilute color (gray), you have the less common blue tuxedo cat. Like tabbies, tuxedos are not a specific breed, but a color pattern that occurs naturally in the random-bred cat population.

Calicos and Tortoiseshells

The white spotting factor plays a role in creating calico cats, too. Again, the calico is not a specific breed but a color pattern in which white patches intermingle among blotches of black and orange (red). People often confuse calicos with tortoiseshells, which also have black and reddish orange blotches, but no intermingling white whatsoever. Interestingly, both of these color varieties occur almost exclusively in females because the black-and-orange patchwork effect is sex-linked, produced by genes carried on the female (XX) chromosomes.

E-Fact

In cat fancy terminology, a cat with a coat of two or more colors, such as the tortoiseshell, is called a particolor. A bi-color cat has a coat of two colors, one of which must be white. The tuxedo is an example of a bi-color cat.

The Himalayan Pattern

Most people recognize the darker points on a cat's face, tail, feet, and ears against a lighter body color as the characteristic Siamese-type coloring, even if they don't know what it's called. The colorpoint pattern is actually named for the Himalayan rabbit breed that sports the same exotic coloring. Among cats, the Himalayan pattern appears predictably in several other breeds besides the Siamese, including the Himalayan, the Birman, the Ragdoll, the Balinese, and the Snowshoe. Occasionally, the pattern even crops up in random-bred cats.

The Himalayan pattern is a recessive trait and is linked with another trait that produces the blue eye color that is also common in the colorpoint breeds. Colorpoint kittens are born white, and their points appear after a few weeks and gradually darken with age.

What's interesting about the pattern, too, is that cooler temperatures influence the pigmentation and darkening process. This explains why colorpoint kittens are nearly white when they leave the warmth of their mother's womb. After birth, the extremities normally stay a degree or two cooler than the body's core, so that's why these areas begin to darken into the characteristic points.

Color is restricted to the points—face (mask), ears, paws, and tail—because of a mutant gene that influences an enzyme needed for pigment production. Core areas of the body are too warm to allow enough production of the enzyme for it to work, so these areas remain lighter in color.

Environmental, hormonal, and health factors can cause temporary variations in the coloring as well. Siamese that are allowed outdoors in winter will develop a darker body color. An obese Siamese will also have a darker body color because the thick fatty layer under the skin insulates it from the body heat deeper within. Cats that experience an illness with elevated fever will sometimes sprout lighter, unpigmented hairs among the darker hairs of their face, giving them an old, grizzled-looking countenance until the coat sheds out again and returns to its normal color in that area. Even pregnancy can affect the coloring, as it does most other things.

3 Choosing a Cat Companion

Why choose a cat over a dog, rabbit, bird, turtle, or fish as a pet? What are the distinct advantages and rewards unique to cat ownership? Dogs are among the most popular pets around the world, but they offer a much different relationship than cats do. Rabbits, turtles, and fish are all fine pets, especially for children, but they don't interact with their owners on an intimate level. Birds, of course, can be quite interactive and rewarding, but they can also be extremely noisy. This chapter will answer your questions about choosing a cat as your pet.

The Finer Points of Felines

If you think a cat might be the right pet for you but you're still undecided, there are some more aspects you should consider. The following list contains some of the great benefits of having cats as pets.

- **Cats can live comfortably indoors in small spaces:** Cats are a great fit for the rising urban population, as they can adapt quite well to living in small spaces, such as city apartments. In addition, many pet lovers spend ten to twelve hours per day away from home. Cats can easily tolerate being left alone for that period of time, as long as you provide a litter box and water. They usually sleep the day away until you return home to feed and play with them.
- **Cats are a snap to housebreak:** Cats come equipped with the natural instinct to bury their waste in a litter box (an instinct reinforced by watching their mothers perform the task). They generally go in the right place with little training required, other than showing them where the litter box is. All you need to do is make sure the box stays clean. Since cats are so fastidiously clean, they won't appreciate having to use a filthy litter box and may even refuse to do so.
- **Cats need little exercise:** While cats certainly require some exercise and toys to keep them from turning into tubby tabbies, they do not need to be walked like a dog (most would be insulted if you tried) or taken for regular romps in the park. Being nocturnal creatures by nature, they are generally content to sleep for about two-thirds of the day, waking in time for dinner and an evening prowl through your house.
- **Cats don't need much training:** Most cats catch on to what's expected of them from the start, as long as you are consistent with them. Of course, kittens aren't born knowing that they're not supposed to climb your drapes or claw your furniture, so you do have to set limits on where cats are allowed and provide alternative scratching areas for them to exercise their instinctive clawing behaviors. (This subject is covered more thoroughly in Chapter 5.)
- **Cats are naturally clean creatures:** Cats usually keep themselves quite clean and seldom require bathing, unless you're going to a cat

show. Plus, cats kept strictly indoors don't bring in dirt, fleas, and ticks from outdoors. However, cats do shed their fur on your furnishings, unless you are willing to put in a little time grooming out the loose hairs.

- **Cats are fairly independent:** Mouse-catching seems to be the only job appointed to cats in the service of humans, and it is one that required no instructions, special breeding, or cajoling on our part. In fact, cats would hunt even if humans didn't exist. Their ancient survival instincts have, for the most part, remained intact, leaving them with their characteristic attitudes of independence and aloofness. Some people dislike this enigmatic aspect of the cat persona, while others find it appealing and refreshing.
- **Cats don't require constant attention:** Cats are in control of their own lives, and will seek attention from you when they want it. Of course, some cats desire more attention than others. But generally speaking, there are no ulterior motives, no manipulative head games, no sucking up to the pack leader (unless, of course, you're holding a can of cat food). In the cat's mind, the two of you are equals interacting. Or, your cat may view you as a mother figure, a sibling, the hired help, etc., but forget about being the boss in the relationship. Some people greatly admire and respect this feline attribute.
- **Cats are quiet:** With all due respect to dogs, cats don't bark. If you live in an apartment and have a noisy dog, you stand a good chance of being evicted by your landlord or despised by your neighbors. Indoor cats almost never raise their voices loud enough to upset the neighbors. Intact, free-roaming outdoor cats, on the other hand, will kick up a caterwauling fuss during mating season, which is just one good reason to spay and neuter and keep cats inside.

Important Considerations

Having considered all the good reasons for acquiring a cat, there are some other things you need to consider about your lifestyle and your ability to commit to caring for a cat before you get one. Acquiring a pet should never be an impulsive decision. Ask yourself these questions first:

- Can I afford to own a cat?
- Can I provide a permanent home for a cat?
- Can I give a cat the love and attention it needs and deserves?
- Am I or any of my friends or family allergic to cats?
- Can I commit to caring for a cat for as long as it lives?

If one or two aspects of your lifestyle don't match up, that doesn't necessarily mean that you're unfit to be a cat owner. You might just need to make some adjustments. The following sections will bring more clarity to your answers to the previous questions and help you figure out what needs to be done in order to prepare for a cat.

Consider Costs

Even if you get a free kitten from a friend or neighbor, you will still have to buy cat food and litter, pay for yearly vaccinations and other veterinary care, purchase seasonal flea-control products, and have the cat spayed or neutered. While not a fortune, these costs add up significantly over time. If you're not currently set up to afford these kinds of costs, perhaps you could create a "cat fund" and save up for a few months before bringing a new kitty home. Your transition to pet ownership will go much more smoothly with a bigger budget.

Housing Issues

Make sure your landlord or housing agreement permits cats before you get one. There's nothing worse than getting attached to a new pet only to have to return it to the shelter where you got it or find it a new home. Also, if your job requires you to relocate often, it wouldn't be fair to adopt an animal, only to have to give it up a few months or years later because you can't take it with you.

Time

Sure, cats can be left at home alone for longer periods than dogs, but they still require that daily dose of affection and companionship from their owners. If you travel often, you'll need to have someone else take care of your cat while you're away, or it will suffer from neglect. Not only is this an expense and inconvenience for you, but it will confuse your cat if you're constantly leaving it in the care of another person. Cats are homebodies, and frequent trips to a boarding facility or a friend's house will upset their comfort and routine.

Pet Allergies

Pet allergies are common and uncomfortable, but not impossible to manage. However, many cats are surrendered each year to animal shelters for this reason. Consider this issue carefully, especially if you have children. Also realize that your social life may suffer if friends or family can no longer visit you because of their allergies.

Are hairless cats hypoallergenic?

Some people assume that a virtually hairless breed like the Sphynx should be non-allergenic, but this is not true. Sphynxes produce the Fel d1 protein just like other cats. The difference is, they don't shed dander-laden hair all over your furnishings. So perhaps in that sense, plus the fact that they are easier to bathe with no hair, the Sphynx may make allergy management less of a hassle.

Cat hair is not the actual culprit in cat allergies. Rather, it's the dried "dander" left behind on the hair after cats groom themselves, which they do a lot. Their saliva and sebaceous glands secrete a protein called Fel d1, which cats spread over their fur when they lick themselves. Regular bathing or using antiallergy wipes reduces the protein buildup on the fur and helps manage the severity of allergy symptoms. Frequent vacuuming and replacing carpets with hard floors help control the amount of dander-laced hair that drops off into the environment. Rather than give up their beloved companions, some cat lovers manage their symptoms with allergy medications or desensitizing allergy shots prescribed by their doctors. If this is a major issue for you, you should discuss the matter with your doctor first and research what treatments are available before you get a cat.

Commitment

With better nutrition and medical care available these days, cats can live about twelve to twenty years, or longer. The average lifespan for an indoor cat is approximately fifteen years. So, you need to be prepared to commit to a long-term relationship. Few people know exactly what they'll be doing in ten years, but you should know that your cat will always be a priority before making the decision to get one. If you're not sure you can commit to caring for a cat for as long as it lives, then don't get one. Smaller animals with life spans of three to five years max, like fish or hamsters, are better short-term pet choices.

Mixed Breed or Purebred?

Perhaps, after considering all issues carefully, you've decided that you definitely want to share your life with a cat. That's great! But you still have some decisions to make about what kind of cat you want to be your companion. The first thing you need to decide is whether to adopt a mixed-breed cat from a shelter or private owner, or purchase a purebred. Either one can make a fine companion, but there are some pros and cons to consider for each.

Because random-bred cats draw their genes from a much larger gene pool than purebred cats, they are somewhat less predisposed to developing anatomical, physiological, or behavioral abnormalities. Many breeders, however, do an admirable job of weeding out undesirable traits from their purebred stock, so the health concerns of breeding genetically similar cats aren't nearly as serious as some might make them out to be. The trick is in finding the right breeder, someone more concerned with healthy, quality animals than profit. We'll discuss that issue in greater detail in Chapter 4.

Obviously, a random-bred cat is less costly to acquire (sometimes free), whereas, a purebred can cost anywhere from several hundred to several thousand dollars (for some rarer breeds). Plus, you can only guess what a random-bred kitten will look like when it grows up, or what kind of personality it will have. By opting for a purebred, you can more closely predict just what kind of temperament and physical characteristics the adult will have.

This book and most people use the terms mixed-breed cat and random-bred cat interchangeably to mean a cat of unknown or unverifiable ancestry. Random-bred is the more politically correct term, however, when you're talking about the Heinz-57 variety feline equivalent of the mutt. In some cases, a mixed breed may actually be a deliberate crossbreeding of two different types of purebred cats.

If your heart is set on acquiring a purebred, you need to decide what breed suits you best. Perhaps you prefer a quiet, reserved cat. A Persian or Himalayan will meet this requirement nicely. But maybe you don't want the daily grooming commitment that a longhaired cat demands. If that's the case, consider the shorthaired version of the Persian, the Exotic Shorthair. If you want a more active, feisty cat, purchasing a Siamese or Abyssinian will definitely ensure that this need is met. If you want a cat, but you really don't care whether it's a random-bred or a purebred, perhaps the following discussion of the ethics involved will help you make up your mind.

Every week in the United States, thousands of cats are euthanized (humanely destroyed) at animal shelters because there are simply many more of them than there are potential owners willing to give them homes. It is a tragedy of epic proportions, caused by the ignorance and irresponsibility of current cat owners who neglect to have their pets neutered or spayed and allow them to roam freely and breed indiscriminately.

E-ssential

Cats at shelters are no less smart than their pristine purebred counterparts and are just as likely to be affectionate and charming companions. By purchasing a purebred, you are, as some people would argue, taking away from one of these unlucky shelter cats one chance of finding a home. Therefore, the ethical question to ask yourself is this: "Can I in good conscience purchase a purebred cat, knowing that so many other cats are so badly in need of homes?"

Knowing what's at stake, the decision is a tough one. However, if every owner of a mixed-breed or purebred cat practiced responsible ownership, we could resolve the pet overpopulation problem. Whatever you decide, have your pet spayed or neutered. If your animal is intact (not altered), keep it indoors and do not permit indiscriminate breeding.

One Cat or Two?

Some people solve the dilemma of whether to get a mixed breed or a purebred by acquiring one of each. They buy the purebred they've always dreamed of having, and they give a good home to a stray or shelter cat. This way, the cats can be companions to each other while you are away at work all day.

If you want two cats, it is best to acquire both as kittens at the same time so they can grow up together as friends. It is much harder to introduce a second cat into a household where an adult cat already resides. In general, however, it's not a good idea to adopt more than two cats unless you have a lot of room. The social dynamics change with three or more cats. Although it's certainly possible to keep peace in a multiple-cat household, territorial problems are more likely to crop up, leading to fighting and injury, if not handled strategically. This is especially true if your house or apartment is small. (See Chapter 17 for more information about multi-pet households.)

Adopting a second cat companion really isn't a bad idea, if your finances and living arrangements will allow it. Cats that spend most of the day alone tend to get into things that shouldn't be any of their business. A bored cat may destroy houseplants, rip apart sofas, become overly vocal, or get into all manner of other untold mischief. Although cats seem to adapt well to a predominantly solitary lifestyle, being alone for too long periods can be stressful, even for a cat; and stress and loneliness can eventually result in poor health and behavioral problems.

Consider the following benefits of having two pet cats:

- Two cats will amuse each other, helping to avert property destruction and separation anxiety. Kittens are social creatures and benefit from having a playmate.
- Two cats will learn to be much more sociable than a kitten raised alone. This may make bringing future animals into the home easier.
- Two cats will retain a vestige of kittenhood into adulthood, making them more playful and accepting of strangers.
- Two cats are twice as much fun to watch play and observe their personality differences and interactions.
- Two random-bred kittens won't cost much more than one to acquire. In addition, you will be saving two lives instead of one.

Of course, as with every situation, this one has two sides. From a practical standpoint, two cats mean double the cost of care and work involved. This includes paying for one additional neutering or spaying operation, and two cats to vaccinate each year instead of one. It also means two cats to bathe and de-flea (as needed), more cat food to buy, two litter boxes to keep clean, plus more litter to buy. Then of course there will be more toys, supplies, and an extra scratching post to buy. But even with double the trouble, two cats can also double your fun and enjoyment as you watch them play and interact with each other and marvel at their distinct personality differences.

Male or Female?

The sex of the cat you choose for your companion really doesn't matter. Both sexes make good pets, but they make better pets if altered. So what does matter is that you have your female cat spayed or your male cat neutered. Sometimes when you adopt from a shelter, this will already be done, because both operations can now be safely performed at a much earlier age than was attempted a few years ago.

The female operation costs more because it involves opening the abdomen and removing the reproductive organs inside. But overall, the surgery is less costly (and less hassle) than raising, feeding, and trying to find homes for successive litters of kittens. Male cats spray urine to mark their territory, which can stink up your house badly. Thankfully, neutering tends to curb this natural but distasteful behavior, and it's best to have the operation done before the cat ever starts the habit. Otherwise, it can be harder to break. For more details about spaying and neutering, see Chapter 18.

In addition to the possibility of kittens, your female will go into periodic bouts of heat (estrus) unless you have her spayed. The annoying vocalizations that ensue, and the lineup of yowling toms that are attracted to her scent from far and wide, are usually enough to convince most people to go through with the operation.

Some people think it's okay to leave their male cat unaltered, since they won't be the ones bothered with unwanted kittens. But when you allow an intact cat to roam freely, you are being an irresponsible pet owner. An intact male allowed to roam freely will seek out and mate with as many willing intact females as he can find. An average-size litter comprises about four to seven kittens, and cats can have several litters each year. That's a lot of unwanted kittens. Although you may never see or know about the kittens, you are directly contributing to the suffering and death already rampant in the pet overpopulation crisis. Any cat not intended for use in a professional breeding program should be altered, without question. And, intact cats should not be allowed to roam and breed freely.

Considering an Adult Cat over a Kitten

Most people don't want to miss the adorable antics of the kitten stage, but there are some good reasons for considering an adult cat. If your heart is set on a particularly expensive breed, you may be able to acquire a retired show cat for a more reasonable sum than a kitten costs. From time to time, breeders must sell off some of their adult breeding and show stock and find good homes for these cats. When they do so, they often cut the price and have the cats spayed or neutered prior to placement. And since adult cats should be up-to-date on all vaccinations, you can really hold down your initial acquisition costs this way.

Adopting an adult cat from a shelter or rescue organization is more of a gamble, unless you can gather reliable information about the animal's history, why it was surrendered, what kind of circumstances it lived in before, and so forth. Still, when you adopt any cat from a shelter, you are saving a life and doing a good deed. When adopting from a private owner who is trying to place an adult cat in a good home, it is often easier to obtain more information about the cat's background. (See Chapter 4 for more information about adopting from a shelter or a private owner.)

Advantages of an Adult Cat

There are other advantages to acquiring an adult cat. An adult cat is precisely the size it is going to be; there are no surprises. Plus, an adult cat's personality is already formed, allowing you to know just what that cat is like temperamentally. Because a kitten's temperament is still developing; you may not get a good read on its true personality until it is six to seven months old. Also, an adult cat is more likely to have been trained to use a litter box.

Disadvantages of an Adult Cat

There are disadvantages to adopting an adult cat as well. An adult cat has set behavior patterns that will be very hard to modify. If some of these behaviors are undesirable, you might get stuck with a cat that annoys more than it amuses. If, for example, the cat was surrendered because of unresolved house soiling, these issues are likely to continue under your roof.

Also, if you want two cats, adopting more than one adult cat is not a great idea, as they will be very territorial with each other and could end up fighting constantly. An exception to this would be two adults that have been together for a long time and enjoy each other's company.

The Indoor Versus Outdoor Debate

One of the final and most important things you need to decide before getting a cat is whether it will have access to the outdoors or will be purely an indoor pet. This decision may be made for you if you live in an apartment complex where the rules forbid free-roaming pets. Many people believe the only correct decision here is to keep your cat indoors at all times. However, others would disagree in this debate and feel that it's okay to let cats roam outdoors as long as they are vaccinated and spayed or neutered. In some areas, the law decides this for you, as more and more localities enact leash and licensing requirements for both cats and dogs. Before deciding where you stand in this debate, check the laws where you live.

Is it true that cats kept indoors typically live longer?

Yes. Due to environmental hazards, the average lifespan of an outdoor cat is about three years, compared to twelve to seventeen years or so for one that is well cared for and kept safely indoors. That said, the simplest way to significantly increase your cat's lifespan is to keep it inside your home.

Decades ago, when humans lived more pastoral lives, there weren't nearly as many dangers as there are now threatening the life of an outdoor cat. Although aggressive dogs, parasites, and fights with other cats have always been with us, the outdoor cat population was once much lower and more widely dispersed. Roads were less heavily traveled. And although still not as safe as being strictly indoors, years ago, outdoor living certainly wasn't the proclamation of an early death that it is for cats today. Some people in this debate seem to be still stuck in this bygone era, but times have changed, drastically.

Outdoor Dangers

Most neighborhoods, particularly urban ones, are rife with feline dangers, diseases, and death. Even rural areas that are relatively free from the dangers that a city brings still will have an outdoor cat population that often carries a legion of diseases and parasites, some of which your outdoor cat can bring home to you (see Chapters 13 and 15). Your cat could be bitten, infected, or killed by a dog, raccoon, skunk, or another cat defending its territory.

Then, there are all the dangers that humans have created, namely cars, trucks, buses, poisons, guns, etc.—not to mention the crazies out there who apparently enjoy harming or killing cats just for fun. Countless numbers of cats get killed each year because of the hectic, crazed environment that most humans live in.

Aside from the obvious health and safety issues, keeping your cat indoors will also prevent it from preying on small wild creatures, such as songbirds. These poor creatures have a hard enough time surviving on their own in a habitat that we seem bent on destroying, without our free-roaming pets further upsetting the fragile balance of things.

Outdoor cats suffer more injuries, become much less sociable with people and other animals, and find themselves visiting the veterinarian far more often then they should have to. So, if for no other reason than to help hold down the vet bills, please keep your cat safely inside, where exposure to disease and injury will be much less.

As long as you provide your cat with a safe, stimulating home environment, it will have no need to go outdoors. Cats kept inside from kittenhood on usually develop little or no desire to go outside. Some indoor cats will refuse to go outside into a strange, unfamiliar environment, even when a door is left open. And why should they? The home is their territory. The outside belongs to some other cat. As long as you neuter your cat before it is of breeding age, you won't have the problem of your cat wanting to go outside to mate and fight. Even cats raised outdoors can, in most cases, be acclimated to life indoors.

Converting an Outdoor Cat to the Indoors

Often, when you adopt an older adult cat that has been used to going outside, it will at first insist on having access to an open door. It may sit by a window and meow, or at least stare out all day wondering why it can't get at those starlings drinking out of a puddle across the street. It may try to scoot out of open doors, so be aware of that and inform family and friends to go in and out quickly, looking to see if the cat is underfoot.

E-ssential

When working to make a previously outdoor cat more comfortable indoors, try to make the cat's new indoor environment as fun and inviting as possible. Provide a cat-scratching tree that the cat can climb in place of real trees. Restrict the cat's access to open doors and windows, and just wait it out. After four or five months, the cat is likely to accept the new situation and claim the home as its new territory.

Some people would say that it is cruel to deny such an animal access to the outdoors. Others say it is crueler to cater to the cat's desires, knowing that in doing so you will be reducing his lifespan and quality of life significantly. The perceived cruelty lies in allowing the cat to go out regularly, unsupervised, into a very dangerous and infection-laden world.

You can always allow the cat to experience the outdoors under safe supervision, in an enclosed outdoor run, a screened-in porch, or on a leash. However, you should never tether a cat outside and leave it unattended, because it could quickly become entangled and accidentally hang or strangle itself.

The Compromise: A Pet Door

Owners who insist on allowing their cat free-roaming access to the outdoors often install a pet door through which the cat can come and go as it pleases. Once you have installed the pet door according to the manufacturer's directions, try these tips to train your cat to use it:

- At first, keep the pet door propped open and lure the cat through it several times with a favorite treat. It should soon get the general idea.
- After the cat is regularly going through the door, start to gradually close it a little bit more each day, until after a week or so, the door is completely shut. If you do this gradually enough, the cat will learn that it can push through the door with its head to gain access outside.

The primary disadvantage of having a pet door is that it does not discriminate between your cat and the neighbor's cat, or the area's wildlife. In fact, any animal, including small dogs, raccoons, or squirrels, may figure out how to use it and come inside your home for a visit. Be sure to consider this consequence carefully, plus the fact that your cat will be safer if kept strictly indoors, before you decide to install one of these products.

Pet Identification

Even if you keep your cat indoors all the time, it is still possible for a door or window to be left open accidentally, providing your feline explorer with an avenue to the outside world. To help get your kitty back, make sure it has some form of pet identification. Nowadays, microchip technology is one of the most efficient and unobtrusive means of pet identification. Most veterinarians offer this service, which involves injecting a tiny microchip under the cat's skin at the nape of the neck. The chip does no harm there, and you can't feel its presence. The best time to do this is when the cat is already under anesthesia for spay or neuter surgery. For a modest fee, you can then register the microchip with a database service that specializes in matching up lost pets with their owners. Shelters, animal-control officials, and most veterinarian offices have scanners that can read the ID information contained on the microchip, should your cat ever become lost and later found by one of these agencies.

The old-fashioned form of pet identification is the collar with a clearly legible identification tag on it. However, collars can pose a definite choking hazard, if they are snagged on a tree branch or other obstacle. If you decide to go this route, consider purchasing an elastic or “breakaway” collar to minimize the danger. A pet shop will have what you need. Make sure that you introduce the collar to your cat early in life, so that you don’t encounter lots of resistance. For the cat that doesn’t seem to take to wearing a collar, try putting one on the cat at first for only a minute. During this time, offer the cat her favorite treat or toy, keeping her attention off the collar for the allotted time. Each day repeat the exercise, lengthening the duration of time that the collar is worn.

4 The Right Cat for You

Once you've decided that you want a cat, and what kind of cat you want, the next step is finding the right one. There are several avenues, from buying from a pet shop or a private breeder, to adopting from a shelter, a rescue organization, or a private citizen. Whatever source you choose, you need to make sure it is a reputable one. Every option has its good points and warnings, so you need to be vigilant while you search for your perfect kitty.

Taking in a Stray Cat

Sometimes the right cat finds you, if both of you are lucky. Picture this scenario: You open the door in the morning on your way to work, only to be confronted by a beaten-up adolescent or adult cat meowing at you and rubbing against your legs? You pet the animal (if it allows it), look for tags, and finding none, you usually go inside and get a saucer of milk or some leftover chicken from last night's dinner. You feed the poor wretch, and then go off to work. When you get home that night the cat is there waiting for you, meowing its head off. For a few days, you go through the same routine, giving the cat water and some food, petting it, then leaving it to fend for itself. After a few days, however, all but the most disciplined would weaken. You take the cat into your home, set up an appointment with the veterinarian (which sometimes can be very expensive with strays), name the poor kitty, and go on from there. (In some localities, if you feed a stray for a certain number of days, you're automatically considered the owner.)

If an animal is behaving oddly, or is obviously sick or injured, it is best to contact a local animal-control official for assistance rather than handle the animal yourself. There is always the risk of rabies to consider in an unknown animal. After the animal is examined, if you want to assume responsibility for its welfare, you can work that out with the authorities.

It's a fact that strays often make great pets. They seem to be very appreciative and particularly loyal to the person who saves them. This may be attributing human motivations to an animal, but it often seems quite true in experience. Those who "throw away" these cats usually miss out on having a wonderful and loving companion.

Health Concerns with Strays

There are problems with taking in strays that you need to be aware of. First and foremost in importance is the animal's state of health, as you must assume that the animal has not had any vaccinations. Consider the following possibilities:

- **Contagious diseases:** Many strays are infected with diseases such as feline leukemia virus (FeLV), feline immunodeficiency virus (FIV), and feline infectious peritonitis (FIP), all deadly contagions that can be spread from cat to cat via various modes of transmission. You will need to have the stray tested for FeLV and feline AIDS to determine its status, and then keep the newcomer isolated from your other pets for a while, to rule out other conditions.
- **Parasitic infestations:** Most strays come loaded with internal and external parasites, including various types of worms, fleas, and ticks. These, too, can be passed on to your current house cats or dogs, so you'll need to have the veterinarian check and treat for any infestations.
- **Injuries and infections:** Strays can often have injuries received during fights with other strays or with dogs, including cuts, abscesses from bites, and broken or sprained limbs. They may also be suffering from ear infections, ear mites, intestinal disorders, or eye problems, which will need to be treated.

Handling Strays Safely

Strays usually have not been vaccinated against anything, and may be carrying the rabies virus, which is deadly to all mammals, including humans. This means you must observe appropriate safety precautions when approaching or handling a stray. Wear thick gloves and other protective clothing if you must pick up the animal, because you don't know whether it will bite or scratch. Hard-to-capture animals can be lured into humane traps and transported to a veterinarian for examination.

Behavioral Concerns with Strays

Most strays that have been on their own awhile have gone through a lot of heartache. Owners have abandoned or abused them. Animals have attacked them. Cars have tried to run them over. Consequently, they tend to be much less sociable, and will almost certainly be aggressive toward other pets you may have, at least at first. Life on the streets has probably taught them some hard lessons, and made them less trusting and more fearful. They become timid out of the need to survive. Therefore, strays may not be as open to being touched or held, as would a cat you have raised yourself.

E-ssential

A stray may try to scratch or bite someone who tries to get too chummy too fast. If you have children, think twice before adopting a stray for these reasons. Children do not understand the risks and must be taught how to properly respect, handle, and hold a cat.

Some strays will want continued access to the outdoors, even though it is where they took all their lumps. It's what they know. If you let them out, they will risk getting into more fights or picking up viruses and parasites and bringing them home to your other pets.

A stray may also refuse to use a litter box for a while, due to inexperience or lack of practice, or from having to exert dominance over other strays by leaving feces unburied. It may take some time to get them on the indoor house-cat track.

Age Issues with Strays

Generally, strays are of adolescent or young adult age. Most of them don't survive outdoors beyond three or four years. If you don't know how old the cat is, a veterinarian can approximate the animal's age by examining its teeth. Adult cats do not learn as quickly as kittens. In fact, any adult cat, be it a stray or not, already has some well-established behavior patterns that will be harder to modify, should the need arise. Of course, this is only a problem if the behavior is unacceptable to you. Starting out with a kitten gives you a much better chance at shaping the animal's behavior to suit your desires.

Adopting from a Shelter

Countless strays and unwanted kittens are placed for adoption at animal shelters or rescue organizations each year. If you want a mixed breed, this is the place to look first. But many people are surprised that they can often find purebred cats here that have been surrendered by their owners for various reasons.

Most shelters and rescue organizations, whether private or publicly funded facilities, have an informed, polite staff present to help you choose a kitty, as well as answer any questions you may have regarding procedures, supplies you may need, proper environment for the cat, diet, or where to find a good veterinarian. Some shelters even offer pet counseling and workshops on proper pet ownership.

E-Fact

You may have to complete an adoption application, and some facilities may make you wait twenty-four hours before you can pick up the cat and take it home. This is to ensure that your desire to have the cat isn't just an impulsive decision. Some organizations will even ask to visit your home first, to ensure that you have proper housing for the pet. They want to make sure they place their animals in good homes, so they won't end up tossed out on the streets again.

Both private and public shelters usually provide you with access to low-cost spaying and neutering services (usually a mandatory condition of adoption). If the shelter has already had the animal altered, this cost is included in the overall adoption fee. Shelters charge a reasonable adoption fee not only to recover their costs of the cat's care, but also because they believe people tend to value a pet more if it has a price. Some shelters will also provide you with some food and litter, and perhaps even a litter box and a toy or two.

Choosing a Healthy Cat or Kitten

Everyone wants to adopt the perfect, healthy kitten. But what do you look for? The following list includes different aspects that you should check out in each cat you consider taking home.

- **Age:** Avoid kittens under six weeks old. Kittens that have left their mothers and litters too soon may show profound fear aggression and antisocial behavior toward others for their entire life. Although adorable, a four-week-old kitten is a risky adoption at best.
- **Coat condition:** The kitten's coat should be clean and relatively free of mats. There should be no missing patches of hair or any scabbing, which might indicate parasitic infestations or an allergy problem.
- **Health:** The kitten's eyes should be clear and bright. The eyes, ears, and nose should not show any kind of discharge. Any kitten that is sneezing or scratching incessantly should be passed over, as should one that seems dull, listless, or scrawny or has a bloated belly (which may indicate a worm infestation). Look for any signs of diarrhea in the animals' enclosure, or evidence of dried feces around the anal area.
- **Litter box behavior:** Observe whether the kittens are using their litter box. Choosing one that already has this skill down pat will save you a lot of aggravation at home!
- **Size:** Pay attention to size (relative to age). Does one kitten seem stockier and larger-boned than the others? Does another seem long-legged and thin? Determining what size a mixed-breed kitten will ultimately be is very difficult, but not totally impossible. If you are looking for a particular build of cat, it won't hurt to try to determine this at an early stage.
- **Sociability:** Evaluate each kitten's sociability with others and determine which ones are dominant, submissive, curious, timid, and confident. Consider a kitten only after you have seen it interacting with

other kittens. Avoid selecting any kitten that shows fear of you or the other kittens; this type may wind up with an antisocial behavior problem later on. Avoid any kitten that swats or hisses at you or the other kittens in unprovoked anger or fear.

E-ssential

Look for a kitten that seems to be at ease around others, and shows a relaxed yet inquisitive nature toward you. Ball up a sheet of paper and toss it in among the kittens; see who gets to it first, and what the general reaction of the group is. A kitten that wants to play and shows no concern about the presence of humans is probably a good choice.

Once you've selected a kitten or cat that you like, you need to find out as much as you can about its history before you sign the adoption papers. Granted, a great deal may not be known, but you can at least find out why, when, and how the kitten or cat was surrendered to the shelter. This is especially important when adopting an adult cat, because the reason it was given up may reveal existing behavior problems. For example, was the previous owner forced to give up the cat because of moving away? Or did the cat have destructive behaviors that the owner couldn't cope with?

Find out if the animal has been seen by a veterinarian or has had any of its shots. If so, the shelter should provide you with those records. You should also clarify the shelter's return policy, in case the cat you've selected doesn't work out well in your home.

Finding Kittens Through the Classifieds

Pick up today's paper and turn to the "Classified/Pets" section. You will find a glut of animals up for sale or adoption, from purebred cats and dogs to hamsters, ferrets, and snakes. The abundance of mixed-breed kittens found here is the result of many irresponsible pet owners still not getting the message regarding spaying and neutering their pets. They either don't listen or don't care, or they're simply not willing to spend the money for the operation. They let their unaltered cats roam freely outside and breed, and consequently, those with females soon find themselves caring for five cats instead of one.

Advantages of Adopting from Private Owners

Although not the best way to shop for a purebred (for reasons to be covered shortly), you may find a suitable mixed-breed kitten this way. First, if you go to a private home to adopt or buy a mixed-breed kitten, you will get to see the mother and perhaps the entire litter (the father is usually some cavalier stud roaming the neighborhood, so it's not likely you will ever get to see him). It is a great advantage for you to see the temperament of the mother. If she is extremely timid and antisocial, you might want to consider passing up her kittens, which could easily have inherited her trait for this undesirable behavior. Of course, be aware that the mother will probably be a bit protective and guarded at first, especially if her kittens are only a few weeks old.

Try choosing an ad that offers kittens in the seven- to eight-week-old range. By this time the mother will be attempting to distance herself physically and emotionally from her kittens, which, in the wild, would be self-sufficient by their fourth month. If the mother seems confident, curious, and at ease in your presence, chances are her kittens will reflect that in their behavior later in life.

The ability to see the entire litter of kittens will give you the chance to compare and contrast them behaviorally, allowing you to choose one that seems the most confident, curious, and at ease with you. Observe and evaluate each available kitten, based on the criteria discussed in the previous section.

Going to the home where the kittens were born allows you to see first-hand just what type of conditions they were raised under. If the place is a pigsty and the owners have twelve pregnant females roaming the property, you know this is the place to avoid. If the place is clean and the owners are easy-going and kind to you and the animals, you can probably assume that the kittens have received decent care and will be relatively healthy. Of course, the same is true if you're looking at an adult cat. With kittens at a shelter, you don't get to see any of this. The previous owners might have abused or abandoned the kittens or just dumped them off at the shelter's doorstep.

Disadvantages of Adopting from Private Owners

There are disadvantages to adopting from a private home. First, the owner will not be providing you with free or low-cost neutering services, as most shelters will do. Also, the kittens probably will not have been vaccinated or dewormed. If, however, they have had some medical care, be sure to ask for the medical records and veterinarian's name. (This information is especially important if you're looking at an adult cat.)

Finally, a lot of private owners (except those involved in the cat fancy) know little or nothing about feline illness or disease; therefore, their kittens might be infectious and pose a possible threat to your other pets at home. They probably will not have been tested for FeLV or feline AIDS. Most shelters, on the other hand, screen out sick kittens.

Hallmarks of a Good Breeder

If you decide that you prefer the predictability and unique characteristics of a particular type of purebred cat (and are prepared to fork over the bucks for one), your next step is to find a reputable breeder. If you haven't made up your mind about what breed you want, it is recommended that you look at popular cat magazines (listed in the back of this book) and attend a few cat shows to better acquaint yourself with the breeds that interest you. Attending shows is also a good way to meet breeders and ask questions about their favorite cats. Most will be more than happy to tell you all about their breed's characteristics, especially if you're a prospective buyer.

Once you've decided on a particular breed that interests you, you must then locate a reputable breeder. The following sections describe the hallmarks of a good, conscientious breeder, so you'll know how to avoid the less knowledgeable backyard breeders who are just in it for a quick profit.

Proper Registration

Reputable breeders should have their purebred cats properly registered with a reputable cat association such as the CFA (Cat Fanciers' Association). The CFA will determine whether a breeder's information regarding his pedigrees is accurate, and will also (for a fee) add your kitty's name to its pedigree and send you a registration certificate. If a breeder has not properly registered his cats and will not provide you with a pedigree, politely walk on.

Breed Standards

Reputable breeders should strictly abide by the "standard" for the breed. A standard consists of the physical characteristics of a breed that set it apart from all others. It is a breeder's job to understand the genetics of the breed well enough to maintain this standard in his stock. You should familiarize yourself with the standards of your favorite breeds. If a breeder's cats do not closely match these, move on. Careless or greedy breeders will sell kittens or cats that are bad representatives of the breed, because they generally know very little about the genetics involved. A Siamese with a kinked tail, for example, or a Manx with a slight build do not meet the standards of those breeds.

Looking for Good Owners

Reputable breeders should be as curious about you as you are about their cats. Dedicated breeders want to see their kittens go to people who are capable of caring for them. If a breeder asks you lots of questions and seems to put you through the wringer, be thankful. This means he is a dedicated professional who is looking for more than just a buyer. He's looking to place his cats with a responsible and caring cat owner. If a breeder wants to know nothing about you apart from your payment plans, walk away and look elsewhere.

Well-Socialized Kittens

Reputable breeders should socialize kittens with other cats and people from a very early age, and also handle the kittens from the first week on to ensure that they will be happy and confident with people. Any breeder who seems to have the kittens isolated from human contact (or claims that socializing at an early age is bad) should be avoided.

E-ssential

Reputable breeders should keep cats in a top-notch, clean cattery. Any breeder who allows the cats' environment to become filthy or overcrowded shows a lack of concern and professionalism, and should be avoided.

Involvement in Cat Shows

Reputable breeders should have a history of attending and competing in cat shows on a regular basis. This helps them keep their skills on a competitive level with those of other breeders and remain in touch with the breed trends. Avoid a breeder who shuns cat shows, or who has never even been to one, as this person likely is only interested in profit, and not the welfare and betterment of the breed. It's also a safe bet that this type of person really doesn't know much about the genetics of the breed he purports to represent, and is probably breeding inferior animals.

Finding a Good Breeder

So, where do you find these wonderful, caring, altruistic cat breeders? Aside from visiting cats shows, it may seem like there are few ways to seek out these people. The following list includes several other ways to locate some.

- **Breed clubs and cat registering associations:** Many cat breeds have a club or clubs dedicated to the betterment and discussion of their favorite breed. You can locate clubs for your favorite breeds by contacting one of the well-known cat registries listed in the back of this book. Any breed club should be more than happy to provide you with information on their breed and to give you a list of reputable breeders in or near your area.

- **Cat magazines:** Newsstand publications that cater to cat lovers, such as *Cat Fancy* magazine, always contain a great amount of breeder advertising. Reading cat magazines may help you locate a local breeder of good reputation. These magazines usually also include a calendar of cat shows taking place all over the country.
- **Veterinarians:** Your local vet knows a healthy cat when she sees one. Ask her for a recommendation/referral to a good breeder in the area, or for contact with a client who owns an outstanding representative of the breed you like. That owner might be kind enough to put you in touch with the cat's breeder.
- **Classified ads:** Good breeders as well as lousy ones advertise in the newspaper classifieds, so they are not the best place to begin your search. What you want to avoid in the classifieds are the backyard breeders—people who are more interested in turning a quick profit than in promoting and enhancing the breed they're selling. If you buy from this caliber of breeder, you're more likely to get a cat with genetic problems or other undesirable traits that a more knowledgeable, reputable breeder would be careful to avoid.

E-Fact

You can usually weed out less reputable backyard breeders in an initial phone call by asking a few choice questions about whether their litters are registered and how well their cats do at shows. Most of them don't bother with proper registrations (the fees cut into their profits) and are not or never have been involved in showing—dead giveaways that you're talking to someone who's not seriously into the cat fancy.

Visiting the Breeder

Once you have identified several breeders of good reputation, make an appointment to visit their catteries. Look for cleanliness and professionalism. Observe the adult cats. Are they timid and nervous or friendly and curious? Also, pay attention to your gut instincts regarding the breeder. Does she come off as trustworthy, open, and curious about you, or guarded and rude?

Expect the breeder to ask you a number of questions before she allows you to purchase a kitten. Any good breeder wants to ensure that a potential customer will:

- Be able to properly care for the kitten
- Have an environment suitable for a kitten
- Abide by the breeder's contractual stipulations, which could include clauses requiring spaying or neutering, indoor-only living, and prohibition of declawing

Purebred Pricing

Most breeders will have both "show" quality and "pet" quality kittens for sale to qualified buyers. The show-quality kittens cost more because they are near-perfect examples of their breed. These animals could eventually be entered into competition, and possibly do quite well. The pet-quality kittens, on the other hand, have some minor flaw in structure or appearance that would prevent them from excelling at a show. Perhaps the coat is the wrong color or a bit too long or too coarse. But they are just as healthy and well adjusted as the show kittens and can make great pets, so the breeder offers them for sale at a substantially lower price. If you don't care about showing or breeding your cat, you should seriously consider purchasing a pet-quality cat, provided the "fault" is not severe or debilitating in any way. Any kitten showing pronounced skeletal deformities, for instance, should definitely be passed over.

Questions You Should Ask a Breeder

After you locate a breeder with whom you feel comfortable, you will need to ask some questions to determine availability of kittens and assess the breeder's competence. Some good questions include:

- **When will you have kittens available?** Reputable breeders do not have kittens available year-round. Many typically allow their females to produce only one or two litters per breeding season, so you may have to wait for a purebred kitten to become available. Only the profit-motivated "kitten mills" have animals available year-round, and you really want to avoid these types of facilities.
- **At what age will you let your kittens go home with their new owners?** No reputable breeder will let a kitten go before it is at least ten weeks old. Kittens who leave their mothers and litters before this time do not become properly socialized, and may turn out to be very antisocial adults, particularly with regard to other animals. Also, kittens under ten weeks of age will not have been fully vaccinated or wormed.
- **Are your kittens raised in the home or in cages?** Most good breeders raise their kittens indoors, so they can become accustomed to the goings-on of a normal home. Certainly, they will have cages in their catteries to separate and protect cats, as needed, but this doesn't necessarily mean that the cats aren't handled often. Kittens raised exclusively in cages with little human contact will not be nearly as friendly or well-adjusted as those raised around people and their daily comings and goings.
- **How many breeding adult cats do you have?** Beware of any breeder who has more than eight or ten breeding cats on the premises. Any more than that and you run the risk of dealing with a profit-motivated, kitten-mill operation. Dedicated breeders choose breeding stock very carefully and don't care about the number of kittens produced, only their quality.
- **Do you currently own any breeding Champions or Grand Champions?** A Champion or Grand Champion didn't win such prestige by being a run-of-the-mill cat. You can be sure that kittens produced by prize-

winning cats will be great examples of their breed. Poor breeders, interested only in high volume and profit, will not have decent enough breeding stock on hand to win any cat show, and probably won't be interested in entering anyway.

- **Is your cattery regularly tested for feline leukemia virus?** This fatal infectious disease can wipe out an entire cattery and spread throughout the entire locale. A good breeder will have a veterinarian regularly test for the presence of this killer. Any kitten you purchase should be certified free of this disease, especially if you have other cats at home.
- **What type of guarantees do you give on your kittens?** Any good breeder will provide the buyer with a two- or three-week guarantee for the kitten's general health, and a six-month guarantee against congenital defects. If the breeder will not agree to these terms, move on.
- **Do you fully vaccinate and worm the kittens?** All good breeders see to this. If the breeder says it is your responsibility, and especially if the kittens have had no medical care whatsoever, you should go elsewhere.
- **Will you provide a veterinary health certificate?** All responsible breeders will provide their buyers with veterinary health certificates, which certify that the kittens are healthy and free of diseases such as feline leukemia virus.
- **Will you provide references?** Dedicated breeders will gladly provide you with a list of happy customers. If they hedge on this, don't waste your time. Look elsewhere.
- **May I inspect your cattery?** Good breeders have nothing to hide. As long as you do not disturb nursing mothers, there should be no problem with your inspecting the cattery. A poor breeder may balk at this request because of terrible, crowded, or dirty conditions in the cattery that they don't want you to see.
- **Should I leave a deposit?** You will most likely first see a breeder's available kittens well before they are ready to leave the nest. To ensure that the kitten of your choice is still available when the time comes to take it home, the breeder may reasonably ask you for a

deposit. No breeder should ask for more than one hundred dollars up front, however, unless the kitten is of an extremely rare breed.

- **Will you accept a check or a credit card in lieu of cash?** Be wary of a breeder who does a cash-only business, as this is often the hallmark of a fly-by-night operation. Paying by check or credit card allows you to void the transaction the next day if foul play or fraud is detected.

Questions a Breeder May Ask You

Just as you should ask the breeder lots of questions, make sure the breeder asks you as many questions. Don't be offended if some of the questions seem personal. A responsible breeder who cares for her cats and kittens will want to ensure that you are going to provide a good, stable home to the kitten. Any breeder willing to sell a kitten with no questions asked cannot be providing very high-quality kittens, and certainly doesn't care about them.

Here are some sample questions you might expect a breeder to ask you, all gauged to determine how knowledgeable and responsible you are or will be as a cat owner:

- Have you ever owned a cat?
- If so, what happened to the cat?
- Was the cat spayed or neutered?
- Did the cat receive annual vaccinations?
- Did you (or will you) let the cat go outdoors?
- Have you ever been to a cat show?
- Do you have children?
- Do you have other pets?
- What attracts you about this specific breed of cat?
- Do you intend to have this cat spayed or neutered?
- Do you intend to keep this cat indoors?
- Who is your veterinarian?

The Sales Contract

Once you decide to buy, a responsible breeder should provide you with a comprehensive contract that includes the following:

- A written health guarantee, including a warranty against congenital defects
- The date of birth and a description of the kitten
- A written bill of sale that includes the price paid and the date of purchase
- Registration papers, including the kitten's registration number
- The kitten's pedigree (pedigree and registrations may be withheld until you furnish proof that you have spayed or neutered the cat)
- Any conditional clauses, including those covering altering, declawing, and indoor living only
- Instructions on diet, worming, vaccinations, and general care
- A health record of vaccinations and wormings to date

Buying from a Pet Shop

Warning: Be particularly careful about buying your kitten from a pet shop. Some (but not all) pet shops get their kittens from "kitty mills," large breeding facilities in the Midwest that pump out thousands of poor-quality kittens each year. Because these facilities are more interested in quantity than quality, an animal that comes from such a place is often not as healthy as one you would get from a private breeder. The kittens get to interact with their mothers or littermates for no more than a week or two before they are shipped off, so they are usually antisocial and very stressed. They are usually greatly overpriced as well, compared to what a local, private breeder is likely to charge. Don't be an impulse buyer, and don't support this cruel, breed-destroying business. The pet trade can be a nasty business, so take your time, and don't get taken.

Thankfully, not all pet shops deal with kitten and puppy mills. Some have become more enlightened and get their kittens from local or regional private breeders. The really enlightened ones even reserve a portion of their display areas for homeless cats and kittens that need adopting. Usually, they coordinate this effort with a local shelter, humane society, or rescue organization. Most of the cats offered for adoption are mixed breeds, but sometimes you'll find a purebred that someone has surrendered.

The pet shop staff should appear knowledgeable about their animals and be able to furnish a health history and vaccination record. If asked, they should be able to tell you where their kittens come from, as well as provide references from others who've purchased from the same place. If they seem unwilling to divulge this information, take that as a warning sign and look elsewhere.

5 Preparing for Kitty's Arrival

So, you've found the right kitty—she's adorable!—and you want to take her straight home and start your new life together. Congratulations are in order, but wait! You can't bring her home just like that; there are all sorts of supplies you're going to need and a number of preparations to be made before your new pet comes barreling in and takes over your household. This chapter will help you make the arrangements needed to welcome your new ball of fur into your life.

Pet-Supply Shopping List

Every new pet needs a few essentials to live happily in the home. Before you bring your cat home for the first time, make sure you have all you need on hand. The following is a list of items you will probably want to have around before your kitty's arrival:

- Pet carrier
- Cat food
- Food and water dishes
- Litter box
- Litter scoop
- Cat litter
- Scratching post
- Pet bed
- Grooming supplies
- Toys

Pretty much all of these items come in various styles, types, brands, and price ranges. It's going to take some more reading and research on your part to get what's best for your cat. The following sections are a great place to start, as they will provide you with some specific information about each item.

Pet Carrier

One of the first items you will need is a pet carrier to bring your new cat home in. A cardboard box with air holes will do in a pinch, but cats can eat or claw their way through this material to escape. A sturdy, plastic pet carrier or travel crate is better and provides a safer way to transport a cat in a car. Most cats do not enjoy car rides because of all the unfamiliar sounds around them. Letting your cat loose in a car is dangerous, inviting escape through an open door or window, or even an accident, if the cat gets under the control pedals or otherwise distracts the driver. Putting your cat in a pet carrier for trips to the vet or elsewhere will keep her more relaxed and safely under control. When traveling by car, secure a seatbelt around the carrier so it doesn't get tossed around inside the vehicle if an accident occurs.

E-ssential

You may want to personalize your kitty's carrier to make it more comfortable and appealing to your pet. It's a good idea to place a comfy pad or blanket in the crate for warmth and security. This will also keep your cat from sliding around on the smooth plastic floor of the carrier. As a bonus, you might choose to include a soft toy to occupy and calm your kitty when you must transport her in the carrier.

Have a pet carrier with you when you go to pick up the cat from the breeder, shelter, or private home. Most pet shops sell good-quality, well-ventilated, airline-approved travel crates. You don't necessarily need an airline-approved crate (which meets airline size requirements and fits under an airplane seat), unless you think you'll be flying with your pet. Choose a carrier that's large enough for a full-grown cat, as your kitten will soon grow into it.

Cat Food and Dishes

A good, nutritious cat food is essential to have on hand for your cat when he arrives in his new home. He may not want to eat right away. He'll want to explore his new surroundings first. But having food available will help increase his comfort level and convince him that maybe this new situation isn't so bad after all.

To avoid making a sudden dietary change, ask what the cat has been used to eating and purchase that type of food for starters. After the cat settles in, you can gradually switch to a different brand of food, if you choose. If you're buying from a breeder, she may even give you a small supply of what the kitten has been eating. Because kittens have higher protein, mineral, fat, and vitamin requirements, their food is different from an adult cat's. Nutrition and cat foods will be discussed in more detail in Chapter 8.

Food and Water Dishes

Nothing fancy needed here—a four- to six-inch-diameter bowl for food and the same for water will do just fine. Pet shops sell a variety of pet dishes. Stainless steel or ceramic dishes are preferable to plastic. Plastic dishes tend to scratch easily, and the tiny surface crevices can harbor odors and bacteria, even after washing. Some cats may find this objectionable and refuse to eat, or they may shovel the food onto the floor before eating it.

Another problem with plastic dishes is that they are lightweight and tend to slide across the floor when the cat eats, whereas, stainless steel or ceramic dishes are heavier and will stay put. When selecting ceramic dishes, make sure they're glazed with lead-free paint and food-safe. Food dishes for people meet this requirement.

Most cats prefer to eat from a shallow dish so that their whiskers do not brush the sides of the bowl. For the flat-faced breeds, such as the Persian and Himalayan, a saucer is a good choice.

Bulk Feeders

Some owners opt for an "extended feeder" type apparatus that meters either food or water down into a dish as the cat needs it. Bulk feeding, as this method is called, comes in handy if you go away overnight and can't find anyone to come in and feed the cat. However, it's not recommended for everyday use, because some cats, like some people, tend to overeat if abundant food is available, and they will get too fat when fed this way.

Dish Placement

Consider placing the cat's dishes in a spot that is easy to clean and where there will be as few interruptions as possible. Cats can be finicky eaters, so placing the food dish in a highly trafficked spot may prevent them from eating properly. A quiet corner in the kitchen is fine, as long as the area doesn't receive a lot of regular foot traffic. Do not place the food bowl near the litter box, because cats, being the clean, fastidious creatures they are, don't like to eat near where they eliminate.

Replenish fresh water daily. If you're feeding canned food, wash the food bowl after every meal with regular dishwashing liquid. Do not use bleach cleaners, as any residue could be harmful, and cats detest the lingering odor.

Litter and a Litter Box

Cats prefer to bury their waste. Because of this instinct, most cats take to using a litter box quite naturally. To take advantage, you will need to supply your cat with a litter box filled with litter. The litter box should be made of a durable plastic so that it can be easily cleaned and will not absorb and retain odors from the cat's urine and feces. If you are bringing home a kitten, consider purchasing a box that has low sides, only two to three inches high, so the little one can get in and out of it easily. Adult cats will do better with a box that is four inches high or more, to prevent them from scattering litter all over the room.

With more than one cat, do I need more than one litter box?

Absolutely. If you have more than one cat, you will need more than one litter box in your home. One litter box for each cat is the rule of thumb. This will help prevent territorial spats regarding the box and the housebreaking accidents that can ensue.

Covered litter boxes are also popular, and allow the cat some additional privacy, but many cats do not like being enclosed, probably because they feel trapped. Most covered litter boxes have a removable top, so you can try one and see if your cat likes it. If not, just use it without the top. Consider keeping the top off at first until the cat begins using the box on a regular basis.

Litter works by absorbing and submerging a cat's feces and urine, thereby reducing the growth of odor-causing bacteria. The most convenient litters are the "clumping" type, designed to collect the cat's urine into small clumps that can be scooped out and discarded. This type of litter will be the handiest and most economical for you to use, because it allows you to keep uncontaminated litter in the box while removing only the clumped material. However, clumping litters are not recommended for kittens because they tend to go through an experimentation phase where they will taste their litter. Ingesting too much litter may cause obstructions. Better to start out a kitten on a standard clay litter and switch over later to a clumping variety, when the kitten is a little older. Litter box training and the problems associated are discussed in Chapter 16.

Scratching Post

Cats scratch to shed worn claw coverings and to help visually mark their territories. Outdoor cats scratch on trees. But for an indoor cat, it is essential to provide the cat with something that is sturdy and tip-proof to scratch on a daily basis. If you don't provide an appropriate scratching area, your cat will select something of her own liking to scratch on, and you might not like her choice.

Scratching is a natural, instinctive behavior in the cat that you cannot eradicate, but you can modify and redirect it. To save your sofa or recliner from being the object of your cat's scratching passion, provide her with a tall, stable scratching post—one that is at least three feet high or taller, four to six inches in diameter, and covered with carpet, sisal, or some other textured material that will interest your cat.

Place the scratching post near where the cat sleeps or naps. Cats prefer scratching right after waking up, much the way we like to stretch. People-loving cats will prefer to have their kitty condo in the area where their owner spends the most time, so that everyone can lounge together. If you carefully consider where you place the scratching post, and don't simply stick it in some unseen corner of the basement, you will greatly improve the chances that your cat will use it. (Training a cat to use a scratching post and dealing with inappropriate scratching behaviors are covered in Chapter 16.)

For a scratching post, some owners use a standard six-inch-wide log with the bark left on, screwed down to a square wooden base to keep it vertical. Others take it up a notch and make or purchase a four- to six-foot-high elaborate "kitty condo" structure, a multileveled, carpet-covered playground that most cats love to climb and nap on. If you have room for something this large and can afford it, get one. It's an investment that will help prevent boredom and consequent destructive behaviors.

Cat Beds and Perches

You may want your cat to sleep in your bed with you, and that's fine. But for those of you who prefer not to share the bed, you may want to invest in some type of cat bed—something comfy and warm enough for the cat to want to curl up on. Check out the pet shops, and get something that has a washable cover and is large enough for the cat to stretch out on. Don't spend too much, because cats are finicky and often turn their noses up at beds of our design. They prefer to define what they consider a bed, which is usually yours, or a comfy chair. You don't want to get stuck with a forty-dollar empty cat bed. Cats tend to alternate their sleeping locations from time to time, too.

In addition to a fluffy bed, a great product you might consider is a window perch. This is a nice luxury that gives your cat a convenient way to view the outside world, and it can help prevent wear and tear on your furnishings. Let's face it: indoor cats are going to try to look out any window within reach, whether they have to jump up on your antique table or sofa to do it. Providing them with their own viewing platform, conveniently placed in full view of a bird feeder, will afford hours of stimulation, and a nice napping site.

Most pet stores or pet supply catalogs sell carpeted window perches that mount easily on window sills without need of screws or other hardware. One major caution regarding their use is to avoid letting cats look out on the world through window screens. Most window screening is so flimsy that cats can easily claw through it and escape to the outdoors, if they are motivated strongly enough. At the very least, they will rip holes in the screen while chasing after a fluttering moth on the other side. Every year, cats fall through window screens from high-rise apartments and suffer serious injury or death, so it's best to keep windows closed or brace screens with sturdy, protective grid work.

Toys

An indoor cat will need plenty of stimulation in his new home to keep busy while you are gone. Playing with your cat is also important and fun, as it is a way to bond with your feline friend. Catnip-filled mice, balls, and teaser toys are the usual choices at the pet store. But you don't have to spend a lot of money on toys.

Try giving your cat a cardboard box or paper grocery bag. Most cats love to play hide-and-seek and go nuts for the crunchy sound of the paper. You can even try a wind-up toy that scoots around the floor on its own spring power, but make sure it is nontoxic. My cats loving chasing bottle caps across the kitchen floor, but beware, most of them disappear forever under the refrigerator.

The most important thing to consider about a cat toy is its safety. Cats, like kids, play rough with toys and will swallow things they shouldn't. So avoid toys that appear to be breakable, or that have glued-on buttons for eyes or sewn-on bells, as these items are easily ripped off and swallowed.

Fishing-rod-style toys that you can use to toss a feather lure to your cat and reel her in are fabulous for an interactive play session between yourself and your cat, but these should be shut safely away in a closet or cupboard when you are not present. If left out for cats to play with unsupervised, any toy with string as a component poses a strangulation risk. Plus, there's the possibility of the string getting wrapped too tightly around a tail or leg and cutting off vital circulation.

Never allow your cat to play with balls of yarn or string of any kind. Not only is there danger of entanglement, but once a cat starts swallowing string-like material, he cannot stop until he gets to the end of it. The stuff amasses in the gut and can cause a life-threatening blockage, called string enteritis. Should you discover string dangling from your cat's mouth, resist the urge to pull it out. Pulling on string that is wound among the cat's intestines can cause fatal internal injury. Instead, seek veterinary help immediately.

Catnip-filled toys are a favorite standby for cats, but not all cats care for catnip. Some cats lack the gene that makes them respond to the plant's intoxicating effects, and they show no marked reaction when confronted with it. Cats that have the catnip gene go temporarily wild in the plant's presence, rolling and frolicking ecstatically before dozing off in a state of drunken bliss. The substance in the perennial herb that elicits this peculiar response is called nepetalactone. The effect wears off in a short time and does not appear to be addictive or harmful. Nor does the plant seem to impair a cat's normal senses while under the influence, as an unfamiliar sound or scent will immediately snap a catnip-sloshed cat back to a fully alert state.

Grooming Supplies

Grooming is an important part of cat ownership, especially if you have chosen a longhaired feline. Longhaired cats need daily grooming to prevent their fur from matting into clumps, whereas, shorthaired cats require far less. If you start grooming at an early age, you will help your kitten grow accustomed to being handled and checked for parasites or injury. Approached correctly, this gentle, regular handling often becomes an enjoyable bonding experience for both of you.

The grooming supplies you'll need will depend on whether your cat has long or short hair. These items are discussed in the following sections.

Brushes

Regular brushing helps remove loose, dead hairs from the cat's coat, can reduce the occurrence of hairballs, and helps keep your home hair-free. Choose a soft, slicker-type brush for your shorthaired cat. This will get the job done and not feel harsh on the cat's skin. For a cat with long hair, choose a brush that more closely resembles one that a human with long hair might use. Your local pet shop will have a wide assortment.

Combs

Frequent combing is not necessary for a shorthaired cat, but any long-haired cat will need to be combed out daily after being brushed. Combing removes mats and tangles, which, when not dealt with, can become irritating and painful to the cat's skin, and may have to be cut out with scissors, ruining the look of your cat's coat. Consider getting both a wide-toothed comb and a fine-toothed comb. Use the wide comb first, then follow up with the narrow. Any pet shop will have what you need.

Nail Clippers

Cat claws grow just like our fingernails, and will occasionally need trimming. If left too long, they can unduly damage your furnishings and carpet, and even give you a scratch or two. If you start trimming his nails during kittenhood, your cat will learn to tolerate the process, provided you don't cut the claws too short into the quick, which hurts. You can use "human" nail clippers, but consider purchasing a set specifically designed for cats. How to clip your cat's nails is discussed in Chapter 11.

Scissors

Some active longhaired cats will get mats in their hair, no matter how diligently you brush and comb them. If you cannot split a mat with your fingers, and then gently comb it out, you may need to cut it out with scissors or shave it off with electric pet trimmers. Some people use a mat splitter, which you can buy in pet stores, or a seam ripper, which you can buy at sewing supply stores. Just exercise caution and take great care not to poke, cut, or injure a wriggling cat with these sharp tools while you are working on the mat.

Shampoo and Conditioner

Unless you intend to show your cat, bathing her is not something you'll need to do often. Cats are naturally clean creatures, which is fortunate, because most of them loathe baths anyway. You may need to bathe your kitty, however, if she gets into something particularly dirty or oily, or if she develops a flea infestation. If you decide to forgo hiring a groomer and do it yourself, you will need to have a good cat shampoo on hand. Purchase a shampoo at your pet shop that is labeled for safe use on cats. Do not use products for humans, as they will be irritating to your cat's skin, and may even make your cat sick. Do not use dog products, as these are often too strong for cats and may be harmful as well. How to give your cat a bath is discussed in Chapter 11.

Harness and Leash

Believe it or not, it is possible to teach your cat to walk outside with you on a harness and leash. Doing so will allow your homebound kitty to have supervised access to the outside world. If this is begun during kittenhood, most cats will take to it quite well, especially if you approach the idea with patience and kindness. Consider waiting until your kitten is four to five months old before purchasing a special cat harness. (Don't get a dog harness, because cats easily figure out how to slip out of them.) By then your pet will be feeling safe and secure with you, and will be large enough to fit into an adjustable harness that can be used into its adulthood. The leash should be four to five feet long and made of lightweight material.

6 A Cat-Safe Home

One of the easiest ways to prevent injury and illness in your cat is to ensure that his home environment is safe, secure, clean, and escape proof. A home that has toxic plants, chemicals, and dangerous substances left out in the open is one that will almost certainly cause your cat to become ill at some time. Remember that cats are curious about their environment and will investigate everything, sniffing, touching, and tasting whatever they can. It is your job to protect your cat from harm, just as you would with a child.

A Safe, Clean Environment

Keeping the home clean and free of infectious germs is an important step in preventing poor health in your cat. Here are some simple steps that will go a long way toward safeguarding your cat:

- Dust and vacuum often to help keep infectious spores and parasites at bay.
- Keep the cat's litter box scooped as free of waste as possible.
- Change the litter completely at least once a week.
- Regularly wash the cat's food and water dishes to minimize bacterial buildup.
- Provide clean, fresh water each day.
- Resist the temptation to bring strays into your home, as they can be hosts to diseases and parasites that could infect your resident cat.
- Do not encourage strays to come around your home by leaving food and water out for them (which will also attract rodents, raccoons, possums, and skunks).
- Do not allow your cat to come into contact with any aggressive animals. Even a relative's or neighbor's dog that seems otherwise friendly might not take kindly to your cat.
- Remove glass or breakable items from tables, shelves, and bookcases that an exploring cat might knock over and get cut on. Display fragile keepsakes in glass-encased curio cabinets to keep them and your cat safe.

These are just a few of the preventative measures you can take for your kitty. The following sections will go into more detail about cat-proofing your home and yard.

Cat-Proofing the Indoors

Before bringing a cat into your home, make the home environment safer for a small animal. Cats (especially kittens) are curious creatures and will get into every accessible nook and cranny of your home, including the tops of appliances, cupboards, and pieces of furniture that no puppy or dog could ever dream of getting to. While it's hard to think of everything that could possibly happen, imagine that you are childproofing your home and take similar precautions that you would for a child to ensure your cat's safety.

Following are some steps that you can take to safeguard your feline's new environment before it comes home.

Seal Off Escape Routes

Check all possible escape routes, making sure that the cat has no way of accessing the outdoors. This includes making sure all window and door screens are strong, sturdy, and secure enough to prevent a cat from pushing, clawing, or falling through them. Many screens are made of material that is thin and flimsy enough for a cat to chew or claw through. Unless you can keep the windows closed at all times, you may need to consider bracing flimsy screens or replacing them with a sturdier, more tight-fitting product. This is especially important in high-rise apartment buildings, where cats often fall through windows or off balconies from many stories high and are either killed or sustain serious injuries.

Speaking of open balconies, don't tie your cat out on one to enjoy the outdoors and leave it there unattended. In all likelihood, the cat will fall or leap from the balcony and will certainly hang itself if it is tethered. Never tie a cat anywhere and leave it unattended.

E-Fact

If a cat escapes to the outdoors within the first few days of arriving at its new home, it won't yet have a clear sense of where "home" is. It could easily become lost or get killed. Even a cat that lives strictly indoors can get lost easily outdoors, because the outside is all strange and unfamiliar territory. That's why it's important to microchip your cat or use some other form of pet identification.

Secure Cupboards

Install childproof locks on the cupboards and drawers, even on ones that contain no dangerous materials. You do not want the cat to learn how to open these, or get into something potentially toxic. You also do not want to come home to find the pantry open and flour, sugar, cereal, dry cat food, and a host of other foodstuffs strewn all around the home.

Electrical Hazards

Install baby guard plugs on unused electric sockets. A curious little paw could enter far enough in to get a fatal surprise. Minimize the number and availability of power cords and wires in the home. Kittens will play with and possibly gnaw on them, and in doing so may be shocked or killed by electrocution. Put wires under carpets when possible, or tack them securely along moldings or under furniture. Another solution is to run them through plastic piping available at your local home-improvement store.

String and Strangling Hazards

Few people think of window and drapery cords as hazards, but they can be to a frolicking kitten that becomes entangled in a dangling cord and accidentally hangs or strangles itself. Tie them up out of reach.

Those little basketball nets that fit neatly over trash cans in children's rooms also pose a risk to a curious kitten that might innocently fall or climb into the net and become entangled. Put away such items when not in use, or get rid of them altogether.

Some cats develop a habit of chewing wool and other fabrics. This is sometimes seen in the Siamese, but all breeds (including mixed breeds) are capable of developing this bizarre habit. Although it is not clearly understood why some cats do this, the habit may be initiated by scent deposits left on the fabric. In other words, if your scent has permeated a piece of clothing, your cat may chew on it as a celebration of familiarity. This behavior should be discouraged. As a precaution, do not leave sweaters and other loose clothing lying about the house. If you see your cat going for a sweater or other piece of clothing in this manner, spray the animal with clean water from a spray bottle. Cats that swallow too much fabric can suffer intestinal blockages.

Stow away all sewing supplies, pins, needles, string, yarns, spools of thread, artists' paints, and other crafts when not in use. Cats investigate everything and will play with anything that's easy to bat about. It's up to you to keep them away from objects that could be ingested with potentially deadly consequences.

Chemical Hazards

Everyone has household cleaners, bleach, insecticides, drain cleaners, floor cleaners, or solvents under their kitchen sinks or in their cupboards. Such products are all potentially toxic to your cat, especially bleach and pine-based cleaners. Get in the habit of reading the warning labels on household products. The label typically states the dangers to domestic animals and children. Heed those warnings, and if you're not sure whether a product is toxic, assume that it is.

Remove all potentially toxic chemicals from the cat's domain, or store them securely in locked, inaccessible cabinets. Do not assume that something stored high up on a shelf is out of the cat's reach. New cat owners used to owning only dogs can be especially vulnerable to this mistake. Don't forget, cats can jump and climb!

Cats also lick themselves a lot, being naturally clean creatures. It's relatively easy for them to ingest poisons simply by walking across a freshly mopped or waxed floor, then licking the damp chemical matter off their paws. Or, they may brush against a dirty, leaky container of paint or bleach and then lick the icky substance off their fur. To avoid such incidents, keep cats out of freshly cleaned areas until floors and counters are completely dried. Read labels on all household and chemical products and heed all warnings regarding use around domestic animals.

Pest-Control Products

Don't place bait for snails, insects, or rodents where your cat might get at them and get poisoned. What's bad for pests is generally bad for your cat as well. Rodent baits sometimes contain a chemical called warfarin, which can cause fatal hemorrhaging in animals that ingest it. A cat can still get poisoned if it ingests a mouse that consumed the bait. So read label warnings carefully on all pest-control products before you use them. If you contract with a professional pest-control company for this job, ask if the products they use are safe for pets, and get that in writing.

Cosmetics and Medicines

Keep perfumes, cosmetics, nail-polish removers, vitamins and all medicines tightly closed and put away in a cabinet or medicine chest. Never give any human medications to cats without a veterinarian's supervision. Common over-the-counter preparations such as aspirin and especially acetaminophen can be highly toxic, even deadly, to cats. Don't leave these medications or their containers sitting out on a countertop with loose caps where your cat can knock them over and get to them. If you drop any medicines, including vitamins, on the floor, make sure you pick up the pills or clean up spills immediately. Don't leave them lying around for a curious cat to ingest accidentally.

Household Appliances

Dryers and refrigerators probably pose the greatest hazards to indoor cats, as far as appliances go. Many cats are killed each year after being accidentally trapped inside a dryer, apparently seeking a warm, cozy place to sleep. Refrigerators, of course, entice with the smells of all sorts of food. Before shutting the door of any major appliance, look to make sure your cat hasn't jumped in unnoticed. Unplug small appliances, such as irons and coffee makers, when not in use, and don't allow cords to dangle and tempt a playful cat. The cat could get electrocuted or pull the appliance down on top of itself.

E-ssential

Don't leave hot stove burners, pots cooking, or teakettles boiling unwatched. If your cat should leap up onto the stove when you're not in the kitchen, it may suffer burns or accidentally knock over a hot, scalding pan. To avoid such mishaps, teach your cat to stay off of stovetops and kitchen counters.

Toilets and sump pumps pose a drowning hazard for young kittens that are too small to climb or jump out once they've fallen in. Make it a rule in your household to keep toilet lids down at all times, and cover sump pumps or securely enclose them to prevent your kitten from falling in and drowning.

Trash Receptacles

Even the trash cans in your kitchen and bathroom can harbor potential hazards. Think about the things you discard: old razor blades, broken glass, used dental floss (which poses a string ingestion hazard), spoiled food, chicken bones, jagged-edge tin cans, empty household product containers, and so forth. All of these things can be hazardous to a foraging cat that gets into the leaky, soupy mess. So keep tight-fitting lids on all trash bins, indoors and outdoors.

Toxic Plants

Although carnivorous by nature, cats like to snack on grass and other greenery. There's a common assumption that the roughage helps purge the digestive system of hairballs. True or not, cats will chew on houseplants. While many plants are harmless to cats, others are deadly and can kill, even in small amounts. If you enjoy having both cats and houseplants, you need to know which plants you can have in and around your home safely.

You can help satisfy your cat's urge to nibble on houseplants by providing it with its own planter of cat grass. Pet shops often sell kitty grass seeds and kits for this purpose, or you can simply plant some grass seed in a container and grow it in a sunny window for your cat to nibble at will.

Ingestion of a toxic plant can cause a variety of symptoms, including drooling, vomiting, diarrhea, convulsions, lethargy, and coma. If your cat displays any unusual symptoms after chewing on a houseplant, contact your veterinarian immediately.

Here is a list of some common plants that can poison your cat:

- Azalea
- Bean plants
- Cactus
- Crocus
- Daffodil
- Dieffenbachia
- Hemlock
- Hydrangea
- Ivy
- Lily
- Marijuana
- Mistletoe
- Mushrooms
- Narcissus
- Nightshade
- Oleander
- Philodendron
- Poinsettia
- Potato leaves

- Rhododendron
- Tobacco
- Tomato leaves
- Walnuts
- Yew

If you are unsure about a particular plant's toxicity, ask your veterinarian. The National Animal Poison Control Information Center also offers a comprehensive list of plants toxic to cats on their Web site at *www.aspca.org*. The center's phone number is listed in the reference section in the back of this book.

Dangers in the Yard

If you've made the wise decision to keep your cat safely indoors at all times, you won't need to worry as much about the outdoor hazards. But for cats that go outside, you need to be aware that there are many potential hazards close to home, in your backyard and driveway.

Lawn Chemicals

Freshly applied weed killers, fungicides, fertilizers, and other lawn-care chemicals can poison cats that walk in treated areas, then lick the substance off their paws. If you apply these to your lawn, read the product label for precautions related to domestic animals. Generally, you shouldn't let your cat out on the grass after such a treatment until at least the first rain has rinsed the chemicals into the ground.

Likewise, read outdoor pesticide product labels carefully before using and take note of any precautionary statements pertaining to domestic animals. If you use a professional lawn service, ask if the products they use are harmful to pets, and get their statement in writing.

Outdoor Ponds and Pools

Swimming pools and ponds are just as hazardous for pets as they are for children, so treat them accordingly. While most adult cats can swim, many drown in pools because they can't reach or get a grip on a ledge where they can climb out, and the they drown from the exhaustion of trying to tread water after a long period. Kittens are particularly vulnerable, so closely supervise all pets (and children) around bodies of water. Remember that fencing around a pool doesn't necessarily make it safe, because cats can climb over, under, or through most fences.

Antifreeze

The antifreeze in your car is deadly poisonous to animals, and it only takes a taste of the sweet, deadly substance to kill. Ethylene glycol is the toxic ingredient. Unfortunately, by the time an owner realizes something is wrong with a cat that has ingested antifreeze, grave injury has already been done.

Getting hit by a car is one of the greatest dangers for the outdoor cat. But even parked cars pose a potential hazard that many people are unaware of. Because car engines stay warm for hours after use, some cats in winter will crawl up under the hoods to sleep. When the engine is started, the fan blades and other moving parts can inflict fatal injuries. To prevent such a tragedy, keep your cat safely inside during the winter. Before starting a car on a cold day, knock on the hood a few times to awaken any sleepers.

The so-called safer antifreeze products on the market replace ethylene glycol with propylene glycol, which is still toxic, but significantly less so than ethylene glycol. Use one of these products in your car, if possible, and keep your car's hoses in good repair. Always clean up any fluid leaks and spills right away. In doing so, you'll help protect not only your own cat, but also the other pets and wildlife in your neighborhood that might be tempted to lick the poison.

Holiday Hazards

Holiday decorations, such as poinsettia, holly berries, and mistletoe can be toxic to cats. Your cat won't be as tempted to gnaw on the artificial variety. However, if you must use real decorations, restrict your cat's access to the decorated areas.

Cats will sometimes try to climb the Christmas tree. Again, using an artificial one helps discourage this inclination. Or, you can insert a hook in the wall or ceiling near the tree and tie it so that a climbing cat can't possibly topple it.

If you put up a real tree, do not add any chemicals to the Christmas tree water. Some people add aspirin or commercial preservatives to keep the tree fresh longer, but these chemicals can be lethal to cats if they lap the water from the tree base.

Safer Decorating

Here are some easy ways to help make Christmas-tree decorations safer for your cat:

- Don't hang breakable ornaments on lower branches; cats will playfully bat them off.
- Don't use foil icicles; cats like to eat them, but they're as unsafe as string.
- Avoid angel hair, artificial snow, edible ornaments, and small plastic beads or berries that cats can swallow easily.
- Avoid using wrapping ribbon on packages; again, this poses a danger like string.
- Keep lighting cords out of reach and unplugged when not in use to prevent electrocution.

Holiday Foods and Spirits

If you want your cat to share some Thanksgiving turkey, a few cooked scraps are fine, but remove any bones. Bones can get caught in the throat and cause choking, or jagged pieces can puncture the gut, causing life-threatening complications. Highly seasoned foods may cause diarrhea and stomach upset, so avoid sharing those with your cat.

Alcohol is toxic to cats, even in small amounts, so don't share food scraps cooked in wine or sherry. Also, be mindful of any unattended alcoholic beverages or spiked eggnog left sitting around on tabletops that may tempt your cat to taste. Chocolate also is toxic to cats, so keep desserts and candy dishes covered.

Other Celebrations

Other holidays and special occasions can be hazardous, too. Halloween, for example, is particularly dangerous for black cats allowed to roam outdoors. The Fourth of July fireworks probably scare more dogs than cats, but some cats may panic at the loud noise and run away. Party guests, tipsy or not, may accidentally step on, sit on, or trip over a cat that's underfoot, or let the cat escape out an open door.

At times like this, give your cat's well-being special consideration. If necessary, shut your cat safely away in one room of the house with all its favorite amenities and let it have some time alone until the party is over.

7 Kitty Comes Home

When you first bring your new cat or kitten home, allow yourself and the animal some quiet, quality time together to get acquainted. This will help make your new pet feel at ease before you rush back to work and leave the little tyke alone all day—something a kitten under ten weeks of age has yet to experience. Even an adult cat will need some quality time with you to bond and feel comfortable in its strange new surroundings.

Special Arrangements for the First Few Days

The best possible scenario is to bring the kitten or cat home at the beginning of a vacation. A week or two together will really help the two of you bond. If a week or two is not possible, try to at least have a three-day weekend coincide with the cat's arrival. The cat will have a chance to explore its new environment, while you get to observe its behaviors and begin to know it as an individual. Each cat is unique and will have its own peculiar habits. During this time, the cat will also begin to learn the "dos and don'ts" of living with you. Having a week or two to accomplish this "settling in" will benefit both of you.

E-ssential

One of the first things you will want to do once you get your new pet is check with local law authorities to find out what, if any, licensing requirements exist for cats in your area. Some localities require dog and cat owners to obtain a license for their pets. Licensing fees are usually minimal (in the range of $8 to $25), but costs depend on the area.

You can expect that your new cat or kitten will be confused and lonely at first in its new surroundings. A kitten especially will miss its mother and siblings. If your new pet is having a tough time, try a few of the following methods to make the adjustment period easier:

- Provide toys for it to play with and investigate. Something as simple as a brown paper bag (not plastic, as these pose a suffocation risk) or a large cardboard box will amuse a kitten for hours.
- Offer ample food and fresh water.
- Provide lots of gentle, loving attention if the cat seems open to it.
- Consider allowing the cat to sleep with you, or at least next to your bed on a bed of its own, for the first day or two.

- Keep a radio on while you are gone. Tune it to a talk radio station, and keep the volume low. This will give the cat the feeling that it is not alone.

Showing Your New Cat Where Everything Is

Show the new feline where all the necessities are located. The food and water dishes, which most owners place in a low-traffic corner of the kitchen, should already have some food and water in them to get the cat's attention right off. Place the cat in front of them and let it dig in if it wants to (although it might not at first, due to a slight case of the nerves).

Show the cat where its litter box is located. Most owners place this in a laundry room or bathroom that gets the least amount of use. Set the cat down in the box, then scratch your fingers in it a few times (making sure that the litter is fresh and clean, of course!). Even if your pet is just a ten-week-old kitten, it will almost certainly have already had some experience using a box, and should catch on quickly. Make sure that you leave the door to the room open so the cat has regular access to its litter box. The easiest way to create a house-soiling problem is to forget to leave that door open!

If an Accident Occurs

It's not unusual for a new kitten to have an "accident" in the house before it learns the routine and gets settled in. If this happens, don't get too upset about it. Just clean up the mess right away, and remove the odor so the scent won't continue to attract the cat back to the same spot.

To do this, you'll need to visit your local pet supply store and select one of several odor neutralizing enzymatic products available. These products are specifically formulated to remove pet stains and dissolve house-soiling odors. You can also mix some white vinegar with warm water, rub it well into the area, and blot dry. If the carpet is soiled, make sure you deep clean enough to reach the mat underneath, where the urine soaked through. Avoid using ammonia-based household cleaners, as ammonia is a urine by-product, and that scent will attract the cat back to the spot.

Sleeping Quarters

Show the cat where its new bed is. Many cats take quickly to a nice, soft cat bed, while others decide on some other spot to snooze in(often they pick your bed or your favorite chair). Cats also tend to rotate their sleeping spots from time to time. If you don't want the cat to sleep on the sofa or other particular furnishings, make these areas off limits from the outset, or cover them until the cat settles into a sleeping place and routine of its own. If you don't want the cat to sleep with you, keep your bedroom door shut.

Scratching Post

Show the cat where its scratching post is and start training the cat to use it from day one. Place the cat on the post and gently pump its paws back and forth in a mock scratching motion. If necessary, rub some dried catnip on the post to entice the cat to use it. If you catch the cat scratching somewhere else, say "No" sharply and loudly to startle it and make it stop. Then pick up the cat and carry it to its scratching post. Do not punish the cat or continue to scold as you carry it to the scratching post, or it will develop a negative association with the very place where you want it to scratch. Pet, praise, and reward the cat when it uses the scratching post appropriately. The key is to give the scratching post a positive association.

Family Introductions

Talk to your children before the cat's arrival and teach them to quietly and gently approach the cat, only if it seems open to the attention. An adult cat especially will not appreciate small, unpredictable children running around nosily, teasing, and pulling at its tail. The cat may even scratch or bite in self-defense if it is handled too roughly.

Children

Children can offer the cat a choice treat or a cat toy. If the cat seems tentative, just let it investigate its new home while you and your children watch passively. The goal here is to start the child/cat relationship off on the right foot. If the cat is frightened or mishandled on the first day, it will not forget it, and may never be open to contact with children again.

E-ssential

Try to have your home as quiet as possible for the new cat's arrival. Do not have the radio or television blaring, and don't throw a wild party or host a family reunion. Avoid bringing the cat home on a day that construction workers with jackhammers are thundering away right outside. Finally, do not bring kitty home on the day that the gardeners are out in full force with their lawnmowers and annoying leaf blowers.

Kittens will be more playful and open to contact, but remember that they are small and frail, and can be easily panicked or injured if dropped or handled carelessly. That's why it's important to supervise all contact between cats and kids, until you're certain that they've adjusted and know how to interact properly.

Resident Pets

It is a good idea to temporarily restrict any pets you currently have to a part of the home away from where the new cat will first be kept. They will be curious and probably concerned in a territorial sense, but if introduced too soon, they may fight, frighten, or hurt the newcomer. When you bring the cat home, release it in a separate room and let it live there for a day or two. Provide food, water, and a litter box and make it comfortable, but restrict the new pet to this smaller area temporarily. This mini quarantine period allows time for the house smell to settle on the new cat, masking the other strange odors from where it was previously. This tactic will help make the newcomer more acceptable to your resident pets when the time comes to introduce them.

Resident Cats

After a few days, consider briefly introducing the new cat to the resident cats for about ten or fifteen minutes, with the new cat secured safely in its travel crate. This allows the resident animals to become accustomed to the new cat's smell and vice versa. Repeat this procedure several times over the next few days, gradually lengthening the contact period. During this time, the new cat should be living in the restricted room, still separated from the others.

Finally, when it seems that everyone is calm and accustomed to each other's presence, begin letting the animals interact for brief periods with the new cat out of the crate. Supervise all contact during these times, but be careful. If they fight, you could get scratched or bitten. During the brief initial interactions, have a large glass of water handy to douse the animals if they really get into it. That normally breaks up most fights. Do not expect them to be best buddies right away; however, they should begin to at least tolerate each other's presence after a few weeks.

At some point, there likely will be territorial conflicts between the resident cats and the new cat, particularly if the new cat is an adult. They will need to readjust their hierarchy to fit the new cat into their ranks. This is why it is generally much easier to introduce a kitten into a household with other resident cats. A kitten always ranks subordinate to the adults and, therefore, is perceived as less of a threat. In most cases, adult cats will not harm a kitten; however, you must still supervise all physical contact until it's clear that they've accepted one another.

The Resident Dog

Always consider your motivations with care if you plan to bring a cat into a home with a resident dog, even if that dog has had previous good experience with cats. Chances are that the cat has not had any exposure to dogs, and will be terrified and very hostile. A kitten will have a better chance of bonding with a cat-friendly dog, but it still can be risky, particularly with certain breeds of dogs that are naturally more aggressive or that have strong predatory instincts toward small animals.

If the resident dog is a puppy, or was raised from puppyhood with cats, then you have a better chance of getting him and the new cat to bond. Otherwise, you may wind up with a badly hurt kitty. And by all means do not get a new cat if you know the resident dog is aggressive to other animals! If you have any doubts as to whether your dog will tolerate a cat, consult a professional dog trainer for advice.

Allow the dog to see and sniff the new cat in its crate at first. Then, when it's time to let the new cat venture out of the crate, keep the dog on a leash and under your control for all initial physical contact for a while. To avoid any food squabbles, do not feed the cat near the dog. Never leave the two alone together unsupervised until you are certain that they have adjusted and accepted one another as friends.

Certain breeds of dogs are highly prey-driven and should not be trusted with a cat companion, even from late puppyhood. Of course, there are many exceptions, and many dogs become lifelong friends with cats. However, you should carefully weigh your decision to get a cat, have a professional dog trainer evaluate your dog's temperament before you do so, and proceed with great caution if you own one of the following dog breeds:

- Afghan
- Akbash
- Akita
- Australian Cattle Dog
- Bedlington Terrier
- Borzoi
- Chesapeake Bay Retriever
- Chow Chow
- German Shepherd
- Great Dane
- Great Pyrenees
- Greyhound

- Komondor
- Kuvasz
- Malamute
- Mastiff
- Pitbull
- Puli
- Rottweiler
- Shar-Pei
- Siberian Husky
- Terriers (most breeds)

Setting a Basic Routine

Cats like routine. Being creatures of habit, they depend on their environment being predictable and safe, with no hidden surprises or unexpected trauma. To that end, try to establish a predictable, scheduled routine for your cat, after all the initial introductions and adjustments are completed.

What's in a Routine?

Here are some things you can do to create a routine for your cat and make it feel more secure and comfortable:

- Feed the cat at the same time and place each day.
- Groom your cat at the same time and place each day.
- Play with your cat at about the same time each day, when you come home from work or when you get up in the morning.
- Try to wake up and go to sleep at fairly predictable times.
- Be fair and consistent about house rules.

Once you have your new cat settled in at home, you will want to begin establishing some basic behavior patterns for it. The cat won't magically know how you expect it to behave in your home. As discussed, you will have to show it where the litter box is located. You will have to teach it to use a scratching post, instead of shredding your sofa. If you do not want the cat in the room with the four thousand dollar sofa, never allow the cat access to that room. That's only fair. If you don't like for your cat to jump on the kitchen table or counters, you'll have to teach it that these are forbidden areas.

E-Fact

Several feline behavior-modification sprays and cat repellents are available at pet stores or through veterinarians to help you keep your cat off of furniture and other areas. Some of these products use herbal ingredients, while others use pheromones, natural chemicals that influence animal behavior. Used as directed, such products may sometimes be helpful in halting inappropriate scratching and urine spraying, or in calming cats in stressful situations.

Quiet Time

Allow the cat some privacy when needed (your cat will let you know when it wants to be alone). Although activity is important to keep your cat fit and alert, rest is also essential. Cats, especially kittens, need a good amount of sleep, usually over fourteen hours each day, to prevent illness and stress. Typically, they do not sleep straight through, but rather in short "cat naps" throughout the day.

Some cats like to sleep in a sunny location, while others opt for a darker spot. Try not to disturb a sleeping cat. You wouldn't want to be rudely awakened, so have the same respect for your cat. If you have children, explain to them that the cat needs rest just as they do, and tell them not to bother the cat while it's sleeping.

Providing a Stable Environment

Cats do not like surprises. They like a safe, predictable environment free of any perceived dangers. They like to know their home is just the way they left it the day before. Cats do not respond well to new, unusual, or unpredictable events. They get stressed out by moving, remodeling, or other changes in their environment. This dislike of unexpected events is a key ingredient in the feline psyche, and must be appeased by the owner in order to keep a happy, stress-free pet. For instance, if you regularly foster strange animals for short periods of time, it can be very upsetting to your kitty and may result in fighting and other displacement behaviors, such as scratching furniture, marking, and soiling outside the litter box.

Likewise, inviting a host of human guests into your home too frequently can confuse and upset your cat, who won't be expecting the intrusion on its territory. Try to avoid blaring music and raucous parties, and your cat will be happier. On those occasions when you must entertain, tuck your cat safely away in a quiet, secluded area of the house, and do not let your guests bother it.

You will want to create an atmosphere of mutual trust and cooperation, and have as little friction as possible between you. Keep an eye on your cat's health. Try to develop a bond with it and be there for it when it wants your affection or attention. In return, your cat will give you years of satisfying companionship, trust, and respect.

When Things Don't Work Out

Sometimes, despite your best efforts to introduce a new pet into your household, things just don't work out as planned. If the problem involves some undesirable behavior on the cat's part that you can't cope with, consult a professional for advice before you give up on the cat completely. Your veterinarian can help or can recommend an animal behaviorist. Often, owners really don't understand how to train their cats, or they are inconsistent in their methods, which serves only to confuse the cat and make the problem worse. A discussion with your veterinarian or an animal behaviorist can sometimes help unravel what's really happening and get both you and your pet headed down a better path together.

Finding a New Home

If you decide that you and the cat must part ways for whatever reason, make every effort to place the cat in a good home before you surrender it to a shelter. Advertise the cat in your local newspaper classifieds, or put a photo and description on the bulletin board at your office. Ask a friend or relative to consider giving the cat a good home. Or, if your cat is a purebred, contact a breed rescue organization specific to your cat's breed. Information about breed rescue organizations is usually available on the Internet, or you can try calling one of the cat registering associations. If you purchased the cat from a breeder or pet shop, there should be a return agreement of some sort. Reputable breeders will nearly always take back cats from their bloodlines, regardless of how much time has passed, so make sure you keep the seller's contact information.

Putting the Cat Up for Adoption

As a last resort, surrender the cat to an animal shelter for adoption, but don't just dump it off there without first attempting to place the cat yourself. Select a no-kill shelter, if your area has one. These types of shelters do not euthanize animals after a period of time, but instead put them in foster homes until they can be adopted. Give the shelter personnel as much history and background on the cat as you can, which may improve its chances of being adopted by someone else. And please, never abandon a cat or drop it by the roadside and expect it to be able to survive on its own. Doing so only condemns the animal to a cruel death.

8 Feline Feeding Basics

Cats are carnivorous by nature, meaning that they must eat meat to survive and remain healthy. In the wild, much of a cat's energy is directed toward hunting. Obtaining food is an elemental part of the cat's psyche. In homes with multiple cats, owners must often place more than one food dish down in order to avoid problems with food aggression. But equally as important in the way you feed your cat is what you feed your cat, the quality of the food and your knowledge of how your cat's nutritional needs will change over the course of its lifetime.

Commercial Cat Foods

Commercial cat foods are formulated to provide complete and balanced nutrition, and there are a variety of different formulas that meet the needs of various life stages of the cat. Cat food comes in three basic types: canned, dry, and semi-moist.

Canned Foods

Canned foods are normally highly nutritious and have a long shelf life. They are more expensive than dry food, however, and tend to be about 70 percent water. If you decide on a supermarket or pet-shop brand of canned food, make sure it has your vet's approval.

Many owners decide to feed their cats dry food and supplement it daily with some canned food to increase the available amounts of protein and fatty acids. This is a less expensive alternative to a canned-only diet and gives the cat some variety. In addition, most cats prefer to nibble throughout the day, unlike dogs, who wolf down their food at one sitting. So leaving out a little dry or semi-moist food for a cat to eat whenever it feels hungry satisfies this tendency. Just be careful not to overfeed.

Dry Foods

Dry food is more economical than canned food. It has a long shelf life owing to its low water content. It will also stay fresher longer (without being smelly) in your cat's bowl than will canned food, making it a better choice if you tend to leave food out all day. Dry food also helps keep your cat's teeth somewhat cleaner, due to its abrasive quality.

If you choose to feed your kitten or cat a dry food, opt for the higher-quality premium brands, rather than a generic store brand. The premium brands cost more, but their ingredients are generally more stable, of higher quality, and overall more digestible.

Semi-Moist Foods

Semi-moist foods are often used as an alternative to canned. They are lighter and easier to store, and very palatable to most cats. These foods tend to be on the expensive side, however, and often contain preservatives, artificial coloring, binders, and sugar. In addition, they do not help scour the cat's teeth the way dry foods do.

Are pet foods regulated?

Yes. The Association of American Feed Control Officials (AAFCO) establishes nutrient and labeling requirements for pet foods and works closely with the Food and Drug Administration's Center for Veterinary Medicine (FDA-CVM) to set standards for the production and quality of animal foods. The AAFCO's labeling guidelines help ensure that the information stated on pet-food labels is accurate and not misleading to consumers. The AAFCO's Web site is *www.aafco.org*.

What to Look for on a Label

Most people don't read cat-food labels when making a selection for their pet, but a lot of effort goes into making sure that information is as accurate as possible. When selecting a food, it helps to know what certain words and phrases mean. The statement, "100% complete and balanced nutrition for adult cats and kittens" means, by AAFCO labeling standards, that the food contains all nutrients (it is complete) cats and kittens need in the right proportions (it is balanced). If some variation of a "complete and balanced" claim does not appear on the label, assume the food isn't.

Pet-food companies must be able to back up any claim they make on the label. They can substantiate their statements of nutritional adequacy through live animal feeding trials governed by AAFCO standards, or they can adhere to a recipe that's already been tested and proven. The method used must be disclosed on the label in some variation of, "Animal feeding tests using AAFCO procedures substantiate that (this product name) provides complete and balanced nutrition for the growth and maintenance of cats." This information is important because it helps the consumer determine what life stage the food is formulated for, in this case, growing kittens and adult cats.

E-Fact

Commercial cat foods are made of the byproducts of the human food industry. Typically, the term "by-products" refers to cuts of meat or parts of animals not used for human consumption. For example, poultry by-products might include the heads, necks, feet, and internal organs of chickens and turkeys that people do not eat. Most cat foods also include some type of cereal grains as filler and fiber, plus vitamin and mineral supplements to compensate for what's lost during processing and storage.

Life Stage Feeding

As with other mammals, the cat's nutritional needs change as it grows and ages. Growing kittens and pregnant or nursing queens need more protein and energy to sustain the extra demands being placed on their bodies, while older, nonbreeding cats usually require fewer calories and less protein. As a cat progresses through various life stages, its dietary needs should be re-evaluated and adjusted accordingly. Some commercial cat foods are formulated to meet all life stages of cats, while others are intended only for certain stages of a cat's life, which is why it's important to read the label when selecting a food for your cat.

Feeding Kittens

A kitten that is six or eight months old should probably eat at least twice per day. A very young kitten (ten to eighteen weeks) might do better with three or even four meals per day, as much as it wants to eat. Because they are growing, kittens need higher amounts of protein than adult cats. That's why it is best to select a commercial cat food specifically designed for a kitten, and to feed that diet for the kitten's first full year. These special kitten foods usually state on the label that they are formulated for kittens, or for "growth and reproduction." Your veterinarian can recommend a suitable product for your growing kitten.

Feeding the Adult Cat

Although adult cats require a higher amount of animal protein in their diet than do dogs or humans, a relatively inactive indoor cat typically needs somewhat less protein than a kitten. When your cat is at least a full year old, ask your veterinarian if you should switch to an "adult maintenance" food. These foods have a little less protein and fewer calories for the adult cat that is no longer growing and, therefore, doesn't need the extra energy for growth that a kitten needs. Do not feed an adult maintenance product to a growing kitten or a pregnant cat.

Do not feed your cat dog food. Dog food does not contain enough protein and other essential nutrients to keep a cat in good health. Nor does dog food contain enough taurine, an important nutrient that cats need to keep their eyes and hearts healthy. Too little taurine has been associated with a heart muscle condition in cats called cardiomyopathy, and with eye problems.

Consider feeding your adult cat twice per day at regular times, morning and evening. Read the feeding guidelines on the package or can for how much you need to feed. Remember, however, that these instructions are just guidelines. The amount to feed can vary according to each individual cat's weight and activity level. Certain breeds of cats are more active than others, and a lazy, relaxed animal needs less food for energy than a hyperactive one.

Feeding the Older Cat

As your cat ages, its metabolism will begin to slow down. If the cat continues to eat the same quantity of food when it is nine years old as it did when it was three, it will gain weight, something that can put undue stress on joints and organs. The older cat may need to begin eating a lower-calorie food formulated for weight control, to help maintain a healthy weight. The older cat may also need a food that is more easily digestible, because as time goes on, the body does a less efficient job of extracting nutrients rom food. For this reason, some "senior" foods are formulated for greater digestibility.

Be sure to take your aging cat in to the vet for a checkup at least once a year, and continue to monitor its weight. If you begin to see a steady weight gain, or weight loss, report these findings to your veterinarian.

E-ssential

To track any weight loss or gain, get into the habit of weighing your cat once a month or so. Ask your veterinarian what an ideal weight for your cat would be, then try to keep as close to that figure as possible. If your cat starts to get a little too hefty, gradually cut back just a little on the amount you're feeding. Weigh both of you on a home scale, then subtract yourself from the total.

Also, be on the lookout for constipation in the older cat, caused by reduced motility in the intestines, decreased liver function, and an increasing inability to absorb nutrients. After you consult your veterinarian about this problem, she may recommend the addition of more fiber to the cat's diet.

Feeding Strategies

To a cat, food is one of the few behavioral motivators. Using the expectation of a food reward is an excellent way to get your cat to pay attention and perform some desired behavior. For instance, some cats will come running to the sound of a can opener, expecting it to open its favorite brands of food. This cat, whether the owner realizes it or not, has been expertly trained to "come" on command. The command just happens to be the sound of the can opener, rather than the human voice. You can teach your cat many interesting behaviors by first instilling in it a healthy hunger drive. A cat that gets hungry regularly and predictably can be motivated to do many clever things in exchange for a choice tidbit at the right time.

Free-Choice Feeding

The way many owners feed their cats works to reduce a cat's desire for food. Many owners leave dry food out for their cats all the time. Called free-choice feeding, this method allows the cat to eat small amounts throughout the day instead of one or two scheduled meals. Many cats seem to prefer nibbling throughout the day, so this method satisfies them. You can feed your cat free-choice without any ill effects, provided it does not overeat. However, from a training perspective, the cat never really gets hungry, and therefore, will not be too motivated to do anything for a food reward (this is also one of the reasons why some cats can become finicky eaters).

Certainly, this does not mean you should starve your cat between meals. Rather, you should set up some expectation for the cat of when the next meal time is. Many owners accomplish the best of both worlds by using a combination of feeding methods, offering canned food at regularly scheduled times, and supplementing with a little dry food left out for free-choice nibbling.

If you choose to leave some dry food out all day for your cat to nibble, it is better to measure and leave out only a day's ration, or one meal ration (check the package's feeding guidelines for how much that amount should be), rather than a full bulk-feed container that lasts for days. This way, the cat is not as likely to overeat and become obese, and it will maintain a hunger drive by looking forward to the next scheduled meal.

Scheduled Meals

Having a hunger drive and satisfying it is a natural way of life for a cat, and feeding your cat at regular times during the day fulfills this. Your cat will anticipate the arrival of food at a specific time. It will tend to become less finicky and eat the food that is given. Feed your cat twice per day at the same times, perhaps in the morning before you go to work, then in the evening when you come home, and stick to that schedule.

Owners who see an empty cat dish between meals are usually tempted to fill it up, but if you do this, the cat ends up determining how much it gets, not you, and it may overeat and get too fat. Some cats can control their food consumption and will not get fat when fed free-choice. However, others don't seem to have an appetite-off switch, particularly strays that were starved early in life. If your cat is among the latter and tends to put on weight when fed free-choice, stick to regular meal times instead, and your cat will have a better chance of staying at a proper weight. Your cat will also eliminate on a much more predictable schedule when fed this way.

Nutritional Problems

Cats need animal protein to stay healthy, along with a number of other nutrients, including vitamins, minerals, amino acids, carbohydrates, fats, and fiber. An all-meat or all-fish diet is not healthy for cats, nor is a totally vegetarian diet. In the wild, cats consume some plant material from the stomachs of their prey, which adds important nutrients to their diet. Cat-food manufacturers consider this fact when adding cereal content to their pet-food formulas. "Complete and balanced" nutrition is an important concept, because too much of certain nutrients can be just as detrimental as too little. Diagnosis of any nutritional disorder or deficiency involves a physical exam by your vet, numerous blood and urine tests, and careful consideration of the cat's weight and dietary habits. Treatment usually consists of a change in diet, and possibly drug therapy, including nutritional supplements.

Heart Problems

The cat's heart muscle is sensitive to deficiencies in the diet, and can suffer from lack of protein and other important nutrients. In particular, a deficiency in taurine has been implicated in dilated cardiomyopathy, a heart muscle disease in cats, as well as central retinal degeneration, an eye condition that can cause blindness.

Obesity can cause heart disorders, because it places great physical stress on the cat's entire system. An overweight cat can also develop diabetes, which contributes to heart disease and a host of other problems. A fat cat is not cute—it could be in poor health! Always monitor your cat's weight to prevent problems.

Taurine in their diet is essential to cats because they are the only known mammals that cannot manufacture enough of this nutrient in their own bodies. Today's commercial cat foods contain enough taurine to maintain good health in cats, although this wasn't the case decades ago, before the link between taurine and heart disease was understood. Dog food is not suitable fare for cats because it doesn't contain enough taurine, nor do homemade diets, unless a veterinary-approved recipe is followed to the letter.

Kidney Problems

Cats need a lot of animal protein, but excessive amounts of protein in the diet have in the past been associated with a risk of kidney problems later on in life. The kidneys filter and remove waste products from the body. When they can no longer perform this function well, the waste products build up in the blood and eventually lead to death.

Kittens and pregnant cats require more protein, but non-breeding adult cats need less. It's important to select a cat food based on the cat's current life stage, to help ensure that it receives a proper amount of high-quality protein, but neither too much nor too little for its needs at that particular stage in life.

Therapeutic diets are available through veterinarians to help manage cats that already have symptoms of decreased kidney function. These foods have reduced amounts of protein, sodium, and phosphorus to ease the waste-filtering burden on the kidneys. These special diets are sold only by prescription because their restricted nutrient levels make them unsuitable fare for healthy cats.

Urinary Tract Problems

Years ago, when feline lower urinary tract syndrome (FLUTD, also called feline urologic syndrome, FUS) was blamed on high magnesium levels in cat foods, manufacturers reformulated their products with lower levels. More than just magnesium was found to be at fault, however. The overall mineral composition of the food seemed to play a role in the development of stones or crystals that can irritate or block the urethra, which is the tube through which urine is excreted from the body. The food a cat eats affects the pH (degree of acidity or alkalinity) of its urine. More alkaline urine favors the development of crystals, whereas, more acidic urine tends to keep them dissolved. This is why manufacturers added acidifying ingredients to their foods, to help maintain normal pH levels. Today, the condition is not nearly as prevalent as it once was, but it still occurs in some cats, and owners need to be aware of it.

E-Fact

Cats that urinate outside are at highest risk of going unnoticed with this condition, because the owners cannot tell when the cat last relieved itself, or observe its elimination habits. Severe cases often require hospitalization, urinary catheterization, and fluid therapy to flush the kidneys and detoxify the system. Treatment may also include drugs that acidify the urine and a change in diet. Special therapeutic diets are available to manage this problem.

If you notice that your cat is having a hard time passing urine, or is visiting the litter box frequently, see your vet immediately. By palpating the cat's bladder, the veterinarian can check it for fullness and determine if a blockage is present. FLUTD is more common in males than in females because of the male's thinner, longer urethra. A urine test will confirm the presence of mineral crystals as well as an alkaline pH, which is conducive to the formation of stones.

If large enough, the stones can block the passage of urine from the body. Complete urinary obstruction can become a life-threatening condition within forty-eight hours, due to the buildup of toxins in the blood, so this situation is a true emergency.

Don't Forget Water

Water, which accounts for 60 to 70 percent of a cat's body weight, is necessary to all life functions, but owners often overlook the importance of this essential element. Always keep a bowl of clean, fresh water available for your cat, and change the water daily.

Dehydration occurs when an animal's output or expenditure of water exceeds its intake. Total water content must be kept within fairly narrow limits for healthy functioning of tissues and cells. During dehydration, the body also loses essential minerals, including salt.

Your cat will have a normal thirst drive to drink water when it needs to. However, when a cat becomes ill, this drive can become inhibited, leading to dehydration. Fever, infections, or injury can all cause a cat to stop drinking (and eating), a situation that should never be ignored.

In addition, certain conditions can cause the cat's body to actually lose water, resulting in dehydration. These include:

- Diarrhea
- Vomiting
- Diabetes
- Kidney disease
- Overheating

Symptoms of dehydration in a cat can include any or all of the following:

- Severe thirst
- Increased heart rate and respiration
- Dry mucous membranes in the mouth, eyes, and nose
- Decreased skin elasticity
- Decreased efficiency of circulatory system
- Disorientation, owing in part to low blood pressure

Most mild cases of dehydration in your cat can be dealt with by providing ample fresh water and by seeking medical treatment for any accompanying illness that is present. In serious cases, your veterinarian may need to administer fluids to the cat, either subcutaneously (under the skin) or intravenously (in a vein). These fluids contain not only water but also salt and other electrolytes to restore the proper balance in the cat's body.

9 Dealing with Eating Problems

Among the most common problems owners face in feeding their cats are obesity and finicky eating habits. Luckily, both of these problems are preventable, as the owner is usually the cause of them. As an owner, it's important to be alert to changes in your cat's eating habits, to notice weight gains and losses, to know how to prevent problems, and to recognize when you need to intervene. This chapter has valuable information to help you stay on top of your cat's eating routine.

Obesity

The most common nutritional disorder in domestic cats today, obesity is usually the owner's fault, not the cat's. Most often brought on by overfeeding and lack of activity, this problem seems to be an increasingly common one among cats, dogs, and humans.

The owner buys the food and puts it in the cat's dish. The owner determines the structure of the indoor cat's day, with regard to exercise, play, and social interaction. Simply put, weight gain in your cat occurs when its caloric intake exceeds its energy output. If the cat takes in four hundred calories each day and burns only three hundred, it is going to put on some extra weight.

Assessing Weight

If you cannot easily locate and feel your cat's ribs, chances are it is carrying some extra weight. Generally speaking, if a cat is more than 15 to 20 percent over its ideal body weight, it is considered obese. The average cat weighs anywhere from about eight to fifteen pounds, depending on its body frame, but certain breeds, such as the Maine Coon or Norwegian Forest cat, are larger and heavier. Ask your vet what would be a good weight for your cat. Then weigh your cat at least once each month to make sure it stays at that target range. Remember, your veterinarian can best assess your cat's weight and body condition and recommend any necessary dietary changes.

E-Fact

Weighing your cat is easy. Simply step on a set of bathroom scales and weigh yourself first. Then step off, pick up the cat, and reweigh yourself holding the cat. The difference from the first weighing equals the cat's weight.

Medical Conditions

Obesity is hard on a cat. It puts needless stress on the heart, lungs, joints, and muscles, and will result in a lethargic animal incapable of performing the amazing physical feats that we associate with cats. A fat cat might not even be able to jump into your lap for a rub and a nap. Obesity also predisposes a cat to a variety of disorders, including diabetes, liver, and heart problems.

In some cases, obesity can be caused by a medical problem. For example, a cat suffering from hypothyroidism (an underactive thyroid gland) might have enough of a metabolic slowdown to cause weight gain. Your vet can run a blood test to diagnose hypothyroidism and then treat the condition with medication.

Aging also often causes a gradual metabolic slowdown and consequent weight gain in your cat unless you cut back on its food a little. Cats, being creatures of habit, may protest the reduction of rations, so consider slowly changing over to a lower-calorie "senior" food instead. This will provide the cat with the same volume of food, but with less caloric value per ounce.

Putting a Cat on a Weight-Loss Diet

It's not easy putting a fat cat on a weight-loss diet, but it can be done. The key is to make all dietary changes gradually. No crash diets allowed! Cats have a peculiar metabolic response to fasting, and if their food intake is reduced too drastically or too quickly, their liver cannot adequately handle the rapid change. If your cat needs to lose weight, here are the steps you need to take:

- Have a veterinarian examine your cat and rule out any medical conditions that could be causing the weight problem.
- Gradually reduce the amount of food you feed your cat, based on your veterinarian's recommendations.
- If your veterinarian recommends feeding a particular type of food, make the switch gradually, by mixing more and more of the new food in with the old food each day.

- Try to increase the cat's activity level by engaging in more interactive play with it, or enriching the environment with toys and climbing trees.
- Weigh the cat at regular intervals to assess progress, and make gradual adjustments as needed.
- After the cat reaches the target weight, gradually readjust the amount fed to maintain the desired body weight.

Never try to put a fat cat on a crash diet. If a cat loses weight too rapidly, or stops eating altogether, a condition known as fatty liver disease, or hepatic lipidosis, can develop with life-threatening consequences. Consult a veterinarian first, before you embark on any weight-loss program for your cat. And don't ignore a cat's refusal to eat for two or more days.

Preventing Obesity

Of course, it's far easier to prevent obesity than it is to get the weight off. There are numerous steps you can take to prevent or halt an unhealthy weight-gain trend in your kitty. But before you start enforcing a weight-control plan for your pet, honestly evaluate the reasons why your cat may be getting fat in the first place. Perhaps your cat was starved as a youngster and has no "off switch" when it comes to food. Or perhaps you overindulge your pet in too many love offerings of treats and table scraps. When you honestly analyze the reasons behind the problem, sometimes the solution becomes clearer.

Avoid Overfeeding

If you're feeding your cat free-choice, start feeding at regularly scheduled times instead, and do not "top off" the food bowl between meals. Some cats cannot control their food consumption, and if fed free-choice, they will overeat, unless you pay close attention to the portions they are receiving. Adopted stray cats that once had to fight and scavenge for food often grow pudgy due to the sudden availability of unlimited food. Their hardships develop an incredible hunger drive that's hard to turn off, and if fed free-choice, they will gorge as if they're never going to get another meal. By feeding measured amounts at specific times, you will be able to control your cat's intake and know how many calories your cat is taking in each day.

Limit Treats

Giving your cat too many treats during the day can raise its caloric intake and put weight on, slowly but surely. Many owners forget this fact when they choose to express affection to their cats this way. Treats can be useful bribes, however, when training a cat, or when encouraging it to perform some desirable behavior. Just don't overdo the treats.

Always discourage begging, because not only is it an obnoxious habit, it is also a source of unneeded calories. Cats that beg usually get "people food" anyway, which is not necessarily healthy for them either. Offering too many treats and too much people food can turn your cat into a finicky eater. If the cat turns down its own food in favor of yours, it won't get the complete and balanced mix of nutrients it needs to stay healthy.

E-ssential

Whether you're cutting back on your cat's rations or switching to a different type of food, make all dietary changes gradually, over a period of two to three weeks. For example, if changing to a different food, mix a little of the new in with the old at first, gradually adding a bit more of the new food every few days or so, until the changeover is complete.

Keeping Your Cat Active

Getting your cat to burn more calories will keep it trim, get it in better cardiovascular shape, and help stave off boredom. Cats need exercise just as much as humans do. Most people just never think about planning exercise for their cats the way they plan walks for the family dog. Some cat breeds are naturally more active than others. Owners of such breeds as the Abyssinian or the Siamese probably wish that they could slow their little wildcats down. Owners of more sedate, reserved breeds, such as the Persian or Himalayan, might have a harder time getting their pets off their laps to play.

For indoor cats, providing ample exercise opportunities can be a challenge, especially if you live in a small apartment. But there are many pleasurable ways to entice your cat to exercise.

Play with Your Cat

First, give your cat plenty of toys to stimulate play, and engage in interactive play with your cat from time to time. Most kittens show a natural prey instinct to chase after a thrown object, especially if it resembles a small furry animal. Cats with a particularly high stalking drive should take to this game nicely. In place of a ball or toy, you can use a fake mouse or feather on the end of a string. Teasing it along will drive your cat bonkers and get it running around, letting off steam.

Provide a Companion

If you can afford it, consider getting two kittens instead of one so they can grow up together and bond as buddies. They will keep each other company, chase each other, and play together enough to burn some calories. Cats with company are far less likely to get fat.

This technique may not work as well if you try to bring a kitten or adult cat into your older resident cat's home. Remember that cats are very territorial. The resident cat may eventually tolerate the newcomer, but the two may never actually become close enough friends to play together.

Leash Training

Obesity is more prevalent among indoor cats than outdoor cats because of the sedentary lifestyle and fewer exercise opportunities. Yet, an indoor lifestyle is considerably safer and more desirable for your cat. But there are ways to help your indoor pet get the exercise it needs. One of them is take your cat for walks. Yes, it is possible to teach a cat to walk on a leash so that you can take it outside in a supervised situation and get its legs moving. A few tours around the backyard can burn enough calories to offset the six or seven treats you softheartedly gave your cat during the day. Plus, it allows your cat to safely enjoy the outdoors, with you on the other end of the leash taking care that the cat doesn't get into anything it shouldn't.

E-ssential

Cats can be trained to walk on a leash, but you should never tie your cat outdoors and leave it unattended. The cat could easily get tangled in the lead and strangle, or hang itself. The cat also would not be able to escape to safety if a loose dog were to attack.

Start while the cat is young, after it has had all of its mandatory vaccinations. Few adult cats will tolerate wearing a harness and being on the end of a leash. Understand also that some cats will be too naturally timid or nervous to try this, even as kittens. If your cat fits this description, do not force it to comply.

Purchase a cat-walking harness, not a dog harness and not just a collar, from a pet shop. Choose an adjustable harness, so you won't have to buy more than one to compensate for the cat's growth. Once you have the harness, you can use the following tips to leash-train your cat:

- Let the kitten see and sniff the harness, and then put it on loosely. Reward your kitten with a treat. Consider using meat-based baby food on the end of a spoon, as it will take the kitten a while to finish licking this, increasing the time that the harness stays on. This should occur in the quiet safety of your home. Do not attempt to venture outdoors with the cat right away.
- Gradually increase the time that the kitten wears the harness each day. After your kitten can comfortably wear the harness indoors for about twenty minutes, clip a light leash onto it and hold the end.

- Encourage the kitten to walk around on its own in the room, with you holding the leash, but do not drag or try to force the kitten to go where you want to go. Use a toy to coax the kitten into moving, if needed, and simply follow along. Never pull hard on the leash, or yank the kitten around.
- Increase the amount of time each day that your kitten walks around inside the home this way, until it grows accustomed to being on the leash.
- After the kitten is comfortable with walking around the house with the harness and leash on, carry it out into a secluded, quiet yard, and let it walk around and investigate things in the same way, with you holding the leash, but letting the kitten choose the way (within reason, of course). Gradually increase the time spent outside, and see if you can eventually get the kitten to walk back into the home on its own.
- Be patient and consistent. Expect this training to take many weeks.
- Do not rush your cat or try to pull it along with the leash, or it will rebel or react fearfully. Remember, the cat will cooperate only if it wants to do something. So you must make the experience pleasant.
- If at any time the cat resists or panics, end the session. Never continue any behavior that upsets the cat.

Dealing with Finicky Eaters

Dog owners rarely have problems with their pets not eating. Some cats, however, develop quite the reputation for being finicky eaters, especially if their owners unwittingly encourage it.

Cats in the wild are not finicky. They eat what they can kill, and are happy to get a meal. That same leopard does not eat whenever it wants to. There is no magical, always-filled-to-the-brim "prey" dish available to it. Often, a cat in the wild will for go days without a substantial meal. Do you think a three-hundred-pound leopard that hasn't eaten for two days is going to be finicky? Of course not!

The point is, owners can unknowingly make their domestic cats finicky by overfeeding them free-choice, which drastically reduces their hunger drive, and by offering too many treats and people food.

Solutions for the Finicky Cat

Consider this: if a person always has food available and eats a little every forty-five minutes or so, that person would seldom feel hungry and probably wouldn't eat more than a handful each time. The same applies to cats that always have abundant food left out for them. Of course, not all cats fed free-choice become finicky eaters. But if yours does, you can try the following two strategies and see which one works best.

- Continue leaving out food for the cat to eat free-choice during the day, but measure out only the recommended daily amount (refer to the package feeding guidelines). When the food runs out, do not refill the bowl until the same meal time the next day.
- Switch your finicky eater from free-choice feeding to regularly scheduled meal times, twice a day. Give the cat thirty minutes or so to eat for each meal, then take up whatever food is left over. This helps restore the cat's natural hunger drive, as it learns to eat the amount it is given and look forward to the next meal time.

Rule Out Medical Problems

If your normally voracious eater suddenly becomes finicky or stops eating completely, observe the cat carefully and see your veterinarian. There might be some dental or medical problem that needs to be identified and treated. For example, an abscessed tooth or an intestinal blockage, such as a hairball mass, can make a cat stop eating altogether.

Treats

Give your cat treats only when you want it to perform a particular behavior, such as coming when called, walking on a leash, or behaving nicely while being brushed. Although okay once in a while, in general avoid giving the cat random treats without expecting something in return.

Most begging behavior in pets is perpetrated by the owners. If your cat cries loudly for food, do not reward it by feeding it right then. You will succeed only in teaching the cat that if it vocalizes loudly, it will get food. Instead, wait until the cat has a quiet moment, and then offer the food.

Never let your cat eat from your plate, and never give it treats while you are sitting at the dinner table. This will create a beggar, for sure, and while this behavior might seem cute and endearing at first, it can quickly become annoying. If your kitty already has the obnoxious habit of begging while you are at the dinner table, keep a loaded water pistol or spray bottle on the table, filled with clean water, and spray the critter as soon as it starts meowing incessantly or tries to jump up on you or the table. At the same time, utter a loud, sharp-sounding "No!" Eventually, the harsh word will suffice as a correction, and you won't need the sprayer anymore. The sprayer technique is useful for correcting a lot of misbehaviors, but it doesn't work on all cats. Some cats just don't seem to mind getting sprayed by a jet of water, while others detest it.

Feeding in the Multi-Cat Household

If you have more than one cat in the home, provide each with its own food bowl to discourage squabbles at meal time. Each cat will have its own idea of how much food it wants to eat. If one is a real porker and the other is skinny and finicky, the hefty one is very likely to quickly eat all its food and then start on the other's bowl. Some cats are fast eaters and some are slow, and sometimes you have to observe their habits and figure out a way to accommodate both eating styles.

Observe how the two eat together side by side, and if competitive eating seems to be an issue, consider separating the cats at meal time and feeding them in different locations. Often, this is the only way to ensure that each animal gets the right amount of food and is given enough time to finish eating.

You will also need to feed your cats separately if one requires a special or restricted diet. This can become a real challenge, because the one cat will almost certainly want the other cat's food. Depending on the situation, it is sometimes possible to put both cats on the same diet, as long as the special food delivers all of the daily nutrients needed for good health to both. This is an option you can discuss with your veterinarian, if feeding your cats separately proves to be too big a problem.

There are clear instances where feeding the same food will not work. For example, if you are feeding a therapeutic kidney diet to an older cat with kidney dysfunction, and you also have a growing kitten in the house, the specialized kidney diet does not contain enough protein to sustain healthy growth in your kitten. So you can't let the kitten live solely on the older cat's food. In addition, the kitten's food contains too much protein for the older cat's compromised kidneys to handle, although the older cat will probably find the kitten's chow much tastier than its therapeutic diet. Clearly, these two cannot share meals and thrive on the same food. Therefore, you must feed them separately, and take up their bowls after about thirty minutes to ensure that one doesn't clean up the other's leftovers.

10 Feline Dental Care

Being a carnivore, the cat has teeth that are better designed to rip and tear than to chew, perfectly adapted to the role of hunting, catching, and killing prey. Kittens have twenty-six baby teeth, all present by six weeks of age. An adult cat has thirty teeth, including the canines, incisors, pre-molars, and molars. As a responsible pet owner, it is your job to stay on top of your cat's dental health, which includes maintaining both the teeth and the gums on a regular basis.

The Cat's Teeth

The canines are the longer fangs, used for tearing flesh. The incisors are the small teeth easily visible in the front of the mouth between the longer canines. Cats use their incisors to rip flesh from their food source. The premolars and molars are all located toward the back of mouth. However, cats don't use their molars to chew food the way humans do. Instead, feline molars crunch food down into chunks small enough to swallow.

E-Fact

To prevent dental problems, you must remove or prevent plaque buildup. Plaque is a soft, gummy mixture of food particles, bacteria, and saliva minerals, which if not removed on a regular basis, gradually hardens and turns brown. This hardened material on the teeth is called tartar, or calculus. Tartar works its way under the gum line, eventually causing painful gum disease and tooth loss, if left untreated.

Maintaining healthy teeth and gums is important to your cat's well-being. Without strong teeth and healthy gums, eating is difficult and discomfort is frequent, and the cat loses weight and body condition deteriorates. Often, this happens in aging cats, and the owner may not notice until the dental condition is quite advanced. Gum disease or oral infections can allow bacteria to seep into the cat's bloodstream, adversely affecting other body organs.

Common Feline Dental Problems

There are several kinds of dental problems that can occur in cats that you should be aware of in order to help keep your cat in the best of dental, and overall, health. Some of the more common ones include:

- Dental plaque and tartar buildup
- Lost, loose, or broken teeth

- Gingivitis and periodontal disease
- Bad breath

In addition, cavities, although relatively rare in cats, can occur, particularly if excessive plaque buildup is present. Most cavities in cats occur under the gums and often escape notice, unless the cat undergoes a thorough, professional dental inspection. If you suspect that your cat has a dental problem, see your vet, who can treat it and help restore your cat's comfort and well-being.

FORLs

Another dental condition seen in cats is called feline oral resorptive lesion (FORL), a fancy name for a cavity or tooth lesion that usually occurs at the gum line. Many cats show no obvious clinical signs of the condition. But some lesions can progress and become painful to the cat, causing difficulty in eating, excessive salivation, or oral bleeding. Often, the cat will react in pain when touched on the face near the affected area.

Stomatitis

Cats can also experience mouth ulcers and an inflammation of the mouth called stomatitis. Characterized by sores and redness in the mouth, weight loss, and excessive salivation, the condition can be quite painful, sometimes to the point where the cat cannot eat. Treatment may sometimes need to be aggressive and usually involves a follow-up home-dental-care program.

Orthodontic Problems

As with humans, some cats are born with orthodontic problems, such as wry bites, uneven jaws, projecting canines, or teeth that just don't meet and close against each other properly. Certain breeds display these types of problems more than others. The flat-faced Persian cat, for example, will sometimes have a fang that juts out over a lip, reminiscent of its ancient saber-toothed-tiger ancestor. If the defect is severe enough, it may hamper the cat's ability to eat. Many orthodontic problems in cats can be successfully treated these days, so have your veterinarian evaluate anything that seems out of the ordinary.

E-ssential

In order to examine your cat's mouth, place it on a sturdy table in a well-lit area that is free of noise and distractions. Have an assistant help hold the cat for you while you look in the cat's mouth. Examine the cat's face for swellings first, then slightly tilt the cat's head back with one hand, and gently pry open the mouth with the other forefinger. If the cat growls or tries to bite, it is better to stop than to risk injury to yourself or your assistant.

Gum Disease

Gingivitis, an inflammation of the gums, is often caused by bacterial infection. When plaque and tartar build up around the base of the teeth, the bacterial toxins produced cause the gums to become swollen and tender. Symptoms include a reddish-purple color of the gums instead of the normal, healthy pink. In addition, the gums may bleed easily, especially after the cat eats, cleans itself, or chews on a toy.

Preventing gingivitis in your cat is simply a matter of inhibiting the formation of bacteria and plaque in the mouth with regular brushing and cleaning. If your cat is accustomed to having its mouth handled, you can also massage the gums to increase blood flow.

Gingivitis, if left untreated, can develop into periodontal disease, an inflammation of the membranes around the base of the teeth and erosion of the bone holding the teeth in the jaw. Eventually, the teeth will loosen and fall out.

Other effects of gingivitis and periodontal disease include:

- Bad breath
- Infection and abscesses
- Loss of appetite, weight, and healthy body condition
- Pain, possible irritability and aggression

Avoiding plaque buildup and treating gingivitis early can easily prevent this serious condition and its possible detrimental effects on the entire body and overall health of your cat.

For cats that have lost teeth to gum disease or other dental problems, switching from dry food to a soft, canned-food diet will make it easier for the cat to eat.

Signs of Dental Problems

Bad breath is one of the more noticeable signs of dental disease. Also, mouth ulcers, painful teeth, or sore gums can all cause a cat to refuse food. If you notice weight loss in your cat or a decline in eating, look inside the mouth for clues. A cat with a dental problem may flinch when you touch the side of its face or try to open its mouth.

Inside the mouth, healthy gums look pink. Inflamed gums appear red and swollen, and pale gums may be a sign of ill health or anemia, perhaps due to internal parasites. Healthy teeth appear white and clean, not yellow or discolored with brown deposits.

Lost or Broken Teeth

If a cat chews on objects that are harder than the teeth—rocks and bones, for example—a tooth may fracture. Lost, loose, or broken teeth can really create havoc in a cat's mouth, particularly if a nerve is left exposed. Infections and abscesses can easily occur, causing gum problems, pain, and perhaps additional tooth loss or ill health. Sometimes a broken tooth can cause a swelling on top of the nose or an abscess that appears on the cat's face, usually below an eye.

If you suspect your cat has lost or broken a tooth, see your veterinarian right away. Broken teeth can sometimes be repaired with fillings or even installing a crown for protection. Likewise, if you press on the teeth and note any movement, have the loose tooth attended to immediately. Often, a loose tooth must be pulled, but sometimes it can be saved. Regardless, your cat's comfort and overall well-being are paramount, and appropriate treatment should never be delayed or withheld.

Consequences of Delayed Dental Care

In the early stages of dental disease, the condition is usually treatable and the problems often reversible. However, ignoring signs of dental problems or delaying treatment can have serious consequences for your cat's health. These can include receding gums and gum disease, loosened and lost teeth, infection that can enter the bloodstream and spread to other parts of the body, and ultimately a shortened lifespan for your cat. Remember, kidney and heart infections often have their roots in the mouth.

Care of Teeth and Gums

Over time, deposits of plaque can form on your cat's teeth, mostly on the molars and pre-molars. Plaque forms when matter left on the teeth after eating combines with saliva and bacteria. Through regular brushing, you can clean plaque deposits off of your cat's teeth, before they have a chance to form into tartar, a harder substance that you cannot clean off without professional help.

If left to build up over the years, tartar deposits can result in gum disease and loss of teeth, not to mention bad breath. Once tartar buildup is significant, your vet will have to clean it off using an ultrasonic device, with the cat under general anesthesia. Although relatively safe, anesthesia has inherent risks, especially in older cats. So if you can take some simple, inexpensive steps to avoid placing your cat at risk, why not do so?

Controlling Plaque Buildup

You can minimize plaque buildup by feeding the cat a mostly dry-food diet, which has a more abrasive, tooth-scouring quality than does canned food, and by cleaning your cat's teeth on a monthly basis, removing any plaque that has formed. This, of course, involves training the cat to accept your probing in its mouth and brushing its teeth, a very personal procedure as far as most cats are concerned, and not one that many take to readily. As with almost all training procedures, you need to begin this when your cat is a kitten to get it used to the idea. Otherwise, an adult cat will probably strongly resist all efforts related to having its teeth cleaned, and to avoid being scratched or bitten, you'll just have to pay the veterinarian to do it for you.

Training a Kitten to Accept Toothbrushing

While the cat is still young, begin gently opening its mouth and rubbing its gums and teeth with a finger while you pet and praise it. The cat may accept this better if you dip your finger in something tasty, such as the juice from a can of cat food. Do not force the cat to submit to your probing and mouth handling. If you try to force the issue, you will only succeed in making the cat fearful and more resistant to such handling. Strive, instead, to accustom the cat to the idea slowly and gently so that in time, the cat will accept the practice without fear. Try to make each attempt positive and pleasurable for the cat, with lots of petting and praise and a tasty reward.

Be gentle, patient, casual, and confident, and do not let your rubbing last more then five or ten seconds at first. Gradually build up the length of time that you rub the kitten's gums and teeth until you are able to cover all of the cat's teeth and gums. Getting all the way into the back might be difficult with your finger, so don't push it. Just stick with what you can see. You don't have to worry about cleaning both sides of the teeth either, just the front side will do.

After the kitten accepts having your finger in its mouth without fuss, wrap your finger in a piece of gauze, dampened with warm water or juice from canned cat food, and continue the procedure. Or, you can switch to a dry cotton swab and continue the procedure. The swab will allow you easier access to the molars, but don't let the kitten swallow the cotton. Remember to be brief, casual, and confident, and always praise and pet the kitten during and after the procedure. Give the cat a treat when you have finished. Continue this brief, gentle handling once each day for as long as it takes, until the kitten seems to accept it matter-of-factly. There is no need to rush to the next stage, which will involve adding feline toothpaste to the procedure.

Dental-Care Products

After you've gotten your kitten accustomed to having your finger in its mouth in the manner described previously, purchase a feline toothpaste from a pet shop or vet's office and apply a dab to your moistened gauze or swab. This will provide a slight abrasive quality that will help clean the teeth. You do not have to rinse out feline toothpaste. It is designed to be swallowed by the cat. Do not use human toothpaste on cats, as it will burn the cat's throat and may cause digestive upset when swallowed.

Certain diseases, such as feline leukemia virus and feline immunodeficiency virus, are known risk factors for feline dental disease and predispose their victims to future dental problems. In addition, feline calcivirus may cause ulcers on the tongue. If your cat develops mouth sores or other signs of dental problems, your veterinarian will want to check for these diseases and rule them out as an underlying cause.

You can continue using the gauze or swab, or eventually you may wish to purchase a small, soft-bristled toothbrush for cats at your local pet store. You can also use a soft, worn-out human toothbrush (disinfected in hot water), if it's not too large. A small child-size toothbrush works well for cats. Also available are soft rubber or plastic tips that fit over the tip of your finger. These work similar to the gauze-wrap technique described and seem to fit better in the cat's small mouth.

Ask Your Vet

If you are unsure about the whole toothbrushing experience with your cat, ask your veterinarian to demonstrate the procedure. Most are more than happy to educate their clients about this vital health care topic. Some even provide literature and videos on how to take care of your pet's teeth. In addition, your vet can also recommend the latest and most appropriate dental-care products available on the market. These products include oral antibacterial mouth rinses and non-foaming, enzymatic toothpastes made especially for cats, which are designed to dissolve plaque without a lot of tooth scrubbing. These kitty toothpastes are typically fish flavored to please the feline palate and do not require rinsing.

For the cat that refuses to submit to toothbrushing, your vet can also recommend various tartar-control treats, plaque control products, specially formulated dental-care foods, and enzymatic chews that can help. Brushing is best, but if your cat won't allow it, there are alternatives you can use that still help promote good dental health in your cat. So be sure to discuss this important matter with your veterinarian.

Professional Cleaning

Once dental disease is present, proper cleaning of the teeth can only be accomplished while the cat is under general anesthesia. Some owners, especially of older cats, are reluctant to submit their cats to this treatment because of the risks related to anesthesia. When faced with the decision, it's important to put the matter into perspective. Modern anesthesia, while not completely risk free, is considered reasonably safe, especially when weighed against the greater risks to the cat's overall health if you delay treatment. Remember, bacteria from a sore, infected mouth can seep into the bloodstream and silently attack other body systems.

A thorough professional cleaning typically involves several steps. First, the ugly brown tartar buildup is scaled ultrasonically from the teeth, above and below the gum line. Once that step is accomplished, the teeth are polished. A smooth tooth surface tends to slow additional plaque buildup. Then, the mouth is flushed to dislodge bacteria and any remaining tartar from the teeth. Finally, a fluoride coating is applied to the teeth to help strengthen the enamel, decrease tooth sensitivity, and fight off further plaque formation.

Diet and Dental Health

Diet does not play as big a role in delaying dental problems as some people have been led to believe by clever advertising. Certainly, adding dry food to a cat's diet can help promote better dental health because of the abrasive, scouring action on the teeth. However, for some cats that bolt their food with little or no chewing action whatsoever, the beneficial effects are minimal. Dry food does not adhere to the teeth as readily as sticky canned food, so plaque and tartar may not build up quite as rapidly. However, eating dry food will not prevent tartar buildup or remove tartar that has already hardened on the teeth.

There are tartar-control diets available through veterinary clinics that can be fed to cats as a treat or as an adult maintenance diet. While these products will not completely prevent or clean tartar from the teeth, they can help prolong the interval between professional cleanings. Also available are enzyme-treated dental chew biscuits for cats that you can use as an alternative to brushing if your cat refuses to accept being handled in that way. Ask your veterinarian about these and discuss the best course of dental care for your cat at your next visit.

E-Fact

Cats that are recovering from a recent dental procedure may need to be fed a soft, canned-food diet for several days afterward. Cats that have already lost their front canines and incisor teeth to dental disease or old age can usually still chew dry kibble, but if the molars are gone, they may need to have their dry food moistened with warm water, or be fed canned food.

Prevention Is the Best Medicine

All the toothbrushing and attention to dental-care details may seem like a lot of trouble for you as a cat owner. You may even find it a little silly to adapt these human hygiene measures to your little ball of fur. But if you ever have a cat that silently suffers and endures dental disease, bad breath, and bleeding gums for a period of time, you'll know that such preventive measures can save you and your cat lots of pain and anguish, not to mention time and money. Many cats with dental problems can be successfully treated and returned to good health, but it's so much better not to let it get to that point. If you start caring for your kitty's teeth and gums when she's young, she will likely get used to tooth-care time and may even come to value it as a chance to bond with you.

11 Grooming Cats

All cats require some grooming, but some breeds are more high maintenance than others. For example, shorthaired cats require brushing to dislodge loose hairs, but they don't have to be groomed as frequently as the longhairs. And some longhairs aren't as high maintenance as others. For Persians and Himalayans, daily grooming is essential to prevent mats and tangles. Some of the other longhairs, such as the Maine Coon, can generally stay tangle-free with just a few sessions per week. Once a week or so will do for the shorthaired breeds.

Shedding

In addition to the health advantages, frequent grooming also helps minimize the amount of cat hair that rubs off on your clothes and furnishings as a result of your cat's seasonal shedding. Most cats shed a little year-round, but the process is more noticeable in early spring and fall. And yes, shorthaired cats shed as much as longhaired cats, but the shorter fur just seems less obvious because it shows up in lesser amounts.

E-ssential

Aside from keeping the coat clean and mat-free, grooming helps remove loose hairs from the cat's coat and prevent the formation of hairballs, or masses of ingested hair, in the stomach. A cat that is trying to regurgitate a hairball will typically crouch low and cough several times, sometimes swaying the head from side to side as it wheezes. Commonly known as the hairball cough, this motion may be followed by convulsive waves of the cat's body as it heaves and vomits the mass onto the floor.

What Causes Shedding

Shedding of the coat is triggered by changes in the amount of daylight, not temperature changes, as many people mistakenly believe. Lengthening daylight hours in early spring trigger shedding of the winter coat. Likewise, the shortening days in fall cause the summer coat to shed out to make way for the thicker winter coat. Cats that live indoors under artificial lights typically shed a little year-round, but they still undergo the major seasonal coat changes.

About Hairballs

Cats are designed for self-cleaning, equipped with a tongue covered in hooked, abrasive papillae used for grooming their fur. The problem is, cats develop hairballs from licking and ingesting too much loose hair during self-grooming. Actually, the term "hairball" is somewhat of a misnomer, as a hairball is not ball-shaped at all, but is rather a long, tubular-shaped mass of ingested hair in the cat's stomach or intestinal tract.

Cats usually regurgitate these masses with no ill effects; however, on occasion a hairball can cause a potentially life-threatening internal blockage, which requires veterinary treatment or even surgery to remove. Signs of a blockage include general lethargy, refusing to eat, or vomiting food shortly after eating. When you regularly groom your cat, you help minimize the occurrence of hairballs by removing the loose fur that would otherwise be swallowed or shed out on your furnishings.

E-Fact

Eating grass is thought to aid cats in purging themselves of hairballs. That's why it's a good idea to grow your cat its own supply of fresh grass indoors in a container set in a sunny window. Pet stores sell kitty grass kits especially for this purpose. If your cat has its own stash of grass to nibble on, it is also less likely to graze on your houseplants.

Grooming is the least expensive way to prevent hairballs. There are also various commercial cat foods and petrolatum-based hairball remedies on the market that you can buy at pet stores or veterinarians' offices that help control hairballs. If your cat seems to have too-frequent bouts of hairballs, ask your veterinarian to recommend or dispense a suitable remedy. The paste remedies are easy to administer and generally act to lubricate the mass so that it can pass through the cat's intestinal tract more easily. Simply dab some on top of the cat's paw, and the cat will lick it off.

Fur Structure

The cat's fur helps protect it from sunburn, heat, and cold. Depending on the breed, a cat's coat can be made of several layers and types of hair. The longer "guard" hairs lie on top. Sometimes there's a middle layer of "awn" hairs that provides additional insulation. Then, there's usually a soft undercoat of "down" hair next to the skin. Of course, not all cats have each type of hair, nor do all cats have hair. The Sphynx is virtually hairless, although it does have a light coating of down.

Coat Condition

The condition of a cat's coat is a good indication of its overall health. A healthy cat has a clean, shiny coat that lies flat. An unhealthy coat is dull, dry, and brittle. An excessively oily coat, or one that smells bad or looks flaky, may indicate a skin condition that needs treating. A "staring" coat, where the hairs stand out from the body instead of lying flat, can be a subtle sign of illness in the cat. Diet and medical conditions can impact coat health dramatically.

Getting Your Cat Used to Grooming

Grooming is something you need to get your cat accustomed to at a young age. So start gently combing and brushing your kitten as soon as it comes home. Establish a regular routine, grooming the cat in the same place and at the same time each session. For example, when you sit down to watch your favorite TV show in the evening, settle the cat in your lap and groom. Or, it may be easier to conduct your grooming sessions with the cat on a table or countertop. Choose whatever works for you, but do it routinely, so that the cat will know what is expected.

The Tools You'll Need

The types of grooming tools you'll need depend on whether your cat is longhaired or shorthaired. But basically, here's a list of things to buy to get you started:

- Nail clippers (either the pet or human type)
- Steel-toothed pet combs (buy several different sizes)
- Fine-toothed flea comb (helps remove flea dirt)
- Natural bristle brushes (soft and medium)
- Mat splitter or seam ripper (for longhaired cats)

Grooming a Kitten

With your new kitten, begin lightly brushing or combing each day, just for a minute or two. Start the habit early for longhaired cats especially, because if you wait until they are six or seven months old to begin a grooming regimen, you may encounter resistance.

For a kitten, start with a small comb with widely spaced teeth and a soft-bristle brush. Always be very gentle and careful not to comb or brush too hard. At first, the kitten may think you are trying to play and may swat at or mouth the grooming tools. This is okay, as you want the kitten to learn pleasant associations about being groomed. At this stage, the objective isn't so much to render a good grooming, as to get the kitten used to and amenable to the idea.

If you are gentle, patient, and consistent, soon the kitten will become relatively desensitized to the procedure, and may even look forward to it if you talk quietly, offer praise, and perhaps reward it with a tasty treat at the end of each session. After the kitten becomes accustomed to the grooming procedure, you can back off the frequency of the sessions to just a few times a week, or as needed, and establish a set routine.

If you are too rough and vigorous in your brushing, or if you pull the kitten's fur or skin with the comb, the kitten will feel pain and may become fearful or resentful of being groomed. You could also get scratched or bitten in the process. Cats that have had unpleasant grooming experiences will often run and hide when you bring out the comb. This is not the outcome you want, because you will end up having to pay a professional groomer to get the mats out of your cat's coat.

Grooming the Longhaired Cat

Most of the time, you groom a cat with the lay of the fur, and this sufficiently dislodges the loose hair. With longhaired cats, however, there is a special technique used to strip the coat during peak shedding periods, called back combing. This is combing, gently, against the lay of the fur to help dislodge and strip out the loose undercoat trapped closer to the skin. To prevent pulling the cat's skin, part out a section of hair, hold it between two fingers close to the skin, and back comb. Empty the comb frequently as you work, as a buildup of hair on the comb can cause pulling. Don't try to do the whole cat during one session, but rather work a section of a coat at a time, as long as the cat will tolerate it. If the cat wants to move away and go elsewhere, allow it to do so.

E-ssential

Back combing the longhaired cat's tail adds fluff and volume. Start at the tail base and work out to the tip, being extra careful not to pull on the sensitive skin or the tail itself. To prevent stripping out too much hair and ending up with a skinny tail, use only a wide-toothed comb for tail combing.

Trimming Nails

Outdoor cats generally keep their claws worn by climbing trees, but indoor cats need to have their nails trimmed on occasion. Begin nail trimming when the cat is young, too, so that it will get used to having its feet handled. Most adult cats do not tolerate this procedure well if they've never had their claws trimmed. For them, you'll have to pay your veterinarian or a professional groomer to do the work. Kittens, however, generally learn to tolerate the procedure easily enough, provided you never hurt them by cutting the claw too close to the quick. After the cat is used to the procedure, you should trim nails approximately once a month or every other month, and always before a show or before visiting the vet.

Here's how to introduce nail clipping: Every day for about a month, while petting your kitten, briefly and gently handle each paw. Massage each paw between your thumb and forefinger, pressing down gently on the claws to expose the nails.

Once the kitten is thoroughly used to having its feet and nails rubbed and touched, begin lightly touching each nail with the nail clippers once or twice during the handling procedure. Do not trim them yet. Just continue desensitizing the kitten to the metallic feel of the clippers on its sensitive nails.

After your kitten has learned to accept having its nails touched with the clippers, try to clip just one or two. Don't expect to clip all of them at one time. Also, do not take off more than a sixteenth of an inch of nail. Just clip the very tip ends. Trimming off too much will cut into the quick, the pink area of the nail that has a visible blood vessel running down the center. If you do cut into the quick, the cat will feel pain and the nail will bleed. (Apply pressure or some styptic powder to the nail end to stop the bleeding.) If you hurt the kitten, it will lose trust in you and will not want you to handle its feet again anytime soon.

If the nail-trimming procedure makes you nervous, or the desensitization process is ineffective, it's probably best not to attempt the task on your own. A shaky hand is more likely to make a mistake and cause your kitty unnecessary pain and anguish. It's better to take your cat to a professional groomer instead of risking the loss of his trust.

Bathing Your Cat

Unless you are going to show your cat, you should not have to bathe it too often. Cats are naturally clean animals, which is one reason why they make such easy-care pets. However, your cat may occasionally contract fleas or get into a particularly messy substance that would be toxic if the cat tried to clean it off its fur. If your cat is accustomed to being bathed from a young age, it will be easier to deal with such a situation should the need arise. An adult cat that has never been bathed will put up a strong fight. Better to avoid being scratched and let your veterinarian deal with it, so that your pet does not lose trust in you.

Getting a Cat Used to Baths

Don't attempt to bathe very young kittens, unless it's absolutely necessary. Wait until they're at least eight to twelve weeks old, or older. Then, to get a cat accustomed to bathing, place it in a sink or water basin (put a rubber mat in the bottom, so the kitten can hold on with its paws). You may also need an assistant for this task, as bathing a cat is often a two-person job, one to restrain the cat and one to do the bathing and rinsing.

Gently wet the cat from neck to rump with warm, not hot, water poured from a small cup. A kitchen sink with a spray nozzle works best for this job later on, after the cat is used to the idea. But in the beginning, start with a little water from a cup. At this point, simply introduce the concept of getting wet, something that most cats never voluntarily experience.

Work the warm water into the coat, praising the kitten during the procedure. Gently dampen its head as well, but use a moist cloth. Never pour or spray water in the cat's face, or you'll really create a fuss. Dry off the kitten with a soft, dry towel. Consider using a quiet hair dryer, set on low. Doing so from this early age will help desensitize the kitten to the foreign sound.

Applying Shampoo

When needed, follow the initial warm water rinse with an application of a cat-safe shampoo made especially for cats. You can buy these at pet stores or veterinarians' offices.

Do not use human shampoos or detergents when bathing your cat. Remember, any product used on cats, such as a flea shampoo, must be labeled as safe for use on cats. Make sure the label also states at what age the product is safe for use on kittens before you apply it.

Gently work the lather into the cat's coat, then rinse out completely. For longhaired cats, follow up with a cat-safe conditioner, made especially for cats, to minimize tangles. Rinse and dry the kitten thoroughly, then reward the cat with a favorite treat.

Grooming the Older Cat

The aging cat may not groom itself quite as efficiently as it once did, due to stiffening joints and reduced flexibility. You can help by continuing to brush and comb the cat each day. If your senior kitty gets dirty, do not wait for it to clean itself. Help it along with a bath or brushing. When brushing or combing, however, do so a bit more gently than when the cat was young, as the skin may be more sensitive and the coat thinner. When finished, dry the cat thoroughly and settle it in a warm room, to prevent any possibility of chilling.

Older, inactive cats may also need their nails trimmed more frequently to prevent the claws from hooking around and growing into the foot pads. Don't forget the dew claws, which are located a little higher up on the inside of each foreleg, as these have a particular tendency to become ingrown in sedentary animals.

Removing Mats

Longhaired cats need to be combed daily to keep their coats free of mats. Mats develop when the undercoat sheds out and works it way up to the surface, getting tangled in the process. Without routine grooming, some longhaired cats become so severely matted that they must be shaved down completely in order to restore the coat.

What if there are several mats, or most or all of the cat's hair is matted?

When a longhaired cat's coat becomes very matted in several places it is referred to as "felt matted." This is because the hair takes on the texture of a felt pad. When this happens, the only real option is to shave the cat. This will give your cat a fresh start, and it will probably be easier for both of you than trying to break up individual mats. Take the cat to a professional groomer or a vet if you do not want to attempt shaving the cat yourself. And don't try to shave a cat without having someone demonstrate the grooming process for you first.

Mats need to be removed promptly, or they will usually get tighter and tighter, pulling on the cat's skin and causing it pain. If neglected long enough, sometimes sores will even form and fester on the skin beneath tight tangles of hair, necessitating some veterinary treatment.

Obviously, it is far easier to prevent mats with good grooming than it is to remove them. The best way to remove one is to pull it apart with your fingers (or use a mat splitter), as gently as possible, and then work it out of the fur in small sections. If the mat is close and tight against the skin, you may need to snip it loose, carefully, with scissors or a seam ripper, taking great care not to poke or cut the cat's skin with the sharp instrument. You can also shave off mats with electric pet trimmers that you can buy at pet stores. Shaving will leave uneven patches in the fur for a time, until the coat grows out.

You may need an assistant to help hold the cat still for any mat removal procedure, and you will need good lighting to see what you are doing. If you aren't comfortable with removing mats, or if the cat simply won't allow it, take the animal to a veterinarian or a professional groomer.

Cleaning Ears

In addition to combing and brushing, you should train your cat to tolerate having its ears inspected periodically and cleaned as needed. Indoor cats need this far less than outdoor cats, but all owners should be able to check their cat's ears for dirt, wax buildup, and parasites.

To begin this training, stroke the kitten's head, casually rub its ears, then gently rub your pinkie tip around the inside of the ear. Do this with both ears, then praise and reward. Continue this for about a week or so, each time you have the little tyke on your lap. Gradually work up to touching the inside of each ear with a dry cotton ball, just for a few seconds.

Then, if the ears need cleaning, dip the cotton ball in warm water or mineral oil, squeeze out the excess moisture, and swab just the visible part of the ear. Be casual and quick about it. Then dry each ear with a dry cotton ball.

E-Question

Is it okay to use cotton swabs to clean a cat's inner ear?

No. Never stick a cotton swab or anything else down into the cat's ear canal, or you may inadvertently damage the cat's hearing. Simply dab and wipe clean only the visible outer areas of the ears. If you see dirt or wax deep inside the canal, take your kitty to the veterinarian for cleaning. A lot of dark brown, waxy buildup may indicate infection or the presence of ear mites. Head shaking and scratching at the ears are also symptoms of ear mites and demand veterinary treatment.

If the cat simply hates having its ears touched, do not force it to endure the procedure. You could accidentally injure the ear if the cat tends to struggle. It's much safer just to see your veterinarian when your pet's ears require cleaning.

12 Cat Health Care Basics

As a cat owner, you have an almost parental responsibility to understand your cat's basic physiology and health care needs. You should select a veterinarian before you acquire your cat and start building a relationship with that person. And you also need to know how to recognize physical symptoms that could signal a medical problem. An educated, caring owner will help her cat live a longer, healthier life. This chapter covers the basics of a cat's physical makeup and health needs.

The Physical Feline

To fully understand an animal's health care needs, it's helpful to know how its body is put together. Almost everything cats do, from changing direction swiftly and effortlessly to methodically cleaning themselves, is a function of their unique feline anatomy and physiology.

The Skeletal System

The cat's skeleton is somewhat different from that of other animals in its geometry and level of flexibility. A cat has thirty vertebrae in its spinal column, five more than humans. This gives the feline a wider range of movement, allowing it to twist and bend more radically than we ever could. The cat has no functional collarbone, which in humans limits the degree to which the shoulders can move. Also, the cat's shoulder blades are positioned close to its chest, allowing the shoulder joints to rise higher and travel in larger arcs than those in animals with more broadly situated shoulder blades. All of these features combine to give your cat a limber, uninhibited ability to run and jump more efficiently than most other animals.

E-Fact

The skeleton is the underlying superstructure of the body, supporting the skin and muscle tissues and acting as a protective housing for the internal organs and the brain. The feline body has about 244 bones, compared to 206 for the human frame.

The Feline Musculature

Muscles are composed of tiny filaments that move in relation to each other when stimulated by a nerve impulse. This movement accounts for the work a muscle does, be it launching the cat from a dresser to a bed, helping the cat pounce on a mouse, or helping us open a can of cat food. Muscles also allow internal movement—digestion, breathing, blood circulation, and many other functions.

Cat Skin

One of the body's largest organs, the skin is a supple, elastic tissue that protects the cat from infection and injury and helps to conserve moisture and temperature. It helps produce vitamin D (through sun exposure) and serves as an anchor for the cat's insulating coat. In addition, it helps provide the cat with information about its environment through the millions of nerve endings buried within it. And with the exception of the nose and paws, the feline skin does not contain sweat glands.

Your cat's skin is relatively loose on its body, as if there is a bit too much of it to go around. A survival adaptation, this loose skin gives your kitty a better chance to slip out of a hungry predator's mouth.

The Respiratory System

Primarily responsible for supplying oxygen to the body and removing carbon dioxide, the respiratory system—consisting of the lungs, air passages, and diaphragm—also helps regulate the cat's body temperature, and aids the cat in using its sense of smell. Cats normally breathe about twenty to thirty times per minute, a bit faster than we humans. If the cat is hot or has just exerted itself, this rate can go up dramatically. Panting helps cool the cat on hot days.

The Digestive System

Your cat needs a regular supply of nutrients to grow, to replace worn-out tissue, and to supply energy for the normal chemical reactions that occur in its body. These nutrients are extracted from food as it passes through your cat's digestive tract, which is essentially a long tube running from the mouth to the anus, working in conjunction with the digestive glands to take in and break down food into a usable, absorbable form.

The "digestive tube" consists of the mouth, pharynx, esophagus, stomach, small and large intestines, and anus. The digestive glands include the salivary glands, liver, gallbladder, and pancreas.

The cat's digestive tract is designed to efficiently convert a largely meat diet into energy in a fairly short period of time. The feline digestive tract is proportionally much shorter than our own.

E-ssential

Cats are carnivores, and, despite having the occasional odd craving for grass or some other plant material, they need a diet of animal protein. They require substantially more protein than dogs, which is why dog food is not nutritionally suitable for cats. Cats will not remain healthy on a vegetarian diet. They must eat meat.

The Urinary Tract

The urinary system serves to rid the body of waste materials that build up as a result of normal cell metabolism. If these waste products were not removed, they would slowly poison the animal, as happens when the kidneys fail.

Chemical waste products are carried in the bloodstream to the kidneys, where they are filtered out of the blood and combined with excess water to make urine. Urine is stored in the bladder until the cat urinates, which involves passing the urine from the bladder, through a tube called the urethra, out the body.

Kidney failure is commonly seen in older cats, especially those that reach the age of fifteen or older. Many common household chemicals and substances, such as antifreeze, can damage the kidneys or cause kidney failure in cats of any age, which is why it's important to keep your cat away from such toxins.

For cats experiencing kidney failure, a transplant may be an option. Such operations have been performed successfully on cats; however, the surgery costs thousands and requires a donor cat. The owner of the cat undergoing surgery is generally expected to adopt the donor cat afterward and give it a good home.

The Reproductive System

The reproductive system does, of course, differ between the sexes. Much of the male's system is located externally. The testes (sperm-producing organs) are situated inside the scrotum, a pouch of skin visible (in unaltered males) directly below the anus. The penis of the male cat is covered with thorny-looking papillae, which are thought to play some role in stimulating the female cat to ovulate after mating.

The female cat's reproductive system is a bit more complex. It is comprised externally of the vulva and clitoris; the cervix, uterus, fallopian tubes, and ovaries are located internally. The unaltered female regularly undergoes a cyclical reproductive period called the estrus cycle. It is during the stage of estrus that the cat is said to be "in heat." During the breeding season, females stay in estrus for about four days, and will come into heat again every two weeks or so, until allowed to breed. (Feline reproduction is covered in more detail in Chapter 18.)

The Circulatory System

Responsible for the flow of blood through the body, the circulatory system routes blood through the lungs and brings nourishment to all the cells of the body, then transports waste material to the kidneys, where it can be processed and discharged. The driving force of this system is the heart, a four-chambered pump that usually beats from about 125 to 130 times per minute in the cat, circulating blood through the body's network of blood vessels. During times of extreme physical activity, the cat's heart rate can surpass 200 beats per minute.

The Nervous System

The nervous system, consisting of the brain, spinal cord, and an intricate network of nerves, is an information-gathering and storage system, as well as the means of control for the many movements and actions of the body. After the cat's senses gather information about the external environment and internal condition, the nervous system analyzes this data and initiates the responses that will best ensure the animal's survival. Most of these responses, from fleeing a perceived danger to shivering, are begun unconsciously and automatically by the nervous system.

The Endocrine System

This system is comprised of a collection of glands that secrete chemical substances called hormones, which are needed for normal body function. These hormones regulate metabolism, growth, body temperature, stress management, behavior, and sexual functions. The endocrine glands secrete their hormones directly into the bloodstream, which transports them throughout the body.

One of these glands, the thyroid, which helps regulate the body's metabolism, can sometimes cause problems in older cats. The most common condition seen in this gland is when its functioning slows down too much to support good health, called hypothyroidism. The opposite condition, called hyperthyroidism, is when gland functioning speeds up too much. Both are covered in more detail in Chapter 13.

The Lymphatic System

The lymphatic system consists of a network of vessels that drain fluid known as lymph from all over the body and back into the bloodstream. In cats as well as in humans, this system functions as part of the immune system, helping defend against disease and infection.

All of the body tissues are bathed in lymph, which is derived from the blood. This fluid flows through the lymph nodes, which are in effect filtering devices that trap bacteria and other foreign bodies. The lymph nodes destroy or render inactive these unwanted bodies. When a particular area of the body is damaged or infected, the lymph nodes closest to the area often become swollen and tender, a condition that normally subsides as the infection reduces.

The Immune System

The cat's skin is the first line of defense against invading bacteria or viruses, but if any microorganisms manage to breach this, they will have the white blood cells to deal with. These include phagocytes (or engulfing cells), which go to war against the invaders and literally eat them up. Lymphocytes, also known as B or T cells, produce antibodies that search out and find invading organisms according to the special protein cell coverings they have (known as antigens). When located, the infectious agents are destroyed.

The immune system has a "memory" in that once the antigen for a specific infection is recognized and its specific antibodies produced, this information stays with the immune system so that future infections of the same invader can be quickly dealt with. This is how vaccines work—in cats as well as in people—a dead or modified version of a normally dangerous virus is injected into the patient, stimulating the immune system to produce antibodies against that virus. Later, if the patient is infected with the real thing, the body has already built up a resistance to it; the immune system has the right bullets, so to speak, to quickly and efficiently zap the invader before it can do any harm.

What to Look for in a Veterinarian

Choosing a veterinarian for your kitty could be one of the most important decisions you make regarding your pet, and the choice should be made before you need the vet's services. Your cat may at some time need serious medical attention that might just save its life. You want the right professional there deciding what to do. So, what should you look for in a veterinarian?

Convenient Location and Hours

No one wants to drive a sick or injured kitty to a vet's office that is forty-five minutes from home. That ride could be potentially life threatening to your cat. You should be able to locate a capable vet within ten or fifteen minutes of your home. Make sure that the vet's hours are also convenient for you. See if there are at least a few days during the week with evening hours, allowing you to take your cat in for a checkup after you get home from work.

E-ssential

In some larger cities, you may find at least one or two veterinarians with a mobile practice who make house calls. Although a little more expensive, because you're paying a premium for their gas and travel time, a house call can be convenient and less traumatic to your cat, especially if you have multiple animals receiving routine care, such as vaccinations, at the same time.

Emergency Care

Emergencies never happen at convenient times of the day. Your veterinarian should provide convenient, efficient emergency care to his clients, or at least be able to refer you to a nearby emergency clinic when necessary. Jot the emergency number down somewhere you can easily find it when needed.

Office Organization

A well-run veterinarian's office should appear professional and organized. Although some occasional chaos is to be expected when strange animals come face to face with each other, you shouldn't see dogs and cats fighting. Nor should you see obviously sick animals waiting endlessly in the waiting room, possibly infecting other animals. The staff should be efficient and polite, and your appointment time should be honored within reason. The waiting room and clinic should always look and smell clean.

Communication

Stick with a veterinarian who makes you feel at ease and seems easy to talk to and willing to listen. A veterinarian needs to be as good at dealing with people as he is with animals, and able to explain things succinctly and compassionately without getting overly technical. Avoid a vet who seems rushed, impolite, or put off by reasonable questions. Choose someone who seems knowledgeable, kind, and genuinely interested in the health of your pet. If you don't feel comfortable with the veterinarian, find another who is more personable.

A good veterinarian keeps up with the most current medical information and tries to improve his skills through continuing education and training. A good veterinarian also tries to share knowledge and educate owners about their pet's health, without being condescending.

When should the first veterinary visit take place?

You should take your new kitten or cat to the veterinary clinic within a week of bringing it home. You need to determine the cat's general state of health, ensure that there are no infectious diseases or parasites present, get it properly vaccinated, and establish the vet/pet relationship.

Finding a Good Veterinarian

Now that you know what to look for in a veterinarian for your cat, how do you find this wonderful, kind animal doctor? There are three basic ways: through advertisements, referrals from friends or relatives, and recommendations from the shelter or breeder.

Advertisements

Advertisements and phone books are one venue for looking for a veterinarian, but these are not necessarily the best place to start. You can open up the newspapers and Yellow Pages and find a number of veterinarian clinics close to your home. Unfortunately, you will know nothing about them or their reputation. The best you can do is check out a few of them and evaluate what you see and are told.

Referral from a Friend or Relative

A much better method than throwing a dart at the Yellow Pages is asking friends or relatives if they are happy with their veterinarian. The fact that someone has stuck with a vet for a period of time is a good sign. Specifically talk to those people who own cats. Your pal the dog lover and your cousin the rabbit enthusiast can probably give you some general guidance, but the best recommendations come from people in as similar a situation to yours as possible.

Recommendation from the Shelter or Breeder

The shelter from which you adopt your cat can probably recommend one or two reputable vets in your area. Shelters deal with hundreds of animals and often have sick ones in need of medical attention. Their on-call vet just might be the most experienced cat vet in the area, so consider a shelter recommendation seriously.

If you purchased your cat from a breeder, she can definitely recommend a good vet, possibly the one she uses. One drawback to this method is that your breeder might not be located near your home, and won't know a vet that will be convenient for you. Ask anyway. The breeder just might know someone in your area, or her vet might be able to recommend someone close to you.

Annual Checkups

Many illnesses that can hurt or kill your feline friend can often be averted with early diagnosis and proper treatment. Make sure to take your cat in for a routine health checkup at least once each year, even if it appears to be in the peak of health at the time. During these annual checkups, your vet will give your feline a thorough physical exam. She may also take a fecal sample from the cat (often requested beforehand, at the time you make the appointment), and test to determine if there is a parasitic infestation.

If you schedule a visit because of a suspected illness, your vet may also take blood and urine samples for testing (the vet will probably be able to express some urine out of the cat by gently squeezing its bladder).

The annual visit is the time to have any needed vaccinations or booster shots administered to ensure that your feline is protected against potentially life-threatening diseases. Kittens usually receive their first recommended vaccinations at about six to ten weeks of age, and then get boosters about one month later. Boosters are then given annually, or as often as recommended by your vet, for the rest of the cat's life. The rabies vaccine is slightly different. It is given first at about three months of age, boosted at one year, then repeated at either one- or three-year intervals, depending on the product used.

The common vaccinations usually recommended for cats include:

- Rabies
- Feline panleukopenia (feline distemper)
- Feline calicivirus (a respiratory disease)
- Feline viral rhinotracheitis (a respiratory disease)
- Feline leukemia virus
- Feline infectious peritonitis
- Feline Chlamydia (a respiratory disease)

These diseases and others are covered in more detail in Chapter 13. Some vaccinations are recommended for all cats, while others are recommended primarily for those at highest risk of exposure. Your veterinarian can best evaluate your situation and tell you which ones your cat should have, as well as how often they need to be boostered.

How Your Vet Can Help You

Your vet can give you great advice on just about anything to do with cats, including:

- **Diet:** What foods are healthy or unhealthy; if you're feeding too much or too little.
- **Behavior:** What is proper or improper, what is causing it, and how to deal with it. If your vet cannot answer your questions about a behavioral problem, she probably knows someone who can.
- **Environment:** What is safe and unsafe; what is toxic and nontoxic.
- **Flea and tick control:** What products are safe and effective for use on cats.
- **Neutering and spaying:** How important this is to the health of your cat, and why you should have it done.

Keeping Records

Your veterinarian will keep accurate records of your cat's health, including vaccinations, treatments, surgeries, and medications. The cat's weight and body temperature will be recorded each time you visit. All of this is important, as a medical history may help diagnose a pattern of illness or abnormal behavior. These records will also be helpful if you must move and re-establish a relationship with a new veterinarian elsewhere. Your current veterinarian can forward the records to the new vet's office, helping her become familiar with your pet more quickly.

It's a good idea to keep track of your cat's vital signs, whether you take them or your vet does. It's as simple as jotting them down in a notebook. Normal vital signs in the cat are: body temperature, 100 to 102.5°F (37.8 to 39°C); pulse, 100 to 180 beats per minute; respiration, 20 to 30 breaths per minute.

You should keep accurate records as well, including all visits to the vet, vaccinations, any sicknesses or traumas your cat suffers, and what medications were used, along with their effectiveness and side effects, if any. Also, consider writing down your cat's weight on a monthly basis, along with the amount and type of food you're feeding. This will help you detect weight loss or weight gain, which can signal certain health issues that need to be addressed. Often, this type of journal can expose to your vet pertinent clues to a chronic condition, such as an allergy in the making.

Signs of Illness

Heading off serious feline illnesses at the pass involves keen observational skills on the owner's part. Ask your veterinarian to show you how to take your cat's temperature and other vital signs, should the need arise. Often, changes in a cat's appetite or elimination habits are the first signs that something may be wrong. Here are some other important symptoms that every owner should pay attention to and report to a veterinarian:

- A temperature over 102.5 degrees Fahrenheit
- Persistent diarrhea or vomiting, especially in combination with fever or other signs of illness
- Dehydration, evident by lifting and releasing a pinch of skin on the cat's back, and watching to see how quickly it rebounds. If it takes more than a moment, your cat may be dehydrated.
- Persistent lethargy combined with poor appetite and weight loss
- Bad breath, especially if combined with excessive thirst
- A cough or wheeze accompanied by fever
- Runny nose or weepy eyes
- Bloodshot eyes or a prolapsed third eyelid
- Limping or obvious pain in the limbs or spinal column
- Any lumps or swollen areas (could indicate a cancerous growth or trauma)
- Pale gums and lethargy, possibly combined with loss of appetite or fever
- Dry, brittle coat, hair falling out in patches, or dry flaky skin with sores
- Dark, waxy buildup in the ears (indicative of ear mites)
- Changes in sleeping habits

- Excessive vocalization (except for a female in estrus)
- Excessive (or nonexistent) self-grooming
- Personality changes, such as irritability in a normally happy, friendly cat

When Urgent Care Is Needed

Symptoms that warrant an immediate trip to the vet include:

- High fever
- Any type of paralysis, be it partial or complete
- Severe shortness of breath, extreme lethargy, and lack of appetite
- Any signs that your cat may have consumed a toxic substance, including difficulty breathing, persistent drooling, excessive lethargy, vomiting, or diarrhea
- Wounds, especially ones that won't stop bleeding
- Any accidental trauma, as from a fall, an attack by another animal or person, or being hit by a car
- An infected abscess (a common result of cat fights)
- Cessation of breathing or loss of consciousness
- Broken limbs or trauma to the eye
- Persistent bloody diarrhea or vomiting

Changes in Elimination Habits

Sudden changes in your cat's elimination habits, or failure to use the litter box, can indicate an underlying health problem and should always be investigated for medical causes first, before assuming that the problem is behavioral in origin. Any time a cat suddenly begins to urinate or defecate in unusual places or to go more or less frequently than is normal for that individual, suspect some health problem and have your veterinarian check it out right away.

Pain or straining during elimination is also cause for concern. If your cat meows forlornly or rocks slightly from side to side during elimination, these are signs of distress and discomfort and should be investigated promptly.

Changes in Appearance

The appearance of the cat's waste is also a good diagnostic tool. Normal stools are fairly firm and dark brown. If stools suddenly become loose or black in color (indicative of bleeding in the stomach or small intestine), or show blood, suspect a problem. Obviously, worms that appear in the stool point to a parasitic infection. Extremely malodorous stool can point to a bad diet or the presence of some toxic condition.

Normal urine is a pale yellow. If your cat's urine is either clear or a dark, deep yellow, there may be a kidney problem or some other disorder present.

Medicating Cats

If your cat develops an infection or illness, the veterinarian may prescribe medication that you will need to administer at home. Unfortunately, most cats are not very cooperative in this regard, so be sure to ask your veterinarian to describe or demonstrate the best way to medicate your cat.

Giving Pills

Many pills and capsules can be crushed or sprinkled onto a spoon of canned cat food and fed to the unsuspecting cat. When this doesn't work, here's a technique that requires a little practice to master:

1. Hold the pill between the thumb and forefinger of one hand.
2. Place your other hand atop the cat's head. Position the thumb and forefinger of this hand at the corners of the cat's mouth.
3. Tilt the cat's head back until the nose points straight up. The mouth will open at this point.
4. Quickly drop or place the pill onto the back-center portion of the tongue.
5. Close the mouth and hold it shut for a few seconds while you massage the cat's throat, to encourage swallowing.

If you cannot master this technique, or if the cat is very uncooperative, you can purchase a "pill gun" at the pet shop, which will shoot the pill way back into the cat's throat.

Instilling Eye Drops

Aside from giving pills, the other most common thing pet owners need to do at some point is instill ear or eye medications. Your veterinarian will demonstrate the proper procedure for you in the office. When you do it at home, ask an assistant to help restrain the cat while you steady its head with one hand and administer the medication with the other hand. Follow the correct dosing instructions on the medication package.

When instilling eye medication, use your thumb to pull down the lower eye lid so that it forms a little pocket. Then squeeze or drop the correct amount of medication into that lid pocket. If the medication is an ointment, close and open the eyelid to distribute the ointment over the eye.

Instilling Ear Drops

For instilling ear drops, you'll also need an assistant to help restrain the cat. Again, always read and follow the label directions. Hold the cat's head steady with one hand and squeeze the medicine into the ear with the other. Then gently massage the ear for several seconds to ensure that the medication flows down into the ear canal. When you release the cat, be prepared for it to shake its head and fling out some of the medicine.

Health Care for the Aging Cat

Thanks to better nutrition and veterinary care, cats are living longer, often into their late teens or twenties. A healthy, well-cared-for cat can age almost imperceptibly, but if you pay close attention, you will see the telltale signs. Typically considered a "senior" by age ten, an older cat may begin to put on some weight as its metabolism slows. Or, it may begin to lose weight due to some loss of kidney function or a digestive system that doesn't utilize nutrients as well as it used to. Either symptom signals a need for a checkup and maybe a change in diet.

Tooth loss in an older cat may also require some dental care or a change to a softer diet that's easier to chew. There are some therapeutic diets available on the market specially formulated for the needs of senior cats. Ask your veterinarian if she can recommend one for your cat's specific case.

Just as in humans, the cat's senses gradually become less acute over time. Flexibility decreases, and joints become stiffer and susceptible to arthritis. The cat's immune system and general resistance to infectious disease decreases, opening up the way for various disorders, including cancer. The owner should be particularly vigilant about observing and reporting any unusual symptoms or behavioral changes in the older cat.

Euthanasia

The downside of pet ownership is that cats don't live nearly as long as humans do. Inevitably, the time comes to say goodbye. When the cat's bowel and bladder movements fail, when the appetite is gone, and when the senses no longer function, sit down with your vet and have a heart-to-heart talk about your options. Euthanasia is a humane and painless end to life, and it can release your pet from great humiliation and suffering.

Still, the impending loss of a loving companion, regardless of species, is a painful experience, but should not be avoided simply to save yourself from emotional distress. Always remember that an old cat in failing health can often be in great pain that sometimes cannot be eased—for example, the cat whose kidneys completely fail, or one with incurable cancer.

Consider all options carefully before making a final decision. Sometimes a diagnosis of a terminal illness is inaccurate, and sometimes a novel combination of therapies and techniques can relieve a cat's pain and improve its quality of life immensely. Get a second opinion, if you feel you need to.

Once the decision to euthanize is made, your vet will explain the procedure to you and answer any questions. With an anesthetic overdose administered by injection, death comes rapidly and peacefully, without pain or discomfort. Some, but not all, veterinarians are willing to perform this service at your home so your cat can die in familiar surroundings. You have the right to be present during the procedure, although you need not be.

Coping with the Death of Your Pet

Seriously consider having someone, a caring friend or relative, go with you to the clinic for the euthanasia procedure. You will be very emotional, and may not even be capable of driving. During the days and weeks after the death of your cat, you will need to grieve the loss in your own way. Consider making a donation to a local animal shelter in your cat's name or planting a tree in its memory.

Many areas now have support groups to help pet owners cope with the loss of their animal companion. Ask your veterinarian or local animal shelter what's available where you live. Or, call the Association for Pet Loss and Bereavement, Inc. at (718) 382-0690, or visit their Web site at *www.aplb.org*.

Realize that some people have never experienced the human-animal bond and will not understand the depth of your loss. Unaware of their ignorance, they may make comments that seem callous and heartless, such as, "It was only a cat. You can get another one." Ignore these remarks and allow yourself time to grieve and heal. Another cat can never replace the companion you've just lost, but when the time feels right, you may decide to honor your cat by giving another one a loving home.

Opting for Burial or Cremation

Before euthanasia, decide what to do with the cat's remains. Your veterinarian can dispose of the body, if you desire. Most areas have pet undertaking services that can help you with the arrangements, including an appropriate burial plot. Many owners choose to bury their pets on their family property or in a pet cemetery, whereas others choose cremation. Your veterinarian can usually refer you to these types of services available in your area.

13 Common Illnesses

Cats are capable of contracting or developing a wide range of illnesses, just as humans are. Fortunately, many of these can be prevented through routine vaccination. It is extremely important for all cat owners to know about the diseases and disorders that can afflict their animals, and to establish with their veterinarian a good schedule for preventive care and immunizations that will continue throughout the cat's life. This chapter discusses the most common feline diseases and conditions, as well as preventive measures and treatments.

Feline Diseases

Typically, veterinarians recommend vaccinating cats for rabies (required by law in most states), feline distemper, feline herpes virus (rhinotracheitis), and feline calicivirus. These are considered the "core" vaccines that no cat should be without. Often, several vaccines can be combined into one injection, so that the cat gets stuck with only one needle. In addition, your veterinarian may recommend "non-core" (optional) vaccines for certain other diseases, if your cat has a higher risk of exposure because it is used for breeding, travels to cat shows, is allowed outdoors, frequents boarding facilities, or lives in the company of other cats. Booster shots may be needed annually or every three years, depending on the product given, to ensure continued immunity throughout the cat's life. Your veterinarian can tailor a vaccination and booster schedule that best suits your cat's needs.

Rabies

An acute viral infection of the nervous system, rabies is also known as hydrophobia. Transmitted by a bite or a lick on an open sore, the virus travels from the wound site along the nerve pathways to the brain, where it causes inflammation and infection that leads to spasms, pain, drooling, delirium, paralysis, and bizarre or vicious behavior. Once infected with rabies, the cat is doomed to die. Bats, skunks, raccoons, and foxes are all known carriers of the disease, and can infect your cat, or you, with a bite or lick.

The only way to test an animal suspected of rabies is to destroy it and examine its brain tissue. A person who has been bitten by a rabid animal must begin a series of painful injections soon after exposure to prevent the disease from progressing. Otherwise, the disease is nearly always fatal.

Signs of infection usually begin to show four to eight weeks after the initial contact. This can vary widely, however. The first signs in a cat are a general restlessness; a normally curious, confident cat might suddenly begin behaving hesitantly or fearfully, and may choose to isolate itself. In the next stage, a fever sets in and the cat soon loses interest in food. It may show insatiable thirst, but attempts to drink bring on painful throat spasms (hence the term "hydrophobia," or "fear of water"). Extreme aggression, paralysis, coma, and death soon follow.

Vaccination, followed by regular booster shots, is an effective means of preventing rabies in your cat. In addition, if your cat bites someone, and the bite is treated and reported to authorities, you may be asked to furnish proof that your cat has been vaccinated against rabies. Without proof of vaccination, your cat may be quarantined for a period of time for observation, or worse.

Any unvaccinated cat that has been infected with the rabies virus should be euthanized, not only to spare it great suffering, but to prevent other animals or humans from becoming infected. Vaccinating and keeping your cat indoors will prevent rabies. Cats can be vaccinated against rabies by four months of age. Booster shots are necessary throughout the cat's life to maintain immunity.

What is Cat-Scratch Fever?

Some people develop fever, rash, and infection after getting scratched or bitten by a cat. The malady is caused by a bacterium and is usually accompanied by local lymph-node swelling. The injury site may also swell and abscess. Most people recover fully without complication; however, the wound may require medical treatment. To help prevent cat-scratch fever, thoroughly clean all cat bites or scratches promptly and apply a topical disinfectant to the wound.

Feline Distemper

Other names for this highly contagious and often fatal viral disease include feline panleukopenia virus (FPV), feline infectious enteritis, and feline parvovirus (no relation to canine distemper). The term "leukopenia" refers to the characteristically low white blood cell count associated with the condition. The term "enteritis" refers to an infection that attacks the intestinal tract, and the resulting painful abdomen that an afflicted cat sometimes displays. Other symptoms include appetite loss, depression, fever, and vomiting yellow bile.

Prevalent among outdoor and stray cats, the disease spreads from cat to cat through contact with any bodily secretion. It is also a hardy virus that can remain a potent source of infection for weeks outside of a host. Normal disinfecting may not kill it. Only cleaning with a dilute bleach solution seems to render it harmless. Fortunately, the disease is easily prevented by routine vaccination.

E-Fact

Cats do not catch colds like humans do. They can, however, contract several upper respiratory illnesses that look like the common cold, but that are much more deadly to their species. If your cat shows cold-like symptoms such as sneezing, runny nose, and watery eyes, don't wait to see if it gets better in a day or two. You may waste valuable treatment time. Such symptoms in the cat are always cause for concern and demand immediate veterinary attention.

Feline Herpesvirus

Another name for this deadly upper respiratory infection is feline viral rhinotracheitis (FVR). Also referred to simply as rhino, this condition is caused by a herpes virus (not related to the herpes virus in humans), but is easily prevented by routine vaccination. Displaying cold-like symptoms, cats with rhino will sneeze, cough, and have a runny discharge from the eyes and nose. They may have conjunctivitis, fever, and a loss of appetite as well. The disease spreads easily through direct contact and is often fatal in kittens and elderly cats. Cats that have had it can remain carriers for the rest of their lives, which makes them a health risk to other cats.

Feline Calicivirus (FCV)

There are many different strains of FCV, also known as feline flu, making vaccination difficult. Although not normally life-threatening to the adult cat, it can be dangerous for the young or old. Lasting from seven to ten days, the condition causes a fever that may last for several days. Ulcerations of the mouth can also occur, as can breathing difficulties, sneezing, and discharge. Loss of weight and appetite is possible, as is vomiting, diarrhea, and dehydration. FCV can weaken the cat for secondary infections to take hold.

Treatment involves proper diagnosis by your vet, rest, medication to combat infection, and possibly fluids to keep the cat hydrated. Vet-prescribed antidiarrheal medication may be needed as well. You can prevent FCV by getting your cat properly vaccinated on a regular basis.

Chlamydia

Yet another respiratory type illness, this one is less common and usually milder than those previously discussed. Weepy eyes, swollen eyelids, and conjunctivitis are characteristic symptoms. A vaccine is available and often administered in combination with others, but some veterinarians consider this vaccine "non-core" or optional and recommend it only for multi-cat households or for cats with a high risk of exposure.

Feline Leukemia Virus (FeLV)

This particularly nasty viral disease passes from cat to cat primarily through bite wounds and prolonged contact. Its name comes from its tendency to suppress the bone marrow and immune system and cause certain cancers, such as leukemia. Symptoms vary but often include weight loss, anemia, poor appetite, lethargy, diarrhea, incontinence, vomiting, and recurring infections.

Some cats sicken and die quickly from this incurable disease, while others can have it for years without showing outward signs of infection. That's why all kittens and cats should be tested for this disease before they are used for breeding, released for adoption, or brought into a household where other cats reside. If a cat tests positive for FeLV, the owner must decide whether to euthanize the animal or keep it strictly indoors and away from all other healthy cats for the remainder of its life.

There is a vaccine that prevents FeLV, but it has been associated with vaccine-induced cancers that occur at the injection site. For this reason, many veterinarians consider this an optional non-core vaccine and recommend it for cats that go outside and have a higher risk of exposure to the infection. Cats kept strictly indoors have a much lower risk of ever coming into contact with FeLV.

Feline Infectious Peritonitis (FIP)

Another immune-defeating viral condition, FIP also has no cure. Caused by a coronavirus, FIP attacks white blood cells and other tissues, causing a breakdown in the body's disease-fighting capabilities. It is nearly always fatal, although an infected cat may not succumb to the disease right away.

FIP is more common among cats living under crowded conditions (such as a cattery or large kitten mill). The disease is transmitted from cat to cat through contact with urine, feces, saliva, and mucus, and through contact with an infected cat's food or water dish or litter box.

FIP Symptoms

Symptoms can vary depending on whether the cat has the "wet" or the "dry" form of the disease, but often include:

- High, intermittent fever that remains unresponsive to drugs
- Weight loss due to poor appetite, vomiting, and diarrhea
- Anemia
- Lethargy and depression
- Fluid in the lungs or abdominal cavity
- Kidney, pancreas, or liver failure
- Disorientation and dizziness
- Secondary infections
- Skin granulomas
- Overall unhealthy appearance

Treatment and Prevention

Your veterinarian will examine various fluids from the cat, including blood, urine, and abdominal or chest fluids, and perform a complete physical exam to properly diagnose FIP. There is no current effective treatment that can save a cat once it has been infected, although treatment of secondary infections can prolong its life and ease discomfort.

E-ssential

You can help prevent FIP by keeping your cat indoors and away from potential carriers, especially strays. Do not take a stray into your home until it has been checked out and given a clean bill of health by your veterinarian.

A vaccine, administered as nasal drops, exists and is sometimes given in environments that contain many cats, such as large breeding facilities and multiple-cat homes; however, studies have questioned the efficacy of the vaccine. For this reason, many vets do not advise owners of cats at low risk of infection to receive the vaccination. A low-risk cat would be a healthy, indoor-only pet that never comes into contact with other cats, especially strays. Discuss this optional non-core vaccine with your veterinarian.

Feline Immunodeficiency Virus (FIV)

A retrovirus similar in structure to HIV (human immunodeficiency virus), FIV or feline AIDS affects cats worldwide more and more, due to an exploding cat population, inadequate vaccinations, and the irresponsibility of owners who allow their cats to roam freely outdoors and interact with other cats. FIV (which is species-specific and infects only cats, not people) invades the victim's body and tricks the affected cells into producing more viruses. It often remains hidden in the host for years without causing any major signs of illness, but it can cause sickness immediately upon infection.

FIV (like HIV) attacks cells of the immune system, particularly certain white blood cells, known as T cells, that serve an important role in combating infection. By weakening the cat's immune system in this way, FIV opens the cat up to many illnesses that would normally be successfully dealt with by the body's defenses.

Transmission and Symptoms

FIV is transmitted from cat to cat through sharing of bodily fluids, including saliva and blood. It is thought that bite wounds (from cat fights) are the most common form of transmission. Pregnant felines can also transmit the disease to their unborn or nursing kittens. Cats with FIV eventually begin to show signs of infection, including:

- Fever and diarrhea
- Swollen lymph nodes
- Low white blood cell count
- Lethargy and weight loss
- Behavioral changes
- Seizures
- Skin sores that will not heal
- Sores in the mouth

As the virus weakens the cat's immune system, many other symptoms can appear, including secondary viral or bacterial infections, parasites, and cancers. Respiratory problems are common, as are urinary maladies, conjunctivitis, nervous system disorders, and mental deterioration.

Treatment and Prevention

Treatment for this lethal condition can extend the infected cat's life (as well as its quality), but will not save it. Because the disease is so infectious, cats with FIV must be kept indoors, away from other cats. Letting an FIV-infected cat outdoors would be irresponsible, as would adopting any new cat into the home where an infected cat resides.

Preventing FIV in your cat can be as simple as keeping it indoors. As with FeLV, a test can confirm whether a cat is negative or positive for FIV, and all cats should be tested before being used for breeding, released for adoption, or brought into a household with other cats.

A vaccine for FIV is available, but its use is somewhat controversial at this time, because the vaccine causes the cat to test positive for the virus, even though it doesn't have the disease. Most veterinarians recommend it only optionally, for cats that go outdoors or that have a high exposure risk.

Other Common Conditions

Aside from several feline-specific illnesses, cats can suffer from many other familiar-sounding disorders, too, such as cancer, diabetes, arthritis, and even allergies. Too numerous to list all of them here, this section highlights some of the more commonly known conditions. As a cat owner, you should purchase a comprehensive veterinary reference manual on cat health and read as much current information as you can about cat care. Veterinary medicine advances rapidly as new treatments and vaccines are developed, so it's important for pet owners to stay informed by reading and talking with their veterinarians.

Hairballs

Cats are meticulously clean animals, regularly licking and cleaning their bodies to remove dirt, parasites, and loose hair. Unfortunately, cats can swallow too much hair, which often forms balls in the stomach or intestines. This is a common occurrence that usually needs no attention from you. Normally, these hairballs pass harmlessly through the cat or are vomited up. But if they are not passed, they can create blockages and cause intestinal problems. In rare cases, surgery may be necessary to remove the blockage.

Prevention of hairballs is fairly straightforward. Groom your cat often to remove as much loose hair as possible. (See Chapter 11 on grooming.) Any hair you remove is that much less that can find its way into the cat's stomach. If vomiting becomes frequent, see your vet, and consider giving your cat a commercial hairball remedy available at pet shops and your vet's office. When smeared on the cat's paw, the cat will lick the substance off, and then the ingested remedy assists the passage of hairballs through the digestive tract. Some commercial cat foods are also formulated to help prevent internal hairball accumulations.

Vomiting

Cats can vomit at the drop of a hat, it seems. Normally, it is due to a hairball or eating grass and is generally not a cause for great alarm. However, if frequent vomiting persists, you should see your vet. Persistent vomiting by a cat that otherwise seems healthy can lead to malnourishment and dehydration. Your vet will need to help you determine just what in the cat's home environment is creating the problem. In some cases, vomiting can occur due to stress. Sudden changes in the cat's environment, such as a move or a new pet, can cause this problem.

Diarrhea

Occurring in almost every cat at least one time or another, diarrhea usually results from eating or drinking food or water that is either contaminated or is simply not agreeable to that cat's system. While diarrhea can be a symptom of more serious diseases, it is often associated with stress brought on by sudden changes in the cat's environment. A change of a brand of food or litter can cause it, as can relocation to another home. Loud noises or mistreatment by humans can also bring on a bout of diarrhea, as can the sudden introduction of another person or animal into the home. Remember that cats prefer the status quo, so if you must change something in their environment, do so as gradually as possible.

Never use any over-the-counter anti-diarrhea drug for humans, such as Kaopectate or Pepto-Bismol, to treat diarrhea in cats. These drugs contain an aspirin derivative, which can be toxic to cats. Kaopectate was once used to treat diarrhea in small animals, and is sometimes cited as a remedy in older texts; however, the medication was reformulated several years ago and an aspirin derivative was added to it, which makes it unsafe for use in cats.

Diarrhea in kittens is much more serious than in adult cats because it can more quickly cause severe dehydration, often fatal in baby animals. Aging cats will be more severely affected as well. Owners of the very young and the very old must, therefore, be alert to this condition and take seriously any such changes in bowel habits.

Allergies

Cats can develop allergies to certain substances, just as people do. The allergic cat's skin can become itchy, breathing can be labored, the hair can fall out, the eyes and nose can become watery, and the cat can develop severe diarrhea and vomiting. Although rare, cats can also have allergic reactions to vaccinations ranging from mild to life threatening. Any unusual symptoms or behaviors noted shortly after a cat has had its shots should be reported to the veterinarian immediately.

Some cats are allergic to fleas and will develop an itchy skin condition called flea-allergy dermatitis from flea bites. The flea's saliva actually causes the itchy allergic response. This condition can usually be eliminated by appropriate flea-control measures.

In the case of food allergies and allergies related to other substances, such as a particular drug or shampoo, the actual allergen (the offending material) is usually harder to determine and eliminate, and you will need a veterinarian's advice in doing so.

Conjunctivitis

An inflammation of the inner eyelid, conjunctivitis is a common malady in cats. Often seen as a symptom of various respiratory infections, it can, if left untreated, cause permanent damage to the cat's eye.

Initial symptoms include excessive tearing of the affected eye, progressing from a clear to a thicker yellow discharge. The eyelids and white of the eye may appear pinkish-red and swollen. Newborn kittens sometimes suffer from this condition, caused by bacteria in the uterus of the mother, and should be promptly treated by your vet.

Ringworm

A non-core (optional) vaccine is available for this deceptively named skin disorder, which isn't caused by a worm at all, but by a fungus. It spreads easily through physical contact or airborne spores, and humans can get it from an infected animal. Although the symptoms, patchy hair loss and scaly skin, are often confused with other skin conditions, a veterinarian can confirm the diagnosis by examining a skin scraping, and then prescribe appropriate medications. Usually, all animals in the home must be treated, and the home thoroughly cleaned to get rid of the spores. The vaccine is generally only recommended if ringworm has been a problem in the household. Keeping cats indoors helps avoid ever encountering the fungus in the first place.

Cancer

All animals can get cancer, and cats are no exception. Cancers, or malignant growths, can develop anywhere in the cat's body. Although more commonly seen in older cats, cancer can strike at any age.

As in humans, early detection and treatment greatly enhances the cat's chances of surviving cancer. When left unchecked cancer is almost certainly fatal, especially after it spreads to several areas of the body. The range of symptoms is vast, but the most obvious is any unusual growth on the body. When petting your cat, check periodically for lumps or swellings, and waste no time in having any such abnormalities investigated by a veterinarian.

Certain cancers, called fibrosarcomas, appear to be vaccine-induced because they develop at injection sites. Although rare, these tumors have most often been associated with the FeLV and rabies vaccines. Research continues in an effort to find the cancer-causing culprit in these cases and to try to make the vaccines safer. Meanwhile, most veterinarians avoid giving these vaccines between the shoulder blades, because tumors in that area are less operable. Instead, the FeLV injection is generally given in the cat's left rear leg, and the rabies is given in the right rear leg.

Feline Lower Urinary Tract Disease (FLUTD)

In this potentially life-threatening condition, formerly known as feline urologic syndrome (FUS), the formation of stones or crystals in the lower urinary tract (bladder and urethra, which carries urine out of the body) can cause partial or total blockages leading to urine retention and infection. Left untreated, permanent kidney damage or death can result from built-up toxins in the blood.

Symptoms to watch out for include:

- Frequent need to urinate, with only a small amount of urine passed each time
- Urination in unusual places
- Pain during urination, usually indicated by meowing or crying
- Malodorous urine
- Urine tinged with blood
- Frequent licking of the genital areas

The condition occurs more often in male cats, but may also afflict females. Treatment may involve putting the cat on a course of antibiotics and urinary acidifiers. The antibiotics clear up the bacterial infection, while the acidifiers dissolve the crystals in the urinary tract. In some situations, surgery may be needed to remove a blockage or widen the urethral passage. Because certain food ingredients are associated with this condition, your veterinarian may also recommend a change in diet to prevent recurrences. See Chapter 13 for more details about the dietary link with FLUTD.

Kidney Dysfunction

Responsible for filtering the cat's blood as well as excreting waste products and excess water in the form of urine, the cat's kidneys are essential organs. A cat with kidney disease is a very sick cat indeed, for without proper kidney function, the body is quickly overwhelmed by a buildup of toxins in the blood, leading to coma and death. Kidney failure is quite common in the elderly cat and is often what takes a long-lived cat's life in old age. In cats of any age, kidney problems can result from many causes, including congenital defects, infections, metabolic disorders, toxic substances (such as antifreeze), impaired blood supply, and trauma.

Symptoms of kidney dysfunction include:

- Increased thirst
- Increased amounts of clear-colored urine that has little or no odor
- Loss of appetite and weight
- Incontinence and vomiting
- Bad breath
- Overall decline in thriftiness and appearance

Blood work confirms the presence of kidney dysfunction. The disorder is progressive, but measures can be taken to make the cat more comfortable. Depending on the degree of function lost, the veterinarian may recommend administering fluids under the skin at regular intervals. The veterinarian shows the owner how to do this easily at home. The procedure serves as a form of kitty dialysis and seems to make the cat feel better by easing the burden on the kidneys and flushing some of the toxins from the body.

E-Fact

Kidney transplants have been performed successfully in cats and may, in certain cases, be a valid option to consider for cats young enough to survive the surgery, and for owners wealthy enough to afford it. The procedure costs thousands of dollars and requires a healthy kidney from a donor cat. The owner of the sick cat is generally asked to adopt the donor cat afterward and give it a home. Veterinary clinics that perform these transplants are few and far between, so some travel likely would be involved.

Detecting problems with your cat's kidneys is not easy. That's why it's important to pay close attention to your cat's everyday health, and visit the vet at the first sign of trouble. If caught early, kidney disease can often be arrested, or its progression slowed, extending the cat's life.

You can also help minimize the chances of kidney disease in your cat by feeding a well-balanced, well-formulated feline diet that is not excessively high in protein, salt, or phosphorus. Ask your veterinarian to recommend an appropriate diet for your older cat's nutritional needs.

Diabetes

This life-threatening disease is caused by the failure of the pancreas to produce the hormone insulin, which is necessary for the metabolism of glucose (blood sugar), a primary nutrient of the body's cells. By some process that is still not completely understood, the cells of the pancreas responsible for secreting insulin are destroyed. One theory is that the body's immune system goes haywire and attacks these cells under the mistaken impression that they are foreign invaders. Often occurring in the older or obese cat, diabetes is thought to have a hereditary component to it.

A cat suffering from diabetes has skyrocketing blood glucose levels, which can cause:

- Excessive urination, thirst, and hunger
- Weight loss and fatigue
- Degeneration of blood vessels and nerve cells
- Dehydration and diarrhea
- Blindness and kidney damage
- Ulcerated skin
- Coma and death

Treatment involves the administration of insulin to restore the metabolism of glucose in the body. Occasionally, special dietary regimens and oral hypoglycemic agents will suffice in keeping the blood sugar levels stable. Your vet will teach you how to inject insulin, if necessary.

Diabetes is not a disease to be taken lightly; left untreated, it will certainly lead to your cat's death. If you observe any of the aforementioned symptoms, play it safe and see your vet right away. A simple blood or urine test could save your feline friend a lot of suffering. You can help prevent the onset of diabetes by watching your cat's weight and feeding a well-balanced, high-quality, veterinary-approved cat food.

Thyroid Disease

The thyroid is an endocrine gland in the neck area that controls the body's metabolism. When it goes haywire, producing either too much or too little of the necessary thyroid hormones, it can cause a range of symptoms and make the cat seriously ill.

Hyperthyroidism

The overproduction of thyroid hormones, hyperthyroidism, is possibly the most common problem of the feline endocrine system. Usually associated with older cats, it can appear in youngsters as well. Symptoms of hyperthyroidism are numerous, sometimes making it a difficult condition to diagnose. Signs of the problem include:

- Enlarged thyroid gland (felt as a lump in the throat area)
- Weight loss despite ravenous appetite
- Restlessness and irritability
- Diarrhea, vomiting, and excessive urination
- Higher blood pressure and heart rate

The diagnosis of hyperthyroidism is confirmed through physical examination and testing to measure thyroid hormone levels in the blood. Treatment consists of drug therapy that will inhibit the production of thyroid hormones, or, in some cases, the surgical removal of part or all of the thyroid gland. Alternatively, administering a dosage of radioactive iodine, which is absorbed by the thyroid gland and renders it inactive, may be less stressful to an older cat. Not all veterinary clinics are equipped to provide the latter treatment, however, and some travel may be necessary, if this option is chosen.

Once the overactive thyroid gland has been removed or destroyed, the cat will need supplements of thyroid hormone for the rest of its life.

Hypothyroidism

The opposite of an overactive thyroid, hypothyroidism, extremely rare in cats, results from the thyroid gland's not producing enough thyroid hormones. A cat suffering from this problem does not always become lethargic and obese, as one might expect; often the animal becomes unpredictably aggressive, shy, and uneasy, and it may develop abnormal skin and coat problems. Diagnosis of this condition involves a blood test, which will measure the amount of thyroid hormone in the cat's system. Once hypothyroidism is confirmed, hormone supplementation can bring the cat back to normal behavioral and physical health.

Common Conditions in Older Cats

Because of advances in veterinary care and feline nutrition, cats are living longer, healthier lives these days. The average life span for an indoor cat is about fourteen to seventeen years, but many cats are now living into their twenties. (Outdoor cats have a significantly reduced life span, due to the many hazards they are exposed to.) As a result of cats living longer, veterinarians are now treating diseases common in older cats that they didn't see much of just a few decades ago.

Arthritis

A painful disease of the skeletal joints, arthritis is characterized by pain, swelling, stiffness, and inflammation. Arthritis occurs more often in older cats, but is also seen in younger cats with birth defects, and in those that have suffered injuries to skeletal joints. An afflicted cat will not seem as agile and will slow down somewhat over time. It may often come up temporarily lame after exerting itself, and be extremely sensitive to touch in and around the affected areas. In advanced stages of arthritis, the cat may not be able to get around at all. Although not presently curable, arthritis can be treated to make the cat's life a little easier.

Never be tempted to give any over-the-counter drug containing aspirin, acetaminophen, naproxen, or ibuprofen to a cat that appears to be in pain. While these drugs may help ease pain in humans, they can be fatal to cats, even in low dosages, and cause lethal liver damage. If a cat is in pain, consult a veterinarian for appropriate treatment.

Urinary Incontinence

Defined as uncontrolled involuntary urination, incontinence can result from numerous causes, including injury or disease of the urinary tract. This disorder often affects the older cat, partly because the efficiency of the sphincter muscles surrounding the urethra declines with age. Incontinence can also be caused by abnormal stress in the cat's environment at any age. Infections, urinary tract crystals, and tumors can all cause your cat to become incontinent, as can damage to the brain or spinal cord. Trauma or infection involving the pelvic area can also bring on this condition.

If you suspect that your cat is incontinent (and not just house soiling or marking territory), see your vet immediately. He will test a sample of the cat's urine to determine if there is infection, inflammation, diabetes, or crystal formation present. Ultrasound and X-rays can be done to determine if there is some type of obstruction. Physical examination can help tell if the cat's bladder or urethra is damaged or infected.

Liver Disease

The liver is one of the most important organs in the body, regulating the levels of most of the chemicals in the blood. It also produces proteins for the blood plasma, helps regulate the distribution of fats in the body, and stores glycogen, which is used as an energy source when needed. In addition, the liver regulates amino acid levels and helps clear the blood of certain toxins. A resilient organ, the liver can partially regenerate, and will continue to function even after over half of it has been removed.

Disease of the cat's liver is not uncommon, particularly among older cats. It is a serious matter, for without the liver, life is not possible. Signs of liver disease may include:

- Diarrhea and vomiting
- Weight and appetite loss
- Lethargy and irritability
- Seizures

Bacterial or viral infections, parasites, and numerous toxic substances can injure your cat's liver. You can help lessen the chances of your cat's contracting liver disease or damage by keeping your cat indoors, by feeding a vet-approved feline diet, and by keeping toxic plants and other substances out of your cat's reach.

14 First Aid and Emergency Care

Most cats will get sick or injure themselves at one time or another. The owner needs to know what constitutes an emergency and how to respond. Taking the correct action could mean the difference between life and death for your cat. Always be prepared for emergencies and keep your veterinarian's emergency number in a handy place. It's also a good idea to keep a feline first-aid kit on hand, just in case.

First Aid and Vital Signs

One of your first steps toward preserving your cat's health is assembling a feline first-aid kid. Include the following items and keep the kit in an easily accessible location in your home. Keeping another kit in your car is also a good idea, in case you should need any items on the way to the vet or emergency clinic.

- A pediatric rectal or digital thermometer
- A small penlight
- Tweezers
- Syrup of ipecac
- Disinfecting solution (ask your vet for one that is safe for feline use)
- A small blanket
- Gauze pads
- A roll of gauze
- Adhesive tape
- Scissors
- Cotton swabs
- A stethoscope

In addition to having a first-aid kit on hand, every cat owner should know what a cat's normal vital signs are and how to take them. If you can gather this information properly and report it to your veterinarian over the phone, it can be helpful in determing the correct course of action in an emergency.

Taking Kitty's Temperature

A digital thermometer makes the task of taking your cat's temperature much easier. But if using a pediatric-size rectal thermometer, clean it with soap and water, rinse it well, and then shake it down to below 98 degrees Fahrenheit. Apply petroleum jelly to the tip and the first inch or so. Place a small amount of petroleum jelly on the cat's anus. Lift the cat's tail and gently insert the thermometer with a straight push, being careful not to put any sideways pressure on the shaft, which could break the tip. Insert it about one inch, and leave it in for at least one minute. Do not let the cat loose. Remove and read the results. A normal temperature reads anywhere between 101 and 102.5 degrees Fahrenheit.

Taking the Cat's Pulse

The easiest place to feel a cat's pulse is on the inner surface of one of the rear legs, right where the leg meets the body. A large femoral artery passes close to the surface. Count the pulses for fifteen seconds, then multiply by four to get the correct number of beats per minute. A normal pulse rate ranges from 100 to 180 beats per minute.

Respiration

Respiration is the cat's rate of breathing. Normal respiration is between twenty and thirty breaths per minute. You can count these by watching the rise and fall of the cat's sides as it breathes in and out, or feeling the motion with your hand. You can also listen to the cat's lungs with a stethoscope and count the breaths in and out for fifteen seconds, then multiply by four.

Injuries

Some injuries, such as minor cuts and scrapes, can be effectively treated at home. The exceptions include deep wounds, punctures, and those that have severed an artery and will not stop bleeding. Serious burns, breaks in the skin caused by a compound fracture, and animal bites also need the quick attention of a veterinarian, although you can perform preliminary treatment on these injuries to ready the cat for transport to the clinic.

Cuts and Scrapes

A scrape that barely breaks the skin (these will most likely appear on the cat's foot pads) can be cleaned with a disinfecting solution, then treated with an antibiotic ointment (ask your veterinarian what products can be safely used on cats because the cat will lick and ingest it). Often a bandage is unnecessary, although you will want to clean the scrape daily until it begins to heal and the threat of infection has passed. Be sure to reapply the antibiotic ointment each time you clean the wound. If any signs of infection appear, see your veterinarian.

E-ssential

Carefully observe any wounds on your cat's chest, to ensure that there are no air bubbles in them—an indication of a punctured lung. This serious condition will require the immediate services of a veterinarian, who may need to perform surgery to correct the problem.

Cuts that seem to be deep or continue to bleed for more than five straight minutes will probably need veterinary attention, perhaps even stitches. To control the bleeding until you reach the vet's office, apply direct pressure to the wound, by either pressing down directly on it with a gauze pad, or applying a pressure bandage, which is simply a gauze pad held in place with a gauze roll or an elastic bandage. If the wound is on a limb or tail, for example, you can wrap the area several times (not too tightly) and leave it for fifteen minutes, observing whether or not it continues to bleed, or eventually stops. Often this short period of direct pressure will quell the flow of blood and allow clotting to begin.

Sprains and Fractures

Sprains or muscle pulls will not normally call for bandaging or splinting, but may require that the cat be confined to a crate or small room for a few days to limit movement. Even if hairline or simple fractures are present, they may not need splinting right away, but will necessitate a trip to the veterinarian.

In the case of a serious break or fracture of a leg, in which the lower portion of the leg is dangling freely, you will need to stabilize it immediately with a splint. Be aware, however, that an injured cat in pain may bite and scratch, no matter how tame it is or how well it knows you. Take the necessary precautions to protect yourself and anyone else helping you.

This may include wearing thick gloves or gently wrapping the cat in a towel to restrain it.

Do not attempt to straighten or set a fracture yourself. Simply immobilize it for the trip to the veterinary clinic. Find a heavy piece of cardboard or another appropriately sized, stiff object (even a rolled up newspaper works in a pinch) to serve this purpose. Wrap the injured leg carefully (have someone help hold the cat) with cotton padding or a disposable diaper. Secure this lightly with adhesive tape, then tape the splint to the padding. Cover any skin breaks with gauze and tape to limit infection. Then get the cat to the veterinary clinic as quickly as possible.

Tourniquets

Serious bleeding of the limbs or tail that does not respond to a pressure bandage may necessitate the use of a tourniquet, a last-ditch technique you should use while preparing to go to the vet clinic. Never a first choice, tourniquets can, if applied improperly, cut off all blood flow to all areas below the wound, effectively starving those tissues of vital oxygen. Tissue death can result; in severe cases, the affected limb or tail may need to be amputated.

Use a length of rope, surgical tubing, cloth, or even an extension cord, if that is all that's available. Form a loop or slip knot, and tighten it around an area a few inches above the wound. Do not over-tighten. Increase pressure until the bleeding slows to a trickle, and always try to reduce pressure, not increase. Remember to release the tourniquet every ten minutes to allow oxygen to flow to tissues below the wound. After twenty or thirty minutes, try using only a pressure bandage to quell the bleeding. Someone should be driving you to the nearest emergency clinic while this is happening. Remember to take rags and towels with you to catch any blood that spills.

Puncture Wounds

Stop the bleeding first. No puncture wound should go unseen by your vet, owing to the frequency of infections and abscesses. In addition, the injury, especially if it's a bite from another animal, could transmit some viral or bacterial disease that could prove fatal if left untreated.

Falls

Because of their ability to right themselves in midair, cats often survive falls with little or no injury. Sometimes, however, a cat can suffer internal injuries that go unnoticed by its owner. Many cats push or tear through flimsy window screening and fall from high-rise buildings. Veterinarians see injuries from such incidents often enough to call it "high-rise syndrome." If your cat takes a fall of more than fifteen or twenty feet, it is advisable to see your veterinarian right away. Take care to move a fallen cat as little as possible, to prevent possible injury to the spinal cord, as you transport it to the clinic.

Car Accidents

No cat should ever be hit by a car, because no cat should ever be allowed outdoors unsupervised. If, as is all too frequently the case, your cat slips out unnoticed and the inevitable does happen, you will probably have a very serious situation on your hands.

First, do not panic. If you witness your cat being struck by a car, your instinctive reaction might be to become hysterical and to act irrationally. Instead, your cat's chances of survival will depend on you acting calmly and methodically and knowing what to do.

Assess the situation. How badly does the cat seem to be hurt? Is it walking around, or lying on the ground? Conscious or unconscious? Bleeding or not? Do you see evidence of broken bones or compound fractures?

Even if the cat seems fine after a car accident, take it to the veterinarian anyway for an exam. Internal injuries do not always make themselves obvious, but can lead to death within a few days.

Keep the injured cat as still as possible. There could be spinal cord damage, and if so, moving the cat could exacerbate the problem and increase the chances of paralysis. Even a cat that is walking around may have serious internal injuries that can be compounded by excess movement. Do not let the cat run away, whatever you do. It could injure itself further, or disappear for days, returning home only when it is too late for treatment, or dying from its injuries.

Of course, it will be necessary to move the cat to place it in a travel crate, box, or on a blanket for transport to the veterinary hospital. In doing so, try to keep the cat's body in as straight a line as possible, so that you're not bending the spine, and with minimal movement. Also, be mindful of the bites and scratches that a panicky cat in pain could inflict on you and take steps to protect yourself as much as possible.

Shock

An animal is said to be in shock when its tissues are not being adequately supplied with blood and oxygen. Most often caused by a severe drop in blood pressure owing to blood loss from either internal or external bleeding, shock can easily kill a cat if not treated quickly. Signs of shock include:

- Weak, rapid heartbeat that gets weaker with time. Often the pulse will be imperceptible, even though the heart is still beating.
- Falling body temperature. The cat's extremities may feel very cool to the touch.
- Very pale or white gums, indicative of failure of the blood to circulate. If the gums are white, it means that the brain is also being starved of oxygen.
- Disorientation, lethargy, and unresponsiveness to any stimuli. The cat may seem "out of it," and may lapse into a coma.

Any cat showing signs of shock needs to see a veterinarian as soon as possible. Any delay could prove fatal. In the interim, keep the cat as warm as possible.

Animal Attacks

Although this is yet another situation that can be minimized by keeping your cat indoors, your feline may still find itself on the wrong end of a bite one day, perhaps from another cat (or dog) in your own home. Whatever the source, your cat could be seriously hurt or killed by an attack from another animal, not only by direct trauma, but by the passing of infectious diseases such as rabies. Bites from insects or snakes can also be injurious or fatal, and should never be taken lightly.

Snake Bites

A bite from a poisonous snake or reptile can be fatal to your cat. Although rare (few cats hunt these creatures), the occasional unlucky cat does get bitten by a rattlesnake, water moccasin, Gila monster, or other venomous reptile.

Unless you discover your cat immediately after a bite from one of these characters, you may be too late. The bite from a mature rattlesnake can kill an adult human, who can weigh fifteen to twenty times as much as a cat. If you witness the attack or get there right away, you should apply a tourniquet several inches above the bite (unless it is to the face or body), and get to the vet pronto. Remember to loosen the tourniquet every ten minutes, to allow needed oxygen to reach body tissues. If you have a snakebite kit available, you can use it on your cat while someone drives you to the vet. Treatment involves making small X-incisions over each fang wound with a single-edged razor blade, then applying suction cups to each wound to prevent the venom from slowly seeping into the cat's lymph system. The punctures should also be cleaned with an antibacterial solution when possible.

Be forewarned that no cat will remain calm during any of this, especially when you make the X-incisions. You will probably have a panicked, biting cat to deal with, unless it is already in shock. If you are at risk of being bitten or clawed while trying to administer aid, your best option may be to try and keep the cat calm and get to the vet as quickly as possible.

Insect Bites

A cat that is bitten or stung by a venomous insect can sustain pain and swelling but rarely dies, unless it is stung by many bees, wasps, or hornets at one time or suffers a severe allergic reaction to the venom, resulting in what is called "anaphylactic shock," which can lead to death. Insects to be especially concerned about are:

- Bees, wasps, and hornets
- Certain species of ants and spiders
- Scorpions

Black widow spiders and scorpions are capable of killing a nonallergic cat with their venom. Treatment for an insect attack involves fast removal of any stingers and a thorough cleaning of the area. Repeated applications of a cool cloth can help minimize swelling and pain. If you see symptoms such as vomiting, disorientation, or shock, see your vet as soon as possible.

Burns

A cat can suffer burns from contact with a corrosive chemical, from an electrical shock, or from a high heat source, such as a car's engine block. If the burn is serious, shock and death can occur.

Chemical Burns

Chemical burns can result from the cat getting into extremely acidic or alkaline materials, such as pool chemicals, car battery acid, drain cleaners, or furniture strippers. The burned area may or may not appear blistered or bubbled, and often the hair will fall out. The affected skin will in any case be damaged, and may discolor. With any external chemical burn, flush the area with large amounts of cool water, cover it lightly with a bandage, then get to your vet right away.

Electrical Burns

Electrical burns often occur when a cat chews on a power cord, if the cat is lucky enough to survive the electric shock. These burns appear most often on the cat's mouth and head area. The surface burns that result are of secondary importance to the electric shock that occurs. Keep the cat immobile and warm, and get to the veterinary clinic. A cat that has suffered a serious electrical shock may stop breathing, or might go into cardiac arrest. If this occurs, you will need to perform artificial respiration/cardiopulmonary resuscitation (CPR) while on your way to the vet. If the cat seems okay apart from the external burns, treat the area with cold water and cool cloths, and go see the vet immediately.

Other Burns

Burns from a heat source such as a car engine, steam iron, or a fallen pot of boiling water or other liquid can be extremely painful and damaging to the cat's skin and coat. Make immediate applications of cold water and cold compresses, and get to the vet quickly. Serious burns invite systemic infection and, therefore, require extended care, including frequent dressing changes and antibiotic therapy.

Cardiopulmonary Resuscitation (CPR)

A situation may arise when, due to shock, choking, or drowning, it is necessary to perform life-saving CPR on your cat. Signs that CPR is needed include no pulse or heartbeat, unconsciousness, or cessation of breathing. CPR needs to begin no longer than a few minutes after heart or breathing functions cease, or else permanent brain damage and death can result.

If your cat has stopped breathing, complete the following steps:

1. Place the cat on its side, open its mouth, pull the tongue out, and check for any foreign objects that might be stuck inside.
2. Check for mucus or blood buildup, then close the cat's mouth and place your mouth over its muzzle, completely covering the nose.

3. Blow gently and easily into its nose and watch to see the cat's chest expanding. Repeat this twelve times per minute (one breath every five seconds) for as long as necessary.
4. If there is no pulse or heartbeat, then cardiac compression will have to be combined with artificial respiration if the cat is to survive. It will be helpful to have a friend perform the compressions while you continue artificial respiration, but you can perform both if needed. In between each breath, place the middle three fingers of your favored hand over the cat's heart, at about the fifth rib, and press with medium pressure, then release. The ribs should compress about one inch. Compress the chest five times in between breaths.
5. Continue compressions and artificial respiration until you get to the veterinarian's clinic, or until the cat begins breathing on its own again.

Poisoning

If your cat has ingested a poisonous plant or other toxic substance, you may need to act quickly to save its life. The most common treatment is to induce vomiting, which removes the toxin from the cat's stomach before it has the chance to get into the system. The exception to this is when the cat has ingested a very corrosive material such as drain cleaner, acid, chlorine powder, tarnish remover, fertilizer, or fuel of any type. Forcing these harsh substances back up will further damage the cat's esophagus and oral cavity. For this reason, you should not induce vomiting until you call the veterinarian or poison control center first, especially if you do not know what the cat ingested.

If you are advised to induce vomiting, you will probably be told to administer two teaspoons of syrup of ipecac, or, if that is not available, two teaspoons of heavily salted water (this is not as effective, and may need to be repeated). Then get to your vet as soon as possible. Do not attempt to induce vomiting if the cat is losing consciousness or is having seizures. Just get to the vet.

Have a talk with your vet sometime before an emergency occurs about antidotes and emergency treatment for poisoning in your cat. Your vet can tell you what plants and other substances are poisonous to your cat, and how to be prepared for any emergency. Of course, prevention is the key. Simply keep all toxic plants and substances out of your cat's reach!

E-ssential

When you have questions about the toxicity of a plant or substance, or when you need advice on handling a poisoning, you can call the ASPCA Animal Poison Information Center, twenty-four hours a day. Their telephone number is 1-800-548-2423. Normally, there is a charge for the service. Keep this telephone number and the number of an emergency veterinary clinic on hand at all times.

Choking

Choking can occur if a large piece of food or a foreign body becomes firmly lodged in the cat's throat. If your cat is unconscious, you will need to perform artificial respiration and perhaps CPR as well. If the cat is still conscious, however, you should first see if the obstruction can be removed with your fingers or tweezers. If the object cannot be reached or is not visible, lay the cat down on its side, place the heel of your hand just below the last rib (where the diaphragm is located), and give two or three quick pushes, straight down. This is the feline version of the Heimlich maneuver. It should force air up the windpipe and hopefully dislodge or expel the object. As in all emergency situations, get your cat to the veterinary clinic as soon as possible. Ideally, you should be performing first aid on your cat in the back seat of a car while someone else is driving you to the clinic.

Hypo- and Hyperthermia

These two conditions are the result of exposure to extreme temperatures. Hypothermia, a condition resulting in a profoundly reduced body temperature, occurs rarely in cats. Hyperthermia is more common and occurs when a cat becomes overheated from extreme temperatures, often caused by poor ventilation combined with hot weather. Each condition has its own specific symptoms and treatments.

Hypothermia

Normally, a cat that has been exposed to widely varying temperatures during its life will easily deal with temperatures below freezing, often for hours at a time. Cats that have lived all their lives indoors can become seriously cold to the point of mortal danger if suddenly subjected to outdoor winter conditions. Even cats used to cool outdoor temperatures can suffer serious hypothermia when subjected to subzero conditions, especially if they are shorthaired. Kittens and elderly or sickly cats left out in the cold are the most vulnerable. A stray or outdoor female that gives birth outside during a cold winter runs the risk of having her entire litter die from cold exposure.

Symptoms of hypothermia include:

- Reduced body temperature
- Disorientation and lethargy
- Uncontrollable shivering
- Decreased respiration and heart rates
- Possible frostbite

Treatment for hypothermia involves getting the cat's body temperature back up to normal as quickly as possible. In mild cases, simply bringing the cat indoors and wrapping it in a warm blanket should suffice. Try using a heating pad or hot-water bottle to speed up the process. More serious cases may call for the immersion of the cat into a very warm bath (about 105 degrees) for a short period, then drying it with a towel and hair dryer and wrapping it in a blanket. Any cat that does not respond quickly should be taken to the emergency clinic right away.

Hyperthermia

This condition, also known as heat stroke, is just the opposite of hypothermia. The perfect example is an animal left by a thoughtless, ignorant owner in a car on a hot summer day with all the windows closed, something you should never do.

A cat accustomed to cool temperatures can also suffer hyperthermia if suddenly moved to a very hot climate, for example, as a result of a relocation from Maine to Florida. Hyperthermia can kill a cat quickly, especially a longhaired breed.

Symptoms of hyperthermia include:

- High body temperature
- Disorientation and dehydration
- Vomiting
- Accelerated heart rate and respiration
- Panting

Treatment for a severely overheated cat involves getting it into a tub of cool water as soon as possible, or hosing it down with a garden hose. Then get the cat to a veterinarian as soon as possible.

How can I prevent my cat from suffering from hypothermia?

Prevention of hypothermia in your cat is simple: Do not let your cat outside, especially on a frigid winter day. If you insist on letting your cats out, consider having only longhaired breeds.

Prevent hyperthermia by providing your cat with plenty of fresh clean water. Always avoid leaving your cat in a car unattended, especially on warm days. Even with the windows cracked, the air temperature inside the car can climb to unsafe levels in a matter of minutes. Likewise, never leave a cat in a travel crate in a hot, stuffy area for too long. Keep your home at a steady, comfortable temperature. Do not leave your cat cooped up on hot days in a stuffy apartment without air conditioning. On horrendously hot days, your pet will enjoy licking a few ice cubes in its water dish.

Seizures

Identified by sudden uncontrolled movements of the muscles, seizures in a cat can be caused by any number of factors, including poisoning, injury, and epilepsy. Seizures should be investigated by a veterinarian to determine the cause. Depending on the cause, some cats might have only one seizure at a time, spaced out over days or even weeks, whereas others can suffer multiple seizures in a very short period.

A cat in a convulsive seizure can be a great danger to itself and to you. The cat doesn't act rationally during this time; it may not even recognize you. The cat may bite or scratch you or anyone who tries to restrain it. If you can predict when the seizure is about to occur, the best course of action is to either wrap the cat in a blanket or place it in a small travel crate or box to restrict its movement and prevent injury. If you have previous experience with your cat's having seizures and know that it does not become violently aggressive during an episode, then simply restrain the cat in a towel until the seizure is over. Otherwise, let the seizure run its course and keep the cat safe from objects in its environment that it might fall on.

15 Parasites of the Cat

Few things can be as annoying or as threatening to your cat's health and well-being as an infestation of internal or external parasites. A cat that becomes infested with protozoa, worms, fleas, ticks, mites, or lice can develop skin sores, diarrhea, or vomiting. It may also become emaciated and dehydrated, scratch itself bloody, or even have damage done to its internal organs and possibly die. Although most parasitic infestations can be treated successfully, it will be to your and your cat's benefit to maintain as parasite-free an environment as possible.

Parasitic Infections

Cats with access to the outdoors are much more likely than indoor cats to pick up parasites sometime in their lives. It is strongly advisable, therefore, not to let your cat outside. Cats can acquire many internal parasites by consuming infected prey. Contact with the feces of another infected animal can also spread a variety of pests to your cat, as can drinking impure, contaminated water. If you insist on letting your cat outside, realize that you will need to be diligent about checking for and controlling these parasitic pests.

What is a parasite?

Any organism that needs to live in or on another and draw sustenance from it, causing the host harm in the process, is considered a parasite. The parasite satisfies its nutritional needs by feeding on the host's blood or tissues or from the host's diet. The hitchhiker multiplies, and in time may possibly sicken or even kill the host.

If you live in an area of the country that gets warm and humid much of the year, your cat will run some risk of acquiring heartworm, although this malady is much more common in dogs. Talk to your vet about heartworm prevention. He may decide to prescribe a monthly heartworm pill for your cat, which will prevent the deadly worms from ever taking hold.

Preventing parasitic infestations and controlling fleas and ticks on your cat does not necessarily require an arsenal of chemicals. Here are some simple things you can do to help prevent these pesky freeloaders from jumping aboard and living on or in your cat:

- Keep your cat indoors.
- Don't feed your cat raw fish or raw or undercooked meat.
- Don't allow your cat to hunt live prey.
- Don't allow your cat to eat garbage.

- Don't allow your cat to drink dirty water from planters, puddles, ponds, or other outside sources.
- Apply a veterinarian-approved flea-and-tick control product, labeled as safe for use on cats, if you see these parasites on your cat.

Fleas

The most commonly found external parasite on a cat is the flea. Fleas (and ticks) can be quite prolific during the warmer, humid months, and if you allow your cat to go outdoors, it will get them, unless you take preventive measures. Even indoor cats can suffer from fleas, owing to the parasites' ability to jump through screens and hitch rides into your home on the backs of other animals, or on your shoes.

E-Fact

A flea is a tiny, wingless insect that feeds on the blood of its host. Capable of great feats of jumping, the flea lives among its host's jungle of hair, hiding from the light whenever possible. These vampires often congregate at the base of the cat's tail, on the belly, and in the groin area and are easy to detect because of the black "dirt" they leave behind.

Make it a habit to inspect your cat daily for signs of external parasites, especially if you allow your cat to go outdoors. Even if you don't see any fleas in your cat's fur, you'll see signs that they were there. A cat infested with fleas will have the parasites on it, as well as their eggs and excrement (commonly called "flea dirt"), which looks like pepper or grains of black sand in the cat's fur. The white, minute eggs hatch after three to ten days, depending on conditions, including temperature. The larvae can live in your carpet fibers (which resemble grass), feeding on any edible debris they can find, and become adult fleas within two to ten weeks, again depending on conditions.

To prevent your home from becoming a stronghold for these pests, you should discuss the best prevention options with your veterinarian. Forget the old-fashioned flea collars, flea sprays, smelly foggers, and messy powders. These days, flea control is not as difficult and complicated as it was before the one-spot, once-a-month topical flea-control products, such as Advantage and Frontline, came along. You can obtain these medications from your veterinarian, and they are easy to apply and highly effective. They typically come in a small tube and can be conveniently dabbed onto the back of the neck, or as directed, where it is difficult for the cat to reach and lick off the product.

Some of these topical products control ticks as well as fleas, while others work primarily on fleas. If your cat goes outdoors, you'll need protection against both, so ask your vet what product will best suit your situation.

Fleas can wreak havoc on cats, causing poor coat condition, allergic dermatitis, anemia, and tapeworm infestation. Some cats are more sensitive to the bites of fleas than others. If your cat seems always to be scratching, is covered with sores, or has any kind of skin problem, chances are, the lowly flea is at least partially responsible.

Some flea and tick products can fail or even be potentially toxic to your cat if you use them improperly or mix them inappropriately. Here are some important things to remember when using any flea- or tick-control product on your cat:

- Read the entire product label carefully before use.
- Make sure the product label says it is safe for use on cats before you apply it.
- Products for dogs may be too strong or even fatal for cats.
- Don't use a product on kittens unless it is labeled safe for kittens and states an age.

- Don't use a product on sick, elderly, or debilitated cats without first asking your vet if it is safe to do so.
- Don't mix different flea products without first asking your vet if it is safe to do so.

Ticks

Ticks are small, eight-legged creatures closely related to spiders. They inhabit bushes, grasses, and woodland areas, and wait in ambush for any poor unsuspecting warm-blooded creature to come idling by. When one does, the tick drops onto it, attaches itself to the skin with its strong jaws, and feeds on the victim's blood.

Ticks can consume great amounts of blood. The females can often expand to several times their normal size. They can spread infectious diseases to animals and humans via their bites, including Lyme disease and Rocky Mountain spotted fever. A sufficient number of ticks can cause anemia, which can be serious, especially in young kittens. Skin inflammation, allergic dermatitis, and paralysis can all be caused by these blood-sucking devils.

If your cat gets a tick, remove it promptly using a pair of tweezers dipped in rubbing alcohol. Grasp the tick as closely to its point of contact as possible and steadily pull straight out with the tweezers until it releases. Do not try to burn ticks off with a cigarette or match! You'll only succeed in burning your cat.

After removal, swab the bite area with disinfectant and keep an eye on it. Sometimes a small part of the tick's head or mouth stays in and can cause infection. If in doubt, see your veterinarian. Prevention is simple, and your veterinarian can recommend products that are safe to use on cats that kill or repel ticks. The easiest way to prevent ticks is simply to keep your kitty indoors, and away from outdoor animals.

Ear Mites

Ear mites are common in cats or kittens that live outdoors, and any stray you take in is likely to have them. A cat suffering from parasitic ear mites will have wax buildup or even pus in the affected ear, and will incessantly shake the head and scratch at the ear in an effort to relieve its discomfort. The inside of the ear can appear inflamed and red, and may have a bad odor. If you notice any of these symptoms, seek veterinary care right away. The condition can be treated easily with medication, but if left untreated, the infection can spread to the middle and inner ear, causing permanent damage.

The mites can also spread to your other cats and dogs, so if one animal has a bad infestation, you may need to treat them all. Be sure to tell your veterinarian if you have multiple pets, so she can prescribe the best course of treatment for your household. Fortunately, ear-mite infestations are no longer as difficult to treat as they used to be either, but you do need to seek treatment promptly, when symptoms first appear.

Other External Parasites

While fleas, ticks, and ear mites are the most common external parasites seen on cats, some other external parasites can infect our feline friends, feeding on their blood, skin, and tissue fluids.

Lice

These small, wingless insects are slightly larger than fleas. Fairly sedentary, they prefer to stay with one host as long as possible, eating dead skin and hair to survive. Fortunately, these pests are relatively uncommon on cats (perhaps due to their impeccable grooming habits), but when they are present, lice can cause symptoms of dermatitis, dry coat, itching, and irritability. Any good veterinarian-approved flea and tick shampoo labeled as safe for use on cats should rid your friend of these pests.

Mange Mites

These mites inhabit the skin of the cat, and can cause itching, skin rashes, and open sores. The two species of mites responsible for this problem are known as *Demodex* and *Sarcoptes*. Of the two infestations, sarcoptic mange is the more serious, definitely requiring veterinary care. Demodectic mange is caused by a mite that is always present on the cat's skin, but these creatures can only cause your cat distress when some other sickness suppresses the cat's immune system.

Internal Parasites

Several types of internal parasites can infect cats, some more commonly than others. Living in the intestines and other internal organs, these creatures can sometimes exist inside a cat without causing apparent signs of illness, wreaking havoc nonetheless. Even though you may never encounter some of these parasites in your cat, it's important to at least know what they are so you can more readily recognize when your cat may require veterinary treatment.

Tapeworms

Tapeworms live in the cat's intestines. They are often acquired by eating uncooked meat or killed prey, and can also be picked up through flea or lice infestation (flea control at home is an essential part of controlling tapeworms). Each tapeworm attaches itself to the intestinal wall using suckers, or hooks on its head. The rest of the worm consists of a chain of flat segments. Tapeworms feed by absorbing nutrients out of the host's intestines. The eggs laid by tapeworms are defecated out and eaten by rodents or fleas, where they grow into an intermediate form and remain until swallowed by another animal (such as a cat). The intermediate form then becomes an adult tapeworm once again in the cat's digestive tract, and so on.

A cat infested with tapeworms may have no clinical symptoms at all, or it may have a dry patchy coat, poor appetite, diarrhea, and weight loss. You may actually see tapeworm segments on the cat's anus and in its stool. They look like wriggling grains of white rice. Your veterinarian can diagnose the condition by fecal examination and then administer a worm-killing medication to rid the cat of its unwanted boarders.

Ascarids (Roundworms)

Three- to four-inch roundworms that live in the host's intestines, ascarids absorb nutrients directly from the host's digestive tract. Kittens commonly become infected with these worms through their mothers' milk, and need to be dewormed early on, usually at around four to six weeks of age, then again a few weeks later. Although not as serious in adult cats, a bad infestation of ascarids in a kitten can prove lethal.

E-Fact

Symptoms of roundworms include coughing, diarrhea, weakness, a dry, dull coat, and a swollen belly on an otherwise skinny kitty. Your veterinarian can successfully rid your kitten or cat of ascarids though proper medication, and this deworming treatment should be part of every kitten's first checkup.

Flukes

Also known as trematodes, these parasites can infect certain internal organs of the cat's body, including the liver, lungs, and small intestines, and cause a variety of symptoms. Acquired through eating raw fish or drinking contaminated water, flukes can be diagnosed through fecal examination or inspection of respiratory secretions. Your vet can effectively treat the infestation with drugs. Avoid flukes by keeping your cat indoors, not allowing it to kill and eat small animals, and not feeding it raw fish. Do not let it drink water from an outside source such as a pond or lake.

Hookworms

Blood-sucking worms that attach to the lining of the small intestine, hookworms are smaller than tapeworms. A cat can acquire them by eating an infected rodent or by larval penetration of the cat's skin. Diarrhea, lethargy, anemia, and weight and appetite loss can all occur as a result.

Hookworms are sometimes difficult to diagnose; you will need the help of a vet to do so, who will identify the culprits through fecal examination. He will then prescribe medication to help rid your cat of the problem.

Whipworms

A common parasite of the large intestine, these one- to two-inch worms have a whiplike tail, and can cause diarrhea, lethargy, and anemia due to their blood-sucking habits. Infected through ingestion of the larvae, your cat can be diagnosed and cured fairly easily through medication prescribed by your vet. The whipworm's eggs can remain viable for a long time via the cat's feces, however, possibly causing recurrences. Keeping the litter box as clean as possible is crucial.

Threadworms (Pinworms)

The larvae of these parasites can penetrate the host's skin and infest the intestine. The threadworm (also called pinworm) can also migrate to other areas of the body, and can cause diarrhea, coughing, scratching, lethargy, and loss of appetite and weight. Your vet will need to diagnose the condition, as threadworms are normally too small to be seen in the stool. Drug treatment to rid the cat of these pests is effective. As with all parasites, you can minimize the risk of infestation by keeping your cat indoors.

Stomach Worms

Spread to cats through the ingestion of different types of large insects, these small worms live in the host's stomach and feed off the partially digested matter found there. Symptoms of infestation include vomiting and a loss of appetite and weight. Thankfully, as with other worms, your veterinarian can diagnose the condition through fecal examination, and get rid of it through drug treatment.

Parasites Associated with Flies

Although flies are more commonly associated with larger livestock, such as horses, they carry parasites that can plague cats as well. In fact, one very puzzling disease seen in cats is linked with the botfly larvae.

Bots

Horse owners are all too familiar with botflies and the tiny yellow specks they leave behind to hatch on their horses' legs. But bots are also believed to be behind an unusual neurological disease in cats called Feline Ischemic Encephalopathy (FIE). Apparently, cats can contract the botfly larvae from catching rodents and other small mammal prey. The larvae then migrate to the cat's brain and cause lesions, resulting in symptoms such as seizures, walking in circles, and even blindness. Since the disease is incurable and largely untreatable at this time, the best prevention is simply to keep your cat indoors and not allow it to hunt live prey.

Eyeworms

Yes, as gruesome as it sounds, worms can even infect the cat's eyes! Usually less than half an inch long, eyeworms infest the white part of the eye as well as the lining of the inner lids, and can cause redness, discharge, and in serious cases, eye damage. They are transmitted through flies. Your veterinarian can remove them.

Heartworms

In certain areas of the country where the weather stays warm and humid much of the year, your cat will risk acquiring heartworms. A particularly despicable parasite, heartworms can grow up to a foot in length, and are found in the heart and arteries of dogs and, to a lesser extent, cats. Obviously, they can cause life-threatening problems, particularly to the infected host's heart and circulatory system. Acquired through mosquito bites, heartworms are more of a problem in parts of the country where mosquito infestations abound.

Signs of infestation in cats are lethargy, loss of weight and appetite, or (unfortunately) sudden illness or death due to arterial blockage. And due to the cat's smaller heart, it doesn't take many worms to kill. A cough can be present, as can difficulty in breathing. Diagnosed by blood tests and X-rays, heartworm infestations can be treated, but are difficult to destroy completely without serious side effects to the host animal. Therefore, prevention is the key. Discuss this issue with your veterinarian. He may prescribe a heartworm medication for your cat, which will prevent the deadly worms from ever taking hold.

Protozoan Parasites

Protozoan parasites, or coccidia, can infect the intestinal tract of cats—often kittens and young cats raised in less-than-clean surroundings. Once infected with these pesky little creatures your kitty can develop diarrhea and become weak, dehydrated, and underweight. Although uncommon, these parasites can infect a cat, dog, or you.

E-Fact

The most primitive class of animal, protozoans consist of a single cell. All are microscopic, but are larger than bacteria. They normally infect the digestive tract of cats (and other animals). The most common sign of protozoan infection is diarrhea caused by the irritation of the intestinal walls. Common protozoans that can infect cats are giardia and toxoplasma. Your vet can prescribe drugs that will rid your cat of these nasty creatures.

Toxoplasmosis

One particularly obnoxious coccidium is known as *Toxoplasma gondii*, which can cause actual tissue damage and long-lasting illness. Humans can acquire this organism, too, primarily from eating raw or undercooked meat. Most healthy people have had some prior exposure to it and, therefore, possess a degree of immunity to it. However, if a pregnant woman with no prior exposure contracts the organism for the first time through the waste of an infected cat's litter box, she runs the slight risk of her unborn child developing birth defects in utero. Although the odds of this occurring are quite small, experts recommend that a pregnant woman avoid cleaning out the cat's litter box for the duration of her pregnancy, and appoint someone else for this chore.

As a general health precaution, it's a good idea to wear gloves when cleaning out the cat's litter box, and avoid directly touching the wastes, when possible. Afterward, thoroughly wash your hands with an antibacterial soap. Keep small children away from the litter box. Also, cover outdoor sandboxes when vacant to prevent free-roaming cats from using them as giant litter boxes. Wear gloves when gardening in areas where outdoor cats may have eliminated their wastes.

A veterinarian can test your cat for toxoplasmosis and treat the condition with medication, if the cat tests positive for the disease. To prevent you or your cat from being infected, you should, once again, keep your cat indoors. Cats usually acquire this protozoan through killing and eating mice and birds. If your cat is always inside, you will not have to worry about this problem. Also, avoid feeding raw meat to your cat, and don't eat any yourself. Most occurrences of this disease in humans can be traced to eating undercooked meat.

Giardia

Cats that spend a great deal of their lives outdoors may contract a protozoan parasite that causes an intestinal infection called giardiasis. Cats pick up the organism by drinking unclean water, such as sewer water contaminated with fecal matter. Persistent diarrhea, often yellow and foamy in appearance, is the most common symptom of this disease. The infection is treatable but sometimes difficult to diagnose.

Like all of the other parasitic infections discussed in this chapter, giardia is another good reason to keep your cat safely indoors. Your cat will most certainly be healthier for it, and you won't have to worry about your pet bringing home unwanted guests that could possibly make you or your family ill.

16 Cat-Training Basics

No pet-and-owner relationship is problem-free 100 percent of the time. Kittens aren't born knowing that they aren't supposed to climb curtains or jump up on kitchen countertops. As with children, you have to set limits and teach them what they can and cannot do inside your home. And yes, cats can be trained. This chapter discusses how to establish appropriate behaviors in the home and gives you some tools to deal with or minimize inappropriate behaviors that your cat may develop over time.

Scratching Behavior

Often, what's normal for cats is perceived as a nuisance by humans. For example, marking and scratching are completely natural behaviors for cats in the wild. But, of course, their owners become quite upset when they have to reupholster a shredded sofa or clean a soiled carpet. That said, it's important to understand that you cannot totally erase behaviors that are natural to cats, but you can modify them with proper strategies and make them acceptable to live with. For example, you can prevent your cat from clawing your sofa by teaching it to use a cat scratching post instead.

Why Do Cats Scratch?

Cats scratch objects in their environment for several good reasons, including:

- To sharpen and condition their claws
- To defend themselves
- To mark territory with scent from their paws

Cats in the wild scratch their claws on tree trunks, fence posts, or whatever is available to loosen old claws. This natural behavior is, however, largely a marking behavior normally occurring at the outer boundaries of a cat's territory. Raking its claws on an object leaves not only visual evidence of the cat's presence but scent evidence as well, for cats have scent glands in their paws. It is a neat, effective way of broadcasting to other cats that "these are the boundaries of my territory. Keep out." Perfectly normal in the wild, this defacing behavior does not transfer well inside the home. Fortunately, this is not a hard behavior to understand or modify.

Scratching Posts Are Important

The indoor cat needs somewhere to scratch inside the home to accommodate this natural urge. Therefore, you need to provide your cat with an appropriate scratching alternative, or it will use your furnishings. And once the cat establishes the habit (which takes only one or two times) of scratching on furniture, it is much harder to break than taking appropriate steps to modify and prevent the problem in the first place.

E-Fact

Individual cats have their own preferences as to what kind of surface they like to scratch on. Some prefer carpet, some prefer tree bark, some prefer sisal (hemp rope). Some cats like to reach upward and stretch long to scratch, while others prefer scratching on a flat surface. You will need to observe your cat as it scratches to try and determine what its preferences are, and select your scratching posts accordingly.

As soon as you acquire a cat, purchase at least one large, sturdy scratching post. Place one near the cat's sleeping area, for cats love to scratch and stretch when they wake from one of their many naps. Place the other in the room where you spend most of your time, for that is where your cat will want to be most of the time, too. If you have the room, investing in a "kitty condo" scratching structure, a multi-leveled climbing structure with scratching and resting areas for cats, will also pay off, in the long run, by saving wear and tear on your furniture and carpeting. (See Chapter 5 for more on scratching posts.)

Scratching Post Training

Initially, you will need to show the cat or kitten where the scratching posts are located. If the cat tries to scratch elsewhere, pick it up and quietly and calmly carry it to the scratching post, set it down, place its paws up on the structure, and gently knead them back and forth in a scratching motion. To catch the cat's interest, rub some dried-leaf catnip, available at pet stores, on the structure and encourage your cat to climb. When you see your cat using a scratching post, praise it and offer it a nice treat. This will help reinforce the modified behavior. In the case of the kitty condo, you can hide treats up in the top enclosures, or hang teaser toys off it to make the structure even more inviting.

Discouraging Scratching in the Wrong Places

Sometimes, despite all your best efforts to train your cat to use a scratching post, it will try to scratch in inappropriate places. You must correct this unacceptable behavior as soon as you're aware of it and continue reinforcing the cat's use of the scratching post. To reduce or stop improper scratching incidents in the home, try any or all of the following techniques.

- Spray your cat with a stream of clean water from a spray bottle or toy water pistol when you catch it in the act. Do this from six to eight feet away, so that the cat does not directly associate the water with you. The water should hit the cat just as it begins to scratch, so that it will think that scratching the object is actually what caused the unpleasant stream of water.
- Put some gravel or marbles in a tin can and put a lid on it to fashion a loud rattler. Whenever your cat scratches on your furniture, rattle the can loudly to startle the animal. As with the spray bottle technique, the cat will associate the unpleasant noise with the object it is scratching, and not with you.
- Treat the most abused objects in the home with a commercially available cat repellent, which will have an odor unpleasant to the cat, but you won't be able to smell. Pet stores generally carry a variety of such products, many of which are herbal in content. Be sure to read the label and follow the directions precisely, for best results.
- Place double-sided sticky tape on the most commonly scratched areas. Most cats hate the sticky feel of it on their feet, and will simply decide to move on. Sometimes crumpled sheets of newspaper or aluminum foil, which will also impart an undesirable feeling underfoot, work just as well.

Try any or all of these for six to eight weeks before considering alternatives. Remember, none of these deterrents will work properly unless you also provide your cat with a proper alternative, so make sure you have good scratching posts on hand, ones that appeal to the cat's scratching preferences, and always encourage and reward the use of them.

Claw Shields

Plastic claw shields or nail caps glued onto the cat's nails can prevent the claws from doing any damage to your rugs and furnishings. Normally, you only need to apply nail caps to the front claws, not the back ones. Although the product is intended for home application, they are not all that easy to apply, unless you have a very cooperative cat that tolerates having its claws handled. Your vet can attach them for you, or show you how to do it yourself. The shields also need to be replaced about every six to eight weeks, coinciding with the shedding of the old nails. Most cats object to the shields at first but eventually learn to tolerate them. The shields are a humane and valid alternative to declawing surgery.

Declawing

Declawing involves the surgical removal of the cat's nails (often just the front nails). An alternative surgical procedure sometimes performed involves cutting the tendons that control the extension and retraction of the claws; this keeps the nails intact but prevents the cat from using them. In general, you should avoid having this procedure performed on your cat, and opt for it only as a last resort, for several reasons:

- If you plan to show your cat, most registries do not condone declawing and will not allow declawed cats to be shown in championship classes.
- Declawing takes away the cat's ability to defend itself, and removes its ability to escape from a dog by climbing up a tree. (Do not declaw a cat that regularly goes outside unsupervised, or you might be signing its death warrant.)
- Without its claws for defense, some cats resort to biting.
- Some cats develop litter box problems after the surgery, presumably because their paws remain tender for a while, and certain types of litter may exacerbate the soreness.

- The surgery is traumatic to a cat, especially adult cats, and some do not adjust well to life without claws.

Consider declawing only after all other options have been tried. Most people with cats that scratch up their furniture simply do not explore corrective training techniques to minimize the problem. Often, they either don't know how or won't take the time to modify the cat's behavior, or they think the problem can't be corrected any other way. Before you give up or resort to such drastic measures, ask your veterinarian to recommend an animal behaviorist who can help you work through such problems with your cat.

Litter Box Behavior

Cats have an instinctive desire to bury their waste, an instinct that is reinforced by watching their mothers and littermates do so. By the time you bring your kitten home, it should already have this behavior down fairly well. However, a kitten separated from its mother and littermates at too young an age might not have this behavior down pat, which is a good reason for not taking a kitten home too early.

E-ssential

Older cats may need a litter box with lower sides, to make climbing in easier on arthritic legs. Continue to keep the aging cat's litter box as clean as possible. In a dog/cat home where the litter box is situated in a high place, perhaps on the top of a tall piece of furniture, you may need to relocate the box, to accommodate an older cat who cannot jump as high anymore.

The feline habit burying of waste in a litter box is a key reason why cats are such easy companion animals to keep in the home. No midnight walks in the rain! Nevertheless, you will need to show your new kitten or adult cat just where the litter box is located in your home, perhaps even placing the kitten in the box and encouraging her to paw at the litter. Adult cats will likely have this mastered, but kittens may need some initial encouragement at first. If necessary, actually dig into the litter yourself (make sure it's clean, of course!) with the kitten in the box, watching. It shouldn't take long for the little one to get the idea. Quietly praise your cat when it begins to use the box properly, but then respectfully leave it alone to do its business.

Litter Box Rules

To help ensure that your cat uses the litter box regularly, follow these general rules:

- **Keep the box clean.** A dirty litter box is one of the most common reasons for a cat's refusal to use it. Remember, cats are very clean animals, so you should scoop out waste from the box every day. If two cats use the same box, you may need to clean it out more often. At least once each week, completely change the litter in each box, and wash the box with mild non-scented soap and water before refilling it with clean litter.
- **Don't move the box.** Cats are creatures of habit and may become upset or confused if you move the box. Doing so suddenly could actually induce the cat to have accidents. If you must move the litter box, purchase a second box, fill it with the same brand of litter, then place it in the new location, while still keeping the old box right where it is. Bring the cat to the new box and encourage her to use it, then leave the rest to the cat. If the cat seems to get the idea and uses both boxes, try removing the old box after two weeks.
- **Place the box in a quiet location.** Select a low-traffic area in the home where the cat will not be disturbed by humans or other animals walking by. You expect a reasonable amount of privacy, and so does your cat.
- **Make sure the box is accessible to the cat.** A common mistake is placing the litter box in an area of the home that is too out of the way for the cat. An older cat in particular that must negotiate lots of stairs to get to his litter box may choose a convenient location more to his liking.
- **Keep dogs away from the box.** If you have a cat-friendly dog in the home, you may have to locate the litter box outside of the dog's

domain, perhaps on top of a piece of furniture. Or, you could prop open the door to the room just enough to allow access to the cat but not the dog (assuming the dog is larger). This is a matter of respect. Plus, many dogs have an objectionable tendency to eat the feces from the litter box.

- **Don't place the box too close to food dishes or sleeping area.** Cats will not eliminate near where they eat or sleep. Do you blame them? If you have placed the litter box too close to either of these places, you may be asking for trouble.
- **Stick with the same brand of litter.** Cats get used to the texture and odor and often develop strong preferences for one type of litter over another. Changing suddenly can result in the animal's refusing to use the box at all, or choosing to use your flowerpots, closet, or dirty laundry instead. If you must change the brand, do so gradually by mixing the new brand with the old, taking three to four weeks to complete the changeover.

Inappropriate Elimination Behaviors

One of the most common behavioral problems that crops up occasionally with some cats is urinating or defecating outside of the litter box. Aside from ranking right up there as one of the most obnoxious and upsetting experiences an owner can face, the inappropriate behavior can be quite challenging to deal with effectively, especially if you let it go on too long and it becomes a well-established habit.

Never hit your cat with your hand or an object, no matter what it has done, unless you are defending yourself or another. Hitting your cat will destroy the trust you have both developed over the years, and your cat will probably be wary and rather fearful of you for the rest of its life.

There can also be many causes for failure to use the litter box, but the one you should always consider and rule out first is any medical condition. Many odd behaviors that appear suddenly are the result of some physical problem, and can often be corrected with prompt veterinary attention. At the first sign of incontinence, take your cat to the vet to be examined. It could have a lower urinary tract disorder, bladder infection, kidney problem, food allergy, sphincter muscle weakness, or some other condition that causes the animal to soil the house. Ruling out a medical condition first will bring you closer to solving the problem, and is the only fair way to proceed.

Hitting or yelling at your cat for going outside the litter box can actually backfire and make her afraid to go near the box. Instead, it will be fearful when it eliminates and will seek hidden areas of the home where it can do its business unseen. There are other more effective ways to correct problem behaviors. Hitting is just an expression of your frustration and anger, and always compounds existing problems. Don't do it.

Territorial Marking

When a cat does its business outside the litter box, it is important to distinguish whether the animal is improperly eliminating or actually marking territory. Marking territory with urine (and sometimes feces) is a natural behavior for cats (especially unaltered males), although certainly undesirable inside the home. Properly identifying the behavior determines how you deal with it.

Try to catch the cat in the act, if possible, to observe its posture. If the cat squats to eliminate on a flat surface, such as the floor, then it is urinating or defecating, and not marking territory (true for males and females). When a cat marks territory, it usually remains standing, backs up to the surface to be "anointed," and sprays urine. Spraying involves less urine volume than normal elimination, and often is directed higher up on some vertical surface, such as a wall or furniture leg. If you spot a pool of urine at the base of some vertical surface like this, inspect it closely for tell-tale streaks where urine has run down. If it looks like the cat peed on the wall rather than the floor, then it's a safe bet that it is marking territory.

Territorial marking spray is also much more odorous than regular urine, especially when from an intact male cat. The sprayed urine is mixed with glandular secretions called pheromones, which impart a profoundly gamy, acrid smell. Most often, male cats engage in spraying, although some females will do it, too. The problem is more often encountered in a multi-cat household, where animals are vying for individual territory. Altering usually curbs this behavior, which is another good reason to have all your cats spayed or neutered.

Territorial marking through defecation is rare, and will occur indoors only if a blatant challenge to the cat's indoor core territory is offered, either from a new animal in the home, a new person, or some other disruptive event that upsets the cat. Cats that do this are normally nervous and edgy by nature, or else extremely dominant, unneutered males.

Causes and Solutions for House Soiling

If you have ruled out a medical problem and determined that the undesirable house soiling behavior is simply improper elimination and not territorial marking, there are numerous possible causes and solutions to pursue. Remember those litter box rules from the last section? Review them and ask yourself if you've violated any of those rules:

- **Is the litter box dirty?** Your cat's perception of clean may differ from yours. Try cleaning and changing the litter more often to see if this helps the problem.
- **Have you recently changed brands of litter, or switched to a different box, too abruptly?** If so, go back to the old type and see what happens.
- **Is the litter box too close to loud sounds or hectic activity?** If so, place another box in a quieter location and see what happens.
- **Is another pet in the household chasing the cat away from the box or otherwise interfering with the cat's privacy and comfort level?** This requires some patient observation on your part. Try adding a second litter box in another location, or if possible, place a box where the cat has chosen to eliminate, since it apparently feels safe using that spot.

Behavioral Approaches

An unneutered male cat will spray in the home, period, especially when sensing the presence of strangers or other animals, even if they are outside! Dominant females will also sometimes do this. The obvious solution is to get the cat neutered or spayed.

My cat has a favorite spot for soiling. How can I stop this behavior?

If, despite all your attempts to the contrary, your cat soils in a particular spot, for instance on a bed or in a closet, consider denying the cat access to this area permanently. For one reason or another, the cat is drawn to that area and will probably continue marking it unless kept away.

If the problem continues, you may need to reduce the cat's "living" area temporarily by confining him to one room, or by using a wire mesh cage with dimensions of at least 3' × 3' × 5'. Place the litter box in one corner, and make sure there is comfortable flooring in the cage for the cat to walk on, perhaps some carpet remnants. Your cat will want to avoid fouling the small area that he is living and sleeping in. Once he begins to reliably use the litter box again, expand his living space to one room for a few days, then to two, then finally back to the entire home (or whatever portion you desire).

Aversion Therapy Techniques

If your cat has been spraying in the home for a long time and you finally get it neutered, it may continue to spray out of habit. If this is the case, try one or more of the following "aversion therapy" techniques:

- Thoroughly clean the sprayed areas with an odor neutralizer, available at a pet shop.
- Spray your cat with water from a spray bottle, if you catch him in the act.

- Treat the sprayed areas with commercially available cat-repellent scents.
- Place double-sided sticky tape around commonly sprayed areas. Strips of aluminum foil, shallow pans of water, or sheets of crinkly newspaper also work well. These "booby traps" may work to stop the spraying, or may just send the cat off to another spot to spray.
- If the booby traps and repellents fail to stop the spraying, try placing small dishes of dry food near where the cat likes to spray. Cats do not like to spray near food, so this may help break the habit. (Remove the booby traps if you use this food technique.)

E-ssential

Any cat allowed to go outside the home is likely to develop a habit of spraying urine to mark its territory, whether neutered or not. This is natural behavior for free-roaming cats. By allowing your cat to go outside, you inadvertently encourage it to develop the habit of spraying. Although relatively unlikely to spray in the home, especially if neutered, the cat will have the behavior solidly learned, and is more likely to spray inside than a cat that stays exclusively indoors.

Stress as a Cause

Changes in the cat's environment, apart from anything having to do with its litter box, can affect elimination habits as well. When the behavior is caused by stress, the solution can sometimes be more complicated to cure. Here are some common stress factors that can cause problems:

- **Moving to a new home:** If your cat begins to have house-soiling problems immediately after moving to the new place, try confining it to one room for a while until it calms down and gets used to the smell of the new place.

- **Remodeling:** When you change the look of your home, you are changing your cat's territorial layout. Try to keep things as stable as possible and make changes gradually, one room at a time.
- **Going on vacation, changing the cat's routine:** The cat doesn't necessarily understand that you've gone away for only a short time and may suffer stress and separation anxiety during your absence.
- **Boarding:** If at all possible, avoid boarding and opt instead for a cat sitter, someone who can come into your home once or twice each day to feed the cat. Allowing your cat to remain in its "territory" will minimize complications and prevent the stress that results from being around numerous strangers, unknown animals, and foreign sounds.
- **Stray cats outside your home:** The regular presence of cats outside your home may provoke your indoor cat to spray inside as a way of confirming its territorial status in the face of possible "invasion." This spraying will usually occur at or near doors or windows.
- **Invasion of home by strangers:** Even the most confident, secure cat can become an indoor sprayer if a new animal or person (or baby) is suddenly introduced into the home. This is an invasion of the cat's core territory. The cat considers this a major threat, and may spray in response. Any abrupt introduction of a new cat or dog can result in spraying and fighting, so go slowly.

E-Fact

A new roommate or spouse moving into the home can upset your cat's routine and create stress, resulting in unwanted behaviors. Introduce your cat to the new person well before she moves in. Have the new person visit and bond with the cat first, and ask her to leave a piece of clothing behind to introduce the new scent into the cat's world.

Plant-Eating Behavior

Although carnivores by nature, cats do consume some vegetable matter on a fairly regular basis. Cats in the wild sometimes devour portions of their prey's stomach contents, usually partially digested plant material. These most likely provide the cat with vitamins and minerals that it would not normally get elsewhere.

As most cat owners will attest, the domestic kitty often likes to chew on and eat plants, those found both outside in the garden and inside the home. Why cats do this is not completely clear, but they could be taking advantage of the emetic qualities that plants can have on the feline digestive tract. Cats will often vomit after eating vegetation, which may aid in bringing up undesirable substances, such as hairballs. It's also entirely possible that cats eat plants simply because they like their taste, texture, and smell.

A prime example of this is the cat's love for catnip, a mint-like perennial that most cats go gaga for.

Some cats simply love catnip. They will eat it, roll in it, dream of it, and play in it for its apparently pleasurable effects. However, not all cats care for catnip. Some will only react only mildly to it, or not at all. Therefore, do a catnip test run with your cat before stocking up.

Whatever wacky reasons cats have for wanting to occasionally go vegan, the behavior can be annoying and also potentially dangerous, especially to a cat that is allowed unsupervised access to the outside, where the more toxic garden and landscaping plants may be growing in your neighbor's yard. To protect your cat:

- Avoid houseplants that are known to be toxic to cats, such as dieffenbachia, ivy, and philodendron. (See Chapter 6 for more information on toxic plants.) Ask your vet what common local plants are poisonous to cats.

- Provide your cat with its own planter of grass seedlings to chew on to its heart's content. These can be started with regular grass seed in a low rectangular planter.
- Locate what indoor plants you do have up off the floor, preferably in hanging baskets or on tables no wider than the base of the plant's draining dish, so that your cat has as little an area as possible to stand on while trying to munch on a leaf.
- Cover the soil of each plant container with marbles or rocks of at least one-half inch in diameter to prevent your cat from digging in or standing on the soil.
- Purchase one of the cat repellents available in pet shops that are safe for use directly on a plant's leaves.
- If you can catch the cat in the act of eating a plant, spray it with clean water from a spray bottle, or rattle something loudly to startle the cat. Try to remain six to eight feet away when you do so, to prevent your cat from connecting your presence with the unpleasant spray or noise.

Jumping Behavior

Decide from the start what limits you intend to set for your cat. For example, will it bother you if your cat jumps up on tables and kitchen countertops, or sleeps on your bed or a special piece of furniture? Some owners don't care, but to others, nothing is as bad as having the cat jump onto the kitchen counter and shove its whiskers into dinner preparations. Likewise, having the cat leap onto the table during a meal can be annoying and anger-provoking. Some owners unwittingly encourage these behaviors by indulging their cats in table scraps.

Here are some steps you can take to help minimize undesirable jumping behavior:

- Do not encourage begging behavior by feeding the cat from the table or offering people-food scraps.
- Avoid leaving food out on counters and tables, and clean all surfaces thoroughly after you eat to keep down food odors and crumbs.

- Store all food out of the cat's reach, in locked cupboards or in the refrigerator.
- Keep a spray bottle or water pistol handy, filled with clean water, for the times that you catch the cat in the act of jumping up onto some prohibited surface.

Teaching Name Recognition

Many cats do not know their names the way dogs do. This isn't because cats are not smart enough to learn. It's because owners often do not teach their cats to respond to a name the way they do with dogs. You should teach your cat to recognize and respond to its name, so you can call it when you need to. Doing so will expand your cat's intellect and strengthen the bond between you.

While your cat is in front of you or on your lap, speak its name and pet it. Do this each time you pet the cat, feed it, or give it a treat. If you practice this from the time the cat is young, eventually it will associate the sound of its name with something pleasant. It will perk up its ears and pay attention to you, knowing that something good is on its way.

After your cat learns its name, you should teach it to come when called. The first step is to keep your cat on a regular feeding schedule. This will create a well-defined hunger drive, the basis for teaching all tricks. Next, follow these steps:

1. Obtain a toy "clicker" device in a novelty or pet store. You can use a whistle instead, but the clicker seems to create a more sudden, percussive noise that really gets the cat's attention.
2. For one month, when you put food in your cat's dish at feeding time, click the clicker and call the cat's name repeatedly until the cat comes.
3. As the cat catches on, click and call the cat to come to you at times other than meal times.
4. Reward the cat with a treat when it comes when called.
5. After the cat seems to have mastered the behavior, gradually stop using the clicker device, so that eventually all you need do is call the cat's name when you want it to come.

Don't overwork this or any other trick. Cats aren't collies, and they get bored with repetition. Also, don't punish or scold a cat for not performing a trick behavior. This always results in a major loss of trust.

Crate Training

Teaching your cat to spend time in a travel crate or pet carrier will be of great help during the times when you have to transport it in a car or airplane. It is not safe to let a cat be loose while traveling by car. Cats can panic when confronted by all the unpredictable noises involved in driving, and this can distract the driver enough to cause an accident.

E-Fact

The waiting room at the veterinarian's office is another place where you will want to have your kitty safely stowed in a travel crate. Many vets do not segregate dog and cat patients in the waiting room. The crate keeps your cat safe and secure, prevents panic, and may save you or someone else from getting badly scratched or bitten.

Start crate training when the cat is young. Simply pick up the cat, stroke it gently, talk to it reassuringly, then place the cat in the carrier and close the door. After a few minutes take the cat out and give it praise and a great treat, perhaps a spoonful of tasty cat tuna. Practice this regularly, gradually increasing the time the cat spends in the crate. Once you have worked up to fifteen minutes or so, put the cat in the crate, carry it out to the car and go for a short ride around the block. When you return home, let the cat out, and give it a super treat and sincere praise.

Socialization

One of the keys to successful ownership of a cat (or dog) is doing all that you can to ensure that your pet will be confident, calm, and friendly around strangers. There is nothing worse than having your cat hiss, scratch, or bite one of your guests, family members, or your veterinarian, simply because that person tried to pet, examine, or move the little fur ball off the sofa.

Several factors determine an animal's level of sociability. Cats that leave theirs mothers and littermates before the seventh or eighth week of life will have a much higher chance of being timid and antisocial. Those who spend the first eight or more weeks of life interacting with mother and siblings will be more confident and socially aware. Cats made timid by leaving the litter too soon are nearly impossible to rehabilitate.

A cat or kitten that has been abused or neglected in the past will tend to be much less sociable than one that enjoyed good treatment from the start. Most competent breeders handle their kittens from the second or third week on, a little bit every day, to teach affection for human touch.

Socializing with Other People

Once your kitten settles into your home, you should begin having regular handling, petting, and grooming sessions. Include playing with toys as well; kittens love play, and learn to trust their playmates (namely, their owner). After your kitten is fully vaccinated, invite some quiet friends to come over (just one or two at a time, not a party) and practice the same techniques. Include men, women, and responsible children, but to avoid scaring the kitten, do not permit any roughhousing or excessive loudness. Otherwise, let them bond with the little tyke as completely as possible. The more people you can get your kitten to trust, the better.

Do not expect an extremely fearful adult cat to become very sociable. The best you should hope for is the absence of aggression, and an acceptance (on the cat's part) that your friends are not out to hurt it.

If you have adopted a timid, fearful adult cat, do not prematurely try having your friends handle, pet, or groom it. They may get bitten or badly scratched. Instead, simply have one person at a time visit the home for several hours, with the cat present. Have each person stick around long enough for a timid cat in hiding to slowly come out to investigate. Do not have your friends follow the cat or try to pick it up. Just have them there, near you. Also, try having each person drop a particularly great treat near the cat each time it comes near. The cat will slowly begin to associate the presence of this ominous intruder with food that it likes.

Socializing with Other Pets

Socializing your kitten with other animals is a different story. The single best way to get cats to interact peaceably is to raise them together from kittenhood. If you want your kitten to have company while you are gone, bring one of its littermates home, or another kitten of comparable age. They will bond through play and form their own sibling understanding as to who is dominant and who is submissive. If you bring a kitten into a home with an adult cat or cats, it is likely to have a hard time fitting in, and may take more than its share of lumps before being tolerated. Remember that adult cats are extremely territorial. Your resident adult cat has claimed your home as its territory, and will not want to share it with some young upstart.

If you do bring a kitten or cat home into another cat's domain, make sure you pay as much if not more attention to the resident cat, especially when the new boarder is around. The resident cat will slowly begin to realize that even though there's a new joker on the premises, it is getting petted, stroked, and played with more than when it was the only game in town. This will help minimize conflicts.

The same "camaraderie of siblings" rule applies to socializing your cat with dogs. Pups and kittens raised together from a young age often become great friends for life. If either is an adult at the time of meeting, the situation rarely, if ever, works out, and can end disastrously, usually for the cat. An older cat-friendly dog that has lived with cats for its entire life should not have much of a problem adapting to a new kitten. However, make sure that you closely supervise the animals' interactions for the first several months. Never leave a young kitten alone with a dog, no matter how cat-friendly the pooch might be. Even in play, a dog could hurt or kill the small, fragile feline.

17 Understanding Territorial and Aggressive Behavior

Most problems in multi-cat households arise from territorial conflicts and manifest through marking behaviors and aggression. The first step in dealing with them is in understanding what purpose territorial behaviors serve to the cat. A domestic cat will stake out its territory by marking, scratching, or physically intimidating other cats. This chapter discusses the various conflicts between pet cats, the reasons behind them, and how to make peace between your kitties.

Marking Behaviors

Marking behavior in cats developed as a way for them to communicate with others, instead of letting things come to immediate blows. If this long-distance messaging service did not exist, many fights between males (and some females) would ensue, possibly threatening the well-being of the species, at least on a local level. Respect for the territory of the established male ensures that enough prey will be available for all. It is rare to find a male so dominant that he would try to usurp another's claim. Spaying and neutering helps to minimize marking behaviors inside the home.

Marking with Urine

The primary goal of urine marking is to identify and claim a definite territory as the cat's own. The cat will spray its urine onto objects on the territorial perimeter, as well as objects within the territory that might have been contaminated by an intruder. The male cat's urine has a fatty ingredient in it that allows it to adhere to objects and surfaces and last even through a rainfall or two. When another male comes by, it can immediately discern that it has entered another male's territory.

Marking with Feces

In addition to urine, cats will use feces to mark territory. In the wild, dominant cats that are competing for territory often do not bury their waste. Only smaller or more submissive cats do so, a way of ensuring that the dominant cats in the area do not feel challenged. Burying waste is also a way of preventing a predator from tracking the cat and eating it. Your house cat buries its waste not only out of hygienic habits, but also in recognition that you are the dominant "cat" in the home.

Scratching

Scratching is yet another way that cats mark territory. In addition to leaving glandular secretions from between the toes, the scratches left on trees, fences, or (unfortunately) furniture are visible markers of territorial boundaries. Both wild and domestic cats tend to pick a few choice scratching posts and then use them over and over again; this is one of the reasons why breaking a pet's bad scratching habit is so difficult.

Other Means of Marking

Cats also mark by other means. They have scent glands on the chin, around the eyes, below the ears, on the sides of the forehead, in and around the anus, between the toes, and at the base of the tail. Some or all of these glands are used by cats to further define territory, inform other cats of their readiness to mate, or release stress.

E-ssential

Dogs and cats can become peaceable companions when they are raised together. It's certainly possible for cats and other small pets to coexist peacefully as well, as long as you provide each species with safe and separate living quarters, and supervise all physical contact. Birds, hamsters, pet mice, small rabbits, and guinea pigs, which cats will naturally prey upon, should be safely contained behind caged doors. Keep fish and reptile tanks securely covered.

Friendly greetings between cats also involve some exchange of scent secretions, usually from rubbing each other with the glands on the head and face. This action plus the offering up of the anal areas for mutual inspection is normally interpreted as a sign of acceptance and respect (as odd as that sounds to us). So, when your cat greets you by rubbing its head all over you, it is not just because it wants to make contact. It is a gesture of acceptance as well as a way of saying "You are mine, baby."

Aggression and Temperament

Aggression in cats can be upsetting and dangerous to an owner who does not understand it or is not prepared for it. Reacting incorrectly to aggression in your cat can intensify the behavior, rather than reduce it. As aggression is the most common problem behavior next to house soiling, understanding the different types of aggression and why they occur is important in dealing with them correctly.

Some cats are born with more aggressive tendencies than others. In the case of purebred cats, it is generally easy to avoid aggressive temperament by judicious, responsible breeding techniques. Greedy backyard breeders and amateurs who do not know any better are the ones most likely to allow inherently aggressive cats to produce offspring, and then try to sell them to an unsuspecting and uninformed public.

The best way to avoid getting a genetically defective cat is to avoid dishonest or amateur breeders. Stick with professionals who have impeccable reputations and who breed for tractable temperaments and other good qualities. In the case of a mixed-breed cat, try to observe the mother, if possible, as well as the rest of the litter. Watch for any signs of unpredictable, aggressive behavior, or anything out of the ordinary, such as one kitten's desire to be alone or attack the other kittens without justification.

Fear Aggression

When a cat finds itself in what it considers to be a threatening situation, the "fight or flight" instinct of self-preservation automatically engages. Often, just bristling the hair, growling, and showing an impressive display of aggression will be enough to warn and ward off a potential attacker. At other times, fleeing the scene seems the better part of valor.

If your cat is by nature playful, outgoing, and gregarious, chances are it will not often show fear aggression toward you or other persons. But if your cat is by nature timid and reserved, it may become easily daunted by a stranger trying to pet it or pick it up. That well-meaning but naive person could easily be scratched or bitten by such a cat that feels threatened.

Causes

Fear aggression in a cat can stem from many causes. Genetics plays a role to a certain extent in the development of the cat's temperament. Also, how well a cat is socialized as a kitten determines to a great degree what its fear threshold will be later in life. The kitten taken from its mother and littermates too soon has a far greater chance of being antisocial and unaccepting of strangers. The first eight weeks of a kitten's life are perhaps the most important in terms of learning acceptable social skills. If these weeks of social interplay are taken from the animal, the only one the poor kitty will be able to trust will be you, its foster parent. Often, all others who come into the undersocialized cat's life later on will be feared.

Even well-socialized cats can become fear-aggressive if subjected to a traumatic experience. Cats have incredible memories. If someone kicks a four-month-old cat or smacks it for jumping onto a table, for instance, that cat will, ten years later, remember that person and react fearfully whenever they come close. A kitten that is attacked by a dog will most likely never trust dogs again, and will become fear-aggressive in the presence of even the sweetest dog in the world.

Body Language

A fear-aggressive cat will exhibit clear, identifiable body language cues to its perceived enemy. Its ears go flat against its head, its tail lashes back and forth, its pupils dilate, and it hisses and often strikes out with its front paws. Often its hair stands on end and its back arches up, a ruse that makes the cat seem larger than it really is, in the hope of scaring off a potential adversary. Some fearful cats, when feeling that there is no possible escape route, will simply go belly-up and brandish all four paws in the air, ready to rip an attacker to shreds if necessary. Children and dogs often make the mistake of interpreting this belly-up posture as a playful one, and get a rude surprise when they approach to play.

If you know your cat is by nature timid and fearful, do not encourage your friends to handle it at all. Just having a friend over is socialization enough for this type of cat. Children are especially susceptible to an attack from a fear-aggressive cat. Always supervise small children around cats, and teach them that chasing a cat is not okay.

Territorial Aggression

Cats in the wild space themselves so as not to intrude on a neighboring cat's "turf." This voluntary spacing helps prevent conflicts and ensures that all will have adequate access to prey. Domestic cats have the same territorial instincts despite their easy and regular access to food and shelter. The instinct to acquire and covet territory is hardwired into their brains.

Your cat may exhibit signs of territorial aggression even if it is an indoor cat. After all, the home is its territory. Most cats, even outgoing, gregarious ones, will show some initial concern when a strange person comes into the home, and all will be suspicious of any new cat or dog, no matter how friendly. This is normal behavior for a cat. However, a territorially aggressive cat will hiss at, chase, and attack other cats (and sometimes people) that come into its territory. Its ears will be pointed, its tail will lash back and forth, and its hair will stand on end.

So, what can you do about it? Spaying, neutering, and proper socialization all help minimize territorial aggression. Also, introduce other animals into the resident cat's world very slowly and carefully. Or, if the cat is known to be quite aggressive, it may be better off as the only pet in the household, or kept separated from other pets in the household. You may also want to discuss possible drug therapies for the aggressive cat with your veterinarian.

As a last resort, find the overly territorial cat a new home, one in which it will be the only cat or have fewer challenges to its territorial claims. Although a sad alternative, it is better than putting the cat to sleep, or subjecting your other cats to an intolerable living situation.

Maternal and Paternal Aggression

For the owner who adopts a pregnant stray, be forewarned that a feline mother with newborn kittens can be a vengeful spitfire. The female cat must protect her offspring at all cost, or the whole species is endangered. Many otherwise affectionate females will prohibit even their beloved owners from approaching the nest during the first few days after they deliver kittens.

The good news is that maternal aggression is never long-lasting. Normally, the behavior subsides after a few weeks. Behaviorists think that the heightened protectiveness comes as a result of hormonal changes brought on by birthing and nursing. As the kittens draw closer to being weaned, hormonal influences on the mother subside, resulting in reduced aggression.

E-Fact

Avoiding maternal aggression is simple. Having a female cat spayed before her first heat will prevent pregnancy and the maternal aggression that can ensue. If you opt not to spay your female cat, keep her indoors. If you don't, she will get pregnant, and you will soon have kittens and a very protective mother.

Male cats do not participate in the raising of the young. Their job is to spread their genetic material as far as possible to ensure the survival of their traits. In fact, male cats in the wild and in domesticity will often kill the young kittens of a nesting female, provided that they did not sire them. Male lions do this, and will even consume the unfortunate little cubs. The reason for this is simple; by killing the young sired by a competitor, the male prevents his competitors from spreading their genetic traits, and enhances the opportunity to spread his own. When young are killed in this way, the mother will quickly come into heat again, enabling the murderous male to successfully mate with her.

This extremely distasteful form of aggression can be avoided simply by having your male cat neutered. If you cannot do this, keep the cat indoors.

Play Aggression

Kittens learn to stalk and attack prey partially through playing with their littermates. They will sneak up on each other and then pounce. Although this is a game, it teaches the little ones how to be predators. They learn timing, coordination, and stealth, all needed skills for a predator.

Some cats never grow up, and continue this stalking "play" aggression on their owners, who can sometimes be scratched or bitten in the process. These cats are not being truly mean. They are just being overly assertive with you, and seeing you as a littermate, someone to play with. In many instances, they just haven't learned how not to play too rough with their human family.

Cats that get carried away with this type of play aggression are often solitary indoor cats who are simply bored. For lack of anything better to do, they will suddenly appear out of thin air and attack your feet while you are watching television, reading, eating dinner, or trying to rest in bed. They do not really mean to hurt you; they are just being immature and restless. Often a behavior associated with adolescent cats, this type of aggression can be minimized fairly easily with these steps:

- Alter the cat as early as possible.
- Bring home two kittens instead of one, so they will amuse each other all day and stalk each other, not you.
- Provide your cat with as much stimulation as possible indoors—toys, a kitty condo, balls, fake mice, a cardboard box, even a paper grocery bag (not plastic bags).

While providing more for your cat to do, you also need to correct the aggressive attacking behavior when it occurs. Try to anticipate when the cat is most likely to play-attack, and have your water spray bottle ready to zap it. Or, clap your hands together loudly while saying "No!" Do not physically strike the cat with your hand or any object.

Also, do not use your hands to play with your cat. Rather, hold out a toy as an extension to your hand for the cat to play with. Cats should perceive human hands as instruments of pleasurable petting, not as toys to be nipped in play.

Competitive Aggression

As with all animals, competition between cats for anything desirable can often cause conflicts. This happens a lot in multi-cat households, when a choice toy, a treat, or even a pat on the head can cause two cats to show aggression toward each other.

How many cats are too many?

Normally two is all you should try to manage in an apartment or small home. More than that and you run the risk of reducing each cat's territory below their level of comfort. Overcrowding and overlapping territory can cause fiercer competition for attention, objects, and areas than would occur if each cat had more spacious digs.

Normally, when you have more than one cat in the home, they will work out their dominance hierarchy among themselves. The dominant and submissive cats will quickly learn their places and act accordingly, the submissive one backing off when the dominant one really wants something. When two cats are very close in stature, however, aggression can occur over competition for some item or your attention. Behaviorally similar to territorial aggression, competitive aggression replaces the quest for territory with the desire for something else. You can avoid competitive aggression between cats if you abide by the following guidelines:

- Have all your cats, male and female, spayed or neutered.
- Avoid keeping too many cats in a given space.
- If you have two cats, have at least two of everything, including food dishes, scratching posts, toys, and litter boxes.
- Feed in separate areas, if necessary, to avoid competitive eating.
- If your living space is small, try to expand the cats' available territory vertically by adding cat climbing trees and tall scratching post/kitty condos for them to claim.
- Give equal individual time to both cats. Completely ignoring one in favor of another will increase the chances of competitive aggression occurring.

In addition, some experts recommend avoiding owning same-sex cats, whenever possible. Two males or two females will tend to fight more than a male and a female, mainly because the male of the species is in general larger and more dominant than the female. Same-sex cats will be inherently closer to each other in the hierarchy and, therefore, will have more disagreements that could lead to aggression.

Let your cats work out their own dominance hierarchy. Stay out of conflicts unless the cats really lay into each other. Also, once you have determined which cat is the dominant one, support its decisions. For example, if it hisses at the submissive cat for coming too close to its food dish, do not punish or confine it for this normal display of dominance.

Redirected Aggression

Have you ever tried to break up a fight, and gotten hurt worse than either of the combatants? If so, you've been a victim of redirected aggression. Redirected or misplaced aggression can occur after any one of a number of stressful experiences suffered by a cat, including a fearful encounter, sighting a stray cat outside a window, an injury, or even a trip to the vet's office. The afternoon right after a visit to the veterinarian is a prime time for a cat to exhibit redirected aggression toward you, so beware.

The victim of redirected aggression is almost never deserving of it. He just happens to be in the wrong place at the wrong time. Being the first one that a frustrated or angry cat comes into contact with after a bad experience is often just a stroke of bad luck, and not anything that the person did directly to provoke the cat. After your cat has undergone an exam or other traumatic experience, avoid physically comforting it for a while. Just let it be. Trying to pick it up when it is feeling stressed can result in the cat's biting or scratching you badly. It is best to let the cat calm down on its own and wait for it to come to you.

Sickness or Injury-Induced Aggression

This is a form of redirected aggression. A cat that shows hostility due to sickness or injury is just responding to internal rather than external stimuli. Pain can cause the cat to vent its frustrations in the same way that it would right after returning from a visit to the veterinarian. Even something as simple as removing a mat from the coat of a longhaired cat can cause enough discomfort to trigger hostility in some cats.

Cats cannot rationalize pain; they just know it is there and that they want it to stop. The pain of a vaccination regularly causes cats to try to beat up on the well-meaning vet; just ask yours how often each day a cat threatens her.

Serious medical problems can also cause pain and ensuing aggression. For instance:

- A bladder or kidney infection can cause not only a change in house training but pain and discomfort as well.
- An under- or overactive thyroid gland can make a cat restless, nervous, and aggressive.
- Epilepsy, a condition made apparent by dramatic and recurring seizures, can cause extreme aggression in cats that would otherwise act as sweet as can be. During a seizure, the cat can become completely unaware of everything; during this time it is not conscious of its actions, and can become very dangerous.
- Parasitic infestations of fleas, ticks, or worms, and skin problems in general can make a cat sick, uncomfortable, and highly irritated. This irritation can result in frustrated aggressive outbursts.
- Tumorous growths, cancerous or benign, can cause pain and therefore aggression in a cat. The presence of large masses of tissue can also affect the function of other parts of the body such as the thyroid or various regions of the brain, which in turn can affect the cat's behavior.
- Arthritis or musculoskeletal problems can cause great discomfort, especially in the older cat, which will become irritable partly due to pain and partly due to its inability to perform at the same physical level that it used to. A cat that is suffering from a hip, back, or shoulder problem might attempt to leap from a chair to a desk, for example, and suddenly find itself missing the mark and in great pain.
- Aging in general will cause a cat to slow down and feel discomfort. Older cats, in addition to having structural problems, can suffer gastrointestinal problems; urinary tract disease; diminished hearing, eyesight, and sense of smell; and a host of other maladies.

Failing capabilities can upset and disorient a cat, leading to possible aggressive reactions.

- Rabies, a viral disease affecting the nervous system, will cause profound and dire behavioral changes in a cat. It will eventually become withdrawn, irrational, and extremely aggressive, scratching and biting at anything or anyone who comes close. Animals who contract rabies almost never recover, and are routinely destroyed to prevent the disease from spreading.
- Toxic materials can profoundly alter a cat's behavior, in some cases provoking aggressive action. Toxic plants, improper medications, lead, insecticides, antifreeze, and even soap can hurt or kill a cat, or at the very least cause it to react unpredictably and often violently.

If your cat does become sick or injured, first take the appropriate steps to get it treated and back on its feet. Follow your vet's instructions, and make the cat as comfortable and secure as possible. Consider confining it to one room while it is recovering, to prevent it from hurting itself and to minimize any upsetting stimuli that might provoke aggression. Leave the cat alone if it seems irritable or stressed. Do not let other people or animals pester it; keep them at bay until your cat has recovered.

Pain and its resultant aggression can come from sources other than sickness or injury. Owners who mistakenly correct their cats by hitting them are doing more than just creating behavioral nightmares and losing their cats' trust. They are causing their cats pain. Cats do not respond well to physical punishment, so avoid it at all cost unless it is necessary to defend yourself or others. Make sure that no one harms your cat or causes it pain in any way.

Unpredictable Biting or Scratching

Some cats will at first accept and even seem to desire petting and stroking from their owners, only to suddenly and unpredictably lash out or bite them. They seem to suddenly reach a saturation point regarding handling and become overstimulated. Confusing and upsetting to the owner, this type of misplaced aggression occurs occasionally in unneutered male cats that are allowed outdoors, in adopted strays, and in poorly socialized cats.

It may also be helpful to put the cat on a regular feeding schedule instead of free-choice feeding it, then periodically give it treats, especially as a reward after a positive and pleasant handling session. With a particularly timid or unpredictable cat, simply avoid physical contact unless the cat initiates it, by rubbing against you, for instance. Then just give it a gentle pet on the head and a treat, and call it quits.

If your cat displays this type of aggressive behavior, limit petting and grooming sessions to just a minute or so, always stopping before the cat becomes stressed, irritated, or overstimulated. Watch for body language cues. If you see the tail lashing back and forth, or if the ears go back and the body tenses, end the session and walk away from the cat. Allow the cat some time alone to de-stress before you approach it again.

Behavioral problems in cats usually come from a combination of several elements. You may solve one only to discover that another is looming beneath the surface. Aggression in your cat could just be a symptom of a deeper problem, sometimes one as straightforward as an improper diet, other times one as complicated as improper socialization and nurturing at an early age. If you have tried various strategies to cope with or remedy the situation, and your cat still has problem behaviors, consult your veterinarian, who can recommend a qualified animal behaviorist. The two professionals may need to play detective for a while before coming up with a solution to your cat's problem. But don't give up on your cat without pursuing the matter thoroughly.

18 Feline Reproduction

Both male and female cats, if not altered by their owners, will begin to show a desire to mate by the time they are seven to ten months old. An unneutered male allowed outdoors will fight with other males and roam for days in search of females in heat. If kept indoors, he will be extremely vocal and will spray strong-smelling urine inside the home. An unspayed female allowed to roam freely outside will get pregnant. If kept indoors, she, too, will possibly spray and keep you up all night, crying to be let out so she can attract males.

Spaying and Neutering

Traditionally, male cats are neutered at between eight and ten months of age, and females are spayed at six months. However, thanks to safer anesthesia, both surgeries can now be performed on younger kittens without adverse affects, and many shelters will do so, before they release kittens for adoption. This helps prevent the indiscriminate breeding that contributes to the nation's surplus of homeless and unwanted pets. Many humane organizations also offer low-cost spay and neuter programs or discounts that can be redeemed with your own veterinarian.

Does altering make cats fat?

No; this is a myth. Obesity in cats results from the same things that make people fat: too many calories and too little exercise. Dealing with overweight problems in cats is covered in Chapter 9.

Neutering the Male

Some people think they can avoid unwanted litters of kittens simply by getting a male cat and not neutering it. This is totally selfish and irresponsible pet ownership, because that intact male will fight and breed, if allowed to roam freely. After all, many unspayed cats wander loose outside, and they will breed with the ones they encounter, creating more unwanted kittens. The suffering and death rampant in the high numbers of homeless pets is every owner's moral responsibility, and if you can't afford to spay or neuter, or are unwilling to, then don't get a cat.

Aside from being the right thing to do, there are several good reasons to alter your pet. In the male cat, neutering, or the removal of the testicles, curbs the desire to roam and lessens marking behaviors, such as spraying urine, inside the home. It also reduces aggression and eliminates the possibility of certain diseases influenced by sex hormones.

Spaying the Female

In the female cat, spaying eliminates annoying estrus (heat) behaviors, along with her ability to produce kittens. The surgery also decreases her desire to roam in search of a mate and eliminates the possibility of disease in the female organs.

Altering the female is more expensive than in the male because the surgery involves opening the abdomen to remove internal reproductive organs: the ovaries, fallopian tubes, and uterus. Due to the invasive nature of the procedure, the female operation also requires a longer recovery period.

Other Benefits of Altering

Eliminating the biological urge to mate makes a cat, whether male or female, a much nicer house companion and improves its chances of living a longer, healthier life. Cats that roam in search of mates are often injured in fights and exposed to disease and other outdoor hazards. The resulting vet bills can quickly exceed the cost of spaying or neutering, so spaying or neutering your cat and keeping it safely indoors are sensible choices that can benefit your pocketbook in the long run.

All cats should be spayed or neutered unless they will be used in a professional breeding program. And in that case, intact cats should never be allowed to roam freely outside and breed indiscriminately. To allow this is irresponsible pet ownership.

Reproductive Cycles and Mating

The typical breeding season for cats is early spring through early fall. Reproductive cycles appear to coincide with the lengthening daylight hours. This means that cats in the Northern Hemisphere cycle opposite to those south of the equator. And cats kept under artificial lighting conditions can be manipulated into cycling year-round.

The Queen's Estrus

Although some female cats (queens) have silent heats with no outward signs, most undergo not-so-subtle behavioral changes when in season. Signs of a queen in heat can vary, depending somewhat on her breed and temperament, but typically they include:

- Seeking more or less affection from you
- Incessant rolling and grooming
- Thrashing back and forth on the floor
- Spraying urine
- Restlessness and wanting to escape outdoors
- Loud, distinct vocalizations (known as "the call")

Intact males (toms) can detect a queen in heat from near and far and will arrive dutifully on her doorstep, eager to satisfy her urges. The queen will remain in season for a week to ten days, and may come into heat every month or so during the breeding season, until a mating takes place to interrupt the estrus cycle.

The Act of Mating

Prior to mating, the male and female investigate each other, usually sniffing each other's faces and rears. The male is easily aroused by the scent of the queen in heat. He might vocalize, lick himself, or move around restlessly while she rolls on the ground in front of him. After a few flirtatious moves (initially rejected by the queen, and reinforced with a few swats of her front paw), the tom will attempt to grab the queen by the nape of her neck and mount her, thrusting his penis forward to make penetration. He ejaculates within a few seconds and withdraws.

Upon withdrawal, the queen screams and swings around to swat at the male, seemingly in pain. Female cats are known to be "induced ovulators." That is, they do not ovulate (release eggs) until they mate. The male's penis, covered with tiny, curved, barb-like protrusions, is believed to stimulate ovulation, and also cause the female some discomfort upon withdrawal.

E-ssential

After copulation, the queen usually rolls around and licks her vulva. If left together, the two cats may repeat the entire act numerous times. This appears to be necessary to ensure that ovulation is induced.

If a queen mates with more than one male during the same heat cycle, ovulation can take place a second time. Two sets of eggs, with differing genetic makeups, can develop simultaneously. Therefore, it is possible for one litter of kittens, born at the same time, to contain some individuals sired by one male and some by another.

Pregnancy and Gestation

If mating is successful, gestation in the cat usually lasts between sixty-two and seventy days, with sixty-six being the norm. Often the first visible sign of pregnancy is "pinking up" about three weeks after conception. That is, the queen's nipples take on a pinkish color and become firmer and more erect. The pregnant cat's shape does not begin to visibly change until around the end of the fourth week, when the belly begins to swell and become rounder. During the seventh to tenth week, movement of the kittens will become clearly evident.

The queen's nutritional needs are greater while she is pregnant and nursing. During this time, she should be fed a high-quality commercial cat food that is specially formulated and labeled for feline growth and reproduction.

Preparing for Birth

Cats will begin to seek out a nesting area near the end of their pregnancy. You can help by furnishing a maternity box a few weeks in advance. This can be a sturdy cardboard box. Cover the bottom with several inches of shredded newspaper, then cover the newspapers' with a clean, washable cloth. Cut a hole in the side of the box, about five or six inches up from the bottom, so the mother has easy access to the outside. A top for the box will help keep in warmth, which is vital to newborn kittens. Place the box in a quiet, out-of-the-way area that is warm and free of drafts, and let the cat investigate it on her own terms.

Toward the end of the pregnancy, keep a close eye on the mother-to-be, watching for blood spotting or any other abnormal signs that could point to an impending premature birth. Anything out of the ordinary should be reported to your vet as soon as possible. Toward the last few days of the pregnancy, make sure that you keep other animals away from the pregnant female, not only for reasons of cleanliness, but also for the safety of the newborns-to-be. A female about to give birth may also be quite irritable, and could get into a fight with another cat.

Delivery

The following information is intended solely as a general overview of the birthing process, and not as a detailed instruction manual. If you have a pregnant cat, discuss with your veterinarian well in advance how to prepare for delivery, and how to recognize and respond to an emergency. If this is your first time delivering kittens, plan to have another person who is experienced in such matters present during the event.

Signs of Impending Birth

At the onset of delivery (also called parturition), the mother will become restless. Her nipples will be enlarged, and milk will be easily expressed from them. She will lose her appetite, and may become vocal and incessantly lick her genital area. If you have allowed the cat to check out her maternity box, she will probably find it an acceptable place for the birth. She may, however, decide on another location, which could end up being your bed or closet, if you allow her access to these areas at this time.

Stages of Labor

During the first stage of labor, the mother will fuss over her nest. Her pulse and respiration will be elevated. Contractions of the uterus will begin to move the kittens along through the uterus to the cervix. This stage may last over twelve hours, especially with first-time mothers. If this period extends longer than twelve hours, call the veterinarian.

The second stage of labor involves the contraction of abdominal muscles in an attempt to expel the kittens. The membrane (amniotic sac) enclosing each kitten may rupture, causing a flood of fluid from the vulva. The mother may lick herself excessively at this point. This will help stimulate labor-inducing hormones and help relax the tissues. As the young enter the pelvis, the mother will assume a comfortable position, which could be either standing or lying on her side. As the head of the first kitten begins to emerge, the mother may scream (especially if it's her first time). About half of all kittens come out head first, and the rest arrive rear legs first, which is usually not a problem. Delivery takes about ten to fifteen minutes for each kitten.

There should be one placenta for each kitten. Count them to make sure all are delivered with or just after each kitten. A retained placenta can cause a serious life-threatening infection in the queen. Also, never pull on the placenta (or the umbilical cord) before it is completely delivered from the queen. This could damage the queen's uterus and cause serious bleeding.

Once a kitten is delivered, the mother nearly always breaks through the amniotic sac with her teeth to allow the kitten to breathe (if she does not, you will have to). She will then lick the kitten all over, which cleans it and stimulates circulation. The mother will then eat the afterbirth and sever the umbilical cord by biting through it.

If You Have to Cut the Cord

First-time mothers may be bewildered by this new experience and not know what to do. They may not eat the afterbirth or bite through the cord. If this happens, you will need to cut the cord yourself. To do so, wash and disinfect your hands, then wrap clean dental floss tightly around the cord about one inch from the kitten's body. Cut the cord (with disinfected scissors) just beyond this tie, on the mother's or placental side. Trim the dental floss ends short, and dip the severed end that is still attached to the kitten in disinfectant, such as iodine or betadine. The stump will dry up and fall off in a few days.

Postdelivery

The total delivery time can take an average of two to six hours, depending on the cat and the number of kittens. Afterward, most feline mothers instinctively care for their young, but a few may not. In this case, you will have to be the foster mother. The close assistance of your veterinarian (or an experienced breeder) will be necessary so that you use the proper formula, feeding schedules, and so forth. Needless to say, this is quite a grueling, time-consuming task, so hope that the mother will take over this responsibility.

Caring for the Mother and Kittens after Delivery

The mother cat needs specific care after delivery of her kittens. Be sure to follow these guidelines to ensure full recovery.

- Observe any abnormal, long-lasting discharges, which could point to internal bleeding or infection.
- Observe and confirm that she is lactating (nursing) properly, and that all the kittens are nursing and thriving.
- Increase her intake of food to make up for the caloric demands of nursing.
- Watch for any signs of infection.

Continue feeding the mother a high-quality commercial cat food formulated for growth and reproduction while she is nursing her kittens. She will need the extra protein for milk production.

E-ssential

It is essential that kittens nurse their mother's first milk, called colostrum, soon after birth. Colostrum contains antibodies that provide newborn kittens with passive immunity to several diseases. This protection may last anywhere from eight to sixteen weeks, depending on the mother's antibody levels. That's why vaccination should begin at six to eight weeks, to ensure that kittens remain protected.

The kittens need specific care and monitoring as well. Each kitten should weigh between three and four ounces at birth, and should steadily gain weight each day. Keeping a record of the kittens' weights on a daily basis will help you determine if they are all getting enough milk. Keep the maternity ward warm (80 to 85 degrees Fahrenheit) and free from drafts. If necessary, place a heating pad in the box, over to one side, so that not all of the flooring is hot. This will allow the growing kittens to adjust their temperatures by crawling toward or away from the heat source.

Kitten Development

Born blind and deaf, kittens have a functioning sense of smell that allows each to locate a nipple and begin nursing. Their mother must lick their bottoms to stimulate elimination, as the kittens cannot urinate or defecate on their own yet. (Should you ever face the challenge of hand-raising newborn kittens without their mother, you will have to assume her role with this chore by gently massaging the kittens' rears with a warm washcloth, or the kittens will die.)

For the first several days, newborn kittens simply eat and sleep. Their eyes do not completely open until the tenth or eleventh day. Avoid handling the kittens during these first few days, except to remove soiled bedding from the maternity box after delivery. Keep the maternity area quiet and free of disturbances, especially from other animals.

Determining the Sex of a Kitten

It is easiest to determine the sex of kittens either right after they are born, or after they are a couple of weeks old. In between, it can sometimes be difficult to tell the difference, except to an experienced eye. Male kittens have a round opening just below the anus. So when you look under the tail of male kitten, you'll see a round opening for the anus, and just below, another round opening. As the male cat matures, the genitals become more pronounced, as the testicles enlarge in the scrotal sac, until they finally appear as two little swollen bulges side-by-side under the tail.

Female kittens have a slit just below the anus. So when you look under the tail of a female kitten, you'll see the round opening of the anus, and directly under it, a narrow slit, which is the vulva. As the female matures, this slit will get slightly longer so that it is easier to see.

Two to Three Weeks

By this time, kittens can hear and will attempt to walk, albeit clumsily. The kittens' first worming should occur at about this time, or as per your vet's instructions. Most kittens are infected with worms by the mother in utero or through nursing. If worming is not begun, the kittens could weaken and might die. You may begin gently and briefly handling the kittens around this time, a little each day to help socialize them to human touch. The mother should be okay with this by the twelfth day or so, but if not, bow to her wishes.

E-ssential

It's best to wait until the litter is at least two weeks old before registering the kittens with your preferred cat registry. This way, you'll be sure they are all going to survive. Often, information such as color of eyes and coat cannot be reliably reported until the kittens are several weeks old; this information can be sent to the registry later. Be sure to report the name of each kitten (including the name of the breeding stock along with the kitten's own name), the sex of each, date of birth, breed, and initial colors.

Three to Four Weeks

By this age, the kittens become much more mobile. You will now need to secure their territory to prevent them from wandering into danger. Put up boundary fencing of some sort, making sure that the mother can jump over it when necessary. By this time, they are able to eliminate on their own. Place a very low litter box outside of the maternity box for the kittens to practice using.

Four to Six Weeks

By now, the kittens should all be using the litter box. They should all be gaining about three to five ounces each week. You can start introducing them to solid foods by offering them some canned kitten food or dry kitten kibble soaked in warm water. Place the mixture outside the maternity box in a large flat tray, and let the little guys go at it. They will not be neat eaters at first and will probably climb into the tray with all four feet.

The kittens' baby teeth will come in by the fifth week. The mother will gradually reduce nursing time, and the kittens can be completely weaned by the sixth or seventh week.

By weaning time, each kitten should weigh close to a pound.

Play begins in earnest during this time. Play is crucial for the kittens to learn how to move, react, hunt, and stalk, as well as for allowing critical socialization to occur. Do not discourage this process by separating them too early. Through play, kittens learn a rudimentary dominance hierarchy amongst themselves and important developmental skills that they will need in adulthood.

Seven Weeks

An additional worming may be done at this time, as recommended by your veterinarian. Vaccinations may begin as well, on a schedule recommended by your vet. The kittens will be roaming freely now, and should be weaned or close to it. Increase the amount of solid kitten food offered to them, as the mother will become increasingly intolerant of any kittens still wanting to nurse.

Eight Weeks

The colors of the kittens' eyes and coats are becoming increasingly obvious. All kittens' eyes are blue at birth and do not get their true color until adulthood. The kittens are now into everything, and it is perfectly fine for them to explore the home, provided you make sure all is safe and keep an eye on their wanderings.

Ten to Twelve Weeks

More vaccines may be given at this time, depending on your veterinarian's recommendations. The kittens are becoming more and more independent, and may begin to play less with each other. By the twelfth week, you can consider letting the kittens go to their new homes, as they should now be inoculated and properly socialized.

Good Nurturing Means Good Cats

Interaction between the mother cat and littermates is crucial because it teaches the kitten about feline etiquette and relationships, and helps minimize antisocial or fear-aggressive tendencies later in the cat's life. This early nurturing period also provides the kitten with an abiding love for maternal and sibling attention. This love is usually transferred to the kitten's owner. It is the basis for most cats' desire for human contact, for they see us not as competing cats or masters, but as mother figures or siblings. Domestic cats in this way remain somewhat adolescent-minded, staying in a perpetual childlike state when interacting with us. This part of their psyche differs from that of their wild cousins, who grow up quickly and do not usually maintain relations with parents or siblings.

E-ssential

In addition to making sure the kittens have plenty of time with their mother, it's also important that they feel comfortable and safe during this period. You'll probably want to show off the cute little kittens to friends and family, but too much visiting can be stressful for the new arrivals. Lots of activity, noise, or other frequent interruptions will make the kittens anxious and untrusting. It's better to give them their own at least semiprivate space where they can feel secure and protected.

Cats that were not with their mothers and siblings for at least the first eight weeks of life can often turn out to be extremely aggressive to other cats and very timid around other humans later in life. Cats that show an intense fear of guests in your home probably left their litters far too early, usually by the time they were four or five weeks old. It is important for owners to recognize the impact that good nurturing early in a cat's life can have on the adult feline psyche.

19 Breeding Purebreds

Before deciding to enter the world of cat breeding, consider your motivations carefully. There are more cats than there are good homes for, and every purebred that's sold takes away another chance at placing some homeless random-bred cat. As a breeder, you should aim to produce a few quality kittens, not a great quantity with profit as the sole motivation. You should be a serious devotee of your particular breed with the desire to maintain or improve its standards over time. Finally, you must be patient, detail oriented, and possess the financial resources to fund the endeavor.

Cat Shows

All successful breeders show their cats. Attendance at a show, especially if you win, is the best way to advertise your cattery. Having one or more titled cats is one of the keys to developing a good reputation—the key not only to financial success but also to gaining influence over the course that the breed in question will take.

Breeders participate in shows to better their breeds, to enjoy some friendly competition, and to hopefully one day make one or more of their cats Champions or Grand Champions, titles that, when seen on a pedigree, command great respect, fame, and often money. Here are several good reasons why breeders get involved in cat shows:

- To share the free flow of information among colleagues
- To find out if a stud or a queen is currently available, if any worthwhile breeding stock is up for sale, or if any spectacular kittens have been born recently
- To "feel out" the competition
- To compare their own breeding results and progress to others
- To meet qualified prospective buyers for their future kittens

Other owners interested in getting into breeding on the ground floor will compete or simply attend a show in order to learn from those with more experience. Some rookies get turned off by the complexity and competition, while others become fascinated with the whole scene and decide to throw their hats into the competitive show ring.

Breeding and showing can both be expensive avocations, and, contrary to many beginners' beliefs, normally not very profitable. Most breeders are lucky to cover their costs and break even. Breeding and showing are both time- and labor-intensive, requiring hours of grooming, rearing kittens, setting up breeding facilities, birthing, dealing with paperwork, and dealing with buyers, judges, and competitors. But a successful breeder and show person can take pride in her craft, and in knowing that the breed in question has been improved in some way.

Basic Feline Genetics

Breeders must have a good scientific understanding of heredity and genetics before they begin creating breeding stock. The appearance of an animal is determined by its genes, plus the influence of diet, environment, and experience.

Predicting the outcome of a mating between two cats is not easy. Certain desirable traits may have undesirable traits secretly linked to them, showing themselves only when paired with another cat with the same undesirable trait. For example, you may innocently attempt to breed white Persians, and end up with four cute, fluffy, deaf kittens because of hidden genetic traits. That's because white cats have a much higher chance of having some level of genetically linked hearing deficiency than do cats of different colors.

A perfect example of how far a breeder can go in adapting or changing the domestic cat is the case of the Sphynx cat. This "hairless" cat is born with a sparse downy coat that quickly falls out, leaving the animal hairless by the time it is an adolescent. Some hairs do grow, only to quickly fall out. This breed should never be let out, as it cannot survive in the wild without any protection from the cold or from ultraviolet light.

Genes and Chromosomes

Each feline parent passes on its individual characteristics and qualities to kittens via the genes and chromosomes. All body cells, except the sex cells, contain chromosomes that are arranged in pairs. Cats have thirty-eight chromosomes, but the sex cells have just nineteen unpaired. These pair up again to total thirty-eight when an egg and sperm unite to create a new individual. In this way, nature ensures that the new individual receives half of its new genetic blueprint for what it will look like from the father and half from the mother.

Dominant and Recessive Genes

Each gene has a coded trait that it controls, and when that trait shows up, or is "expressed," in the individual, it is said to be dominant. Recessive genes, on the other hand, cannot express their traits when paired with a dominant gene. They can only show their trait when two recessives are paired.

For example, coat length in the cat is controlled by dominant or recessive genes. The shorthair gene is dominant, while the longhair gene is recessive. That's why we have many more shorthaired cats than longhairs. To have a long coat, a kitten must inherit one recessive gene for the trait from each parent.

Occasionally, a random change in the genetic blueprint causes a mutation. Mutations have created several breeds of cats, including the tailless Manx and the hairless Sphynx. Mutations can be good or bad, enabling an animal to adapt and survive better in its natural environment, for example, or making it more visible and vulnerable to predators.

Color Inheritance

The more common markings and colors in cats, such as black and red, are produced by dominant genes, while recessive genes produce the less common dilute shades of these colors, known as blue and cream. In some instances, coat color may be paired with other traits, such as the blue eyes and the pointed color patterns so distinctive in the Siamese and Himalayan. A less desirable trait, deafness, is associated with blue-eyed white cats.

Genes and Gender

Special chromosomes determine whether an unborn kitten is male or female. All females have two sex chromosomes labeled XX, while males' are labeled XY. Again, one comes from each parent, so the kitten always gets an X from its mother, and either an X or a Y from its father. The father, therefore, determines the sex of the kitten.

Sex chromosomes can carry genes for other traits besides gender. Certain colors and patterns are carried only on the X chromosome, such as red tortoiseshell, blue-cream, and calico. Because of the sex-linked trait, cats of these colors are nearly always females.

Creating Breeding Stock

All cats considered for breeding should be carefully screened for good health and proper temperament. These cats must then be examined closely with regard to their pedigrees: what were their parents and grandparents like, as well as their siblings and cousins? Do the cats in question already have offspring? If so, what are they like? If any serious faults are found in a cat's lineage, it is very probable the cat will carry that fault in its genes and produce kittens with the undesirable trait.

Inbreeding

The most significant breeding technique used by professionals today is inbreeding. Done properly, it can produce results not possible with any other method. Inbreeding, or the mating of two closely related animals, father to daughter, for example, is often done to enhance desirable traits in a line of cats. Linebreeding involves the same concept, except more distant relatives are used for the mating. Over time, the genetic makeup of inbred offspring becomes more and more similar, causing the cats produced to be similar in appearance and traits.

Close inbreeding, however, can have dire consequences when not properly controlled, because undesirable traits may be concentrated along with the desirable ones. That's why breeders often outcross to separate bloodlines of the same breed, to add new genes to the pool and keep it healthy.

Crossbreeding

The cross mating of different breeds has produced many breeds known in the cat fancy today and added variety to existing breeds. The Himalayan is one example of a breed created by crossbreeding a Persian with a Siamese.

Also known as hybridization, crossbreeding can work directly against inbreeding, which serves to reduce the variation of gene makeup, and with it the chances of divergence of appearance.

E-ssential

Most breeders cannot afford to maintain more than one line of their favored breed. To create improved kittens, there must be mutual cooperation between successful breeders. Teaming up can benefit both parties, but can be accomplished only if both set long-term goals instead of going for short-term profits.

The Stud

Keeping a stud cat can present the beginning breeder with considerable difficulties. An unneutered male cat can be loud, pushy, and odorous, and can quickly render the inside of your home uninhabitable due to incessant spraying. The stud will be very active, and likely will not be well suited to life in a small apartment, especially after he reaches sexual maturity around eight to ten months of age.

The stud cat will probably fare much better temperamentally if he lives with another cat companion (neutered, of course), preferably a sibling he knows and tolerates. Ideally, his owner should provide him with his own "digs," perhaps a separate room with a large cage that can double as a honeymoon suite.

A stud cat must be in great health, free from parasites, vaccinated, and certified free of feline leukemia virus and feline AIDS. He should match his breed's standard of perfection as closely as possible and should be registered with the appropriate cat associations so that other members can have access to his services (for a fee, of course).

A stud should be allowed to provide his services at least two times each year. His first "love" should be an experienced queen, who will tolerate his initial clumsiness better than a less experienced female. A healthy stud should be able to mate and produce offspring well into old age.

The Queen

Most beginning breeders opt for owning a queen and contracting for a stud service, instead of owning both a stud and a queen. A more fulfilling way to begin, this allows the inexperienced breeder to focus on the care of the pregnant queen, the birthing, and the rearing of the kittens.

Like the stud cat, the queen must be a perfect representative of her breed, and should be fully vaccinated for all infectious diseases (although live vaccines should not be given to a pregnant animal). The queen should be fully vaccinated before breeding occurs, so that she can pass her immunity on to her kittens while nursing. She should be free from parasites or any medical problems that might draw strength away from pregnancy or nursing.

Although some queens may be sexually mature at six or seven months of age, they are not physically or psychologically prepared to give birth at this point. A female who is still maturing physically cannot afford to sap nutrition away from her own growth process in favor of the kittens. It could prove harmful to her health, and might promote sickly offspring. The queen should not be bred until she is fully one year old. Overweight queens, along with those not bred until later in life, statistically have a harder time with pregnancy and birthing.

Arranging a Mating

If you do not own a stud cat, you will need to find one several months before the actual mating takes place. Examine the stud's pedigree in detail, as well as his health records. Also, before the mating takes place, discuss with the stud's owner all of the details pertaining to the arrangement, including the stud fee, arrangements for repeated matings, proper environment for the mating, and so forth.

As soon as all the contractual details are worked out and the queen comes into season, take her to the stud. Ideally, breeding should occur within the first four days of the queen's estrus. The cats should be allowed to copulate several times to ensure ovulation and fertilization. If all goes according to plan, and the queen conceives, she will have a gestation period lasting an average of sixty-five or sixty-six days before the kittens arrive.

The stud is rarely taken to the queen's environment, because he must feel at ease and at home to perform properly. Even if you own both the stud and the queen, you should take her to his "digs." If the stud is not allowed to mate in familiar surroundings, it make take days or even weeks before he feels comfortable enough to do the deed properly.

Selling Kittens

One of the hardest parts about being a breeder is eventually giving up the kittens and making sure they are placed in good, loving homes. A responsible breeder should not simply sell a well-bred pedigreed cat to anyone who walks in the door with the cash. The buyer needs to be able to take care of the cat properly, and must show a willingness to abide by your standards of care for the kitten.

Finding the Right Buyer

Finding the right buyer, one who will give your kitten proper health care and a stable, loving home for the rest of its life, is no easy task. That said, where can qualified buyers be found? Several venues exist for the serious breeder, including:

- Cat and breed clubs, which will often provide qualified buyers with lists of local breeders of good reputation. Belonging to at least one club will allow these match-ups to occur.
- Cat shows, where many serious cat lovers come to scout out good breeders and shop for a particular breed of kitten. If the kittens are old enough and the show owners permit this, you may be able to bring or rent an extra benching cage and hang a "For Sale" sign on it. Always have business cards ready to hand out.

- Cat magazines, which can run your advertisements on a monthly basis. Normally the potential buyers reading these magazines will be serious cat lovers and not impulse buyers.
- Your veterinarian, who can certainly put you in touch with serious, qualified buyers looking for your breed of cat.
- Word of mouth, especially lines of communication between breeders. Once the local "cat" community knows about your healthy, breed-correct kittens, they will probably ring your phone right off the wall. This is one excellent reason for "networking" with other cat aficionados as often as possible.
- Classified sections of the local newspapers, which are always checked by potential buyers. As a word of caution, advertising here may attract many potentially unsuitable buyers, including frequent movers and those who insist on letting their cats go outside. You will need to do some serious screening in order to find the right buyers for your valued kittens.
- The Internet, where many breeders have started their own Web sites to promote their cats and catteries. You'll have the same screening issues here that you would have with classified newspaper ads, and you may not get to meet the prospective buyer in person, if he lives far away.

The Sales Contract

Once you find a qualified buyer, you should provide a purchase agreement (or sales contract). You may need to consult an attorney to draw up a suitable contract, but generally speaking, the contract should include:

- A written health guarantee, including a veterinary health certificate and a warranty against any congenital defects
- A written bill of sale
- The date of purchase
- The kitten's date of birth and physical description, including breed, sex, color, weight, and so forth
- The price of the kitten
- The registration number of the kitten

The Registration Papers

Soon after birth, the breeder registers each litter of purebred kittens, furnishing the registry with the pertinent breed information, registration numbers of the stud and queen, and other details. In return, he receives a litter registration with individual registration forms for each kitten in the litter. Each buyer receives one of these individual registration forms to register the kitten they purchase. The breeder fills in the section of this form about the kitten's sex, breed, color, and other description. Then the buyer will select a name for the kitten and send the form back to the association with the appropriate fee to register the individual. The registry verifies the pedigree and sends the buyer an owner's registration certificate.

E-Fact

If the breeder has an established cattery name, it will appear on the registration form and become part of the kitten's registered "show" name, after the form is sent back to the registry and processed. For example, if the cattery name is "Winston," and the cat's chosen name is "Sammie Dee," the registered name will appear on the owner's certificate as "Winston's Sammie Dee."

Breeders may choose to sell their pet-quality kittens with or without registration papers. If the buyer has purchased the papers, the breeder will need to provide these at some point, along with a pedigree. Sometimes the registration papers are not available at the time of purchase. Often, the registering of cats with the large cat registries can take some time. Or, the breeder has the right to withhold the papers until the buyer furnishes proof that the cat has been spayed or neutered. The terms should be spelled out clearly in the contract as to when the buyer will receive the papers.

Special Contract Conditions

A responsible breeder may choose to specify in the contract what special conditions, if any, are required of the buyer. These may include:

- Having the cat spayed or neutered
- Never using the cat for breeding
- Keeping the cat indoors only
- Never declawing the cat
- A no resale, return-only agreement
- Basic health care requirements

The breeder also should supply the buyer with instructions on diet, vaccination and deworming schedules, and general health care. Supplying the buyer with a record of all vaccinations and dewormings to date is mandatory.

Letting the Kittens Go

Once you have completed the sales transaction with the buyer, it will be time to send the kitten on its way. However, this should not occur until the animal is at least ten weeks old, preferably twelve, and longer if the kitten must be shipped to its new home. Never consider letting a kitten go before the tenth week. It might not yet be properly wormed or vaccinated, and will not be adequately socialized with other cats or humans. Realize that two weeks is a long time at this stage in a kitten's life.

You can, however, allow an interested buyer to come and regularly visit with the kitten of his or her choice for several weeks before taking it home, to experience it at different developmental stages and to begin bonding. Caring breeders will encourage this, and will also, when the time comes, give the buyer a supply of kitten food and some litter (preferably of the type the kitten is used to).

This is the moment of truth for all beginning breeders: once you find responsible, caring buyers, you must trust that all will be fine. After all, bringing these kittens into the world is the very reason you got into breeding in the first place. The objective is not to hoard the kittens selfishly, but to create outstanding examples of the breed and distribute them to well-meaning persons who will care for them and love them. If you cannot find the emotional strength to let the little ones go, then you may need to seriously reconsider your decision to become a breeder. Trust in the buyer's sincerity, and in your ability to match the right kitten with the right person.

20 Showing Cats

Most cat owners are satisfied to interact with their pets on a personal level, simply enjoying their company. For others, however, cats become more than just household pets. They become an avocation, a healthy hobby, or a pleasant obsession, depending on your point of view. Best of all, you don't have to own an expensive purebred cat to get involved in cat shows. Many shows have household pet classes for non-pedigreed cats.

When Did Cat Shows Begin?

As far back as the seventeenth century, cat owners have been flaunting their felines at organized events. Hundreds of years ago, a "show" was not much more than a side exhibit at a local fair, with prizes awarded in categories such as "biggest cat," "most beautiful cat," "best ratter," and so forth.

It was not until the latter part of the nineteenth century that organized cat shows began to skyrocket in popularity. Harrison Weir is credited with staging the first official cat show in 1871 at London's Crystal Palace and with writing the first breed standards by which cats were judged in those days. He also was president of Great Britain's first national cat club, which issued the first feline stud book for registering cats in the late 1800s.

The popularity sparked in England eventually spread to the United States, and the first official all-breed show took place here in 1895 at New York's Madison Square Garden. Nearly two hundred cats were entered in that show, and it sparked a national interest that continues to grow to this day. Local cat clubs began to spring up everywhere, leading to the founding of large national organizations.

E-ssential

To show your cat, you must register it with whatever association is sanctioning the show. There are numerous registries in North America (listed in the back of this book). The association uses the registration information to score and track awards.

Today, hundreds of clubs nationwide serve as the binding force in the nation's growing cat craze. The CFA (Cat Fancier's Association) and other large organizations continue to add new members each year. Together all of these clubs and organizations sponsor cat shows from coast to coast.

Why Do People Show Cats?

Some owners are so appreciative of feline beauty that they choose to contribute to the making of it in some way, or at least demonstrate their favorite breed's beauty through some public venue. Many owners who go on to become professional breeders are particularly enamored of one breed, and feel the need to champion it, ensure its popularity and survival, or even modify and improve the breed somehow, perhaps subtly changing the cat's appearance or temperament through selective breeding. Plus, showing cats is a great way to learn more than the average person will ever know about cats.

Most serious breeders show their cats. Competition in a public forum is one of the best forms of advertisement and will ensure the sale of kittens (provided the queen, stud, or both were at one time successful competitors in the show ring).

Of course, you might own one particularly gorgeous feline that you want to show but not breed, and that is fine. In fact, many shows have classes specifically for spayed and neutered purebreds, called premiership classes, and also household pet categories that honor the random-bred cats that enrich our lives. However, showing any cat still requires more than a passing interest. You must honestly assess whether you have the time and wherewithal to take on the responsibility and commitment involved.

To Show, or Not to Show

Showing cats, like breeding, is not for everyone. Serious competition in cat shows often involves a substantial outlay of money, even if you are not an active breeder. Your cat must be in tip-top physical condition with an impeccable coat (the first thing a judge will see). You must learn to become an expert groomer, especially with longhaired breeds such as the Persian, Maine Coon, and Himalayan. You will sometimes have to travel appreciable distances to get to a particular show. This can cost a good deal of money, and be stressful to both you and the cat.

Before entering your first show, attend one or two with a friend and get a feel for what goes on (leave your cat at home). If it seems like something you might like to try, select a venue close to your home for your first show.

A breed standard is a written ideal description of what representatives of a particular breed are supposed to look like. Each cat registering association adopts their own breed standards and reviews and revises them periodically. Anyone who shows or breeds cats should be familiar with their breed's standard. To obtain a copy, contact the association sponsoring the show.

Cat-Show Classes

Most cat shows take place over a two-day period, and are almost always scheduled on weekends. The largest shows in this country are usually held in the fall and winter. Few shows are held at the height of summer (when most people have vacation). Anywhere from less than 100 to more than 800 cats can be shown, depending on the sponsor and the size of the venue. A few shows specialize in specific breeds, but most will cater to all cats.

Various divisions and classes exist for eligible pedigreed cats and kittens, depending on the association sponsoring the event. Kittens must be at least four months of age to compete in kitten classes. Generally, unaltered, adult pedigreed cats begin their show careers competing in "open" classes against others of their breed, sex, and color. Then, with each show, they accumulate wins and points toward a championship title. Once they've earned this title, they vie with other champions for the more coveted title of grand champion.

Classes for Altered Cats

Altered pedigreed cats compete against other altered cats under the same standards as intact cats and for similar titles, although the names are different. For example, an altered champion is called a "premier," and the grand champion is a "grand premier."

Classes for Experimental Breeds

Experimental breeds and colors that have not yet been recognized are generally exhibited in classes labeled provisional, miscellaneous, new breeds and colors (NBC), or any other variety (AOV). Such classes allow cats that do not conform in some way (usually in color or coat length) to their current breed standard to be shown to the public. Often, this is how new breeds become established. Practices for accepting new breeds and colors vary widely among the cat registering associations.

Classes for Non-Pedigreed Cats

Many major cat shows have classes for mixed-breed or non-pedigreed cats to promote the human/animal bond and to elevate the status of the common alley cat. Called the household pet or HHP category, competition is open to non-pedigreed cats at least four months old. Household pets older than eight months must be spayed or neutered to compete. Some of the sponsoring associations permit declawed households pets to be shown in this category, but not all do, so be sure to check the rules if you consider entering yours.

To further celebrate the value of all pets, regardless of their origins or misfortunes, some associations even allow HHPs with physical handicaps, such as a missing limb or eye, to compete. Otherwise, HHPs can be of any size, color, or hair length.

E-ssential

Although some associations have a general written standard for household pets, HHPs are not judged in the same formal way purebreds are judged. Instead, HHPs are judged on more general and subjective terms for their overall condition, beauty, personality, and an elusive quality called show presence. The more poised and playful they are in the show ring, the better their chances of winning.

HHPs do compete for awards and titles like the purebreds, although the names and titles vary from one association to another. Usually, points scored at each show accumulate toward year-end awards. To have your points and awards recorded and tracked throughout the year, you need to register your household pet with the associations sponsoring the shows you compete in. Several associations maintain registries for non-pedigreed cats. (See Appendix B for a list of associations, organizations, and breed registries.)

Entering a Cat Show

Before entertaining the thought of entering a cat show, consider joining a local cat club to learn how it's done. To locate a club in your area, contact one of the cat registering associations (listed in the back of this book) that sponsors clubs. Choose either a club devoted to your favorite breed or a more generalized one for all cats. This club will be your eyes and ears in the cat world at large, and will provide you with information regarding local and national shows that you and your cat can compete in. You will meet people who are experienced in the world of showing cats, and who can tell you what classes to enter your cat in, what the fees and other entry requirements are, and so forth.

Another way to learn about the cat fancy is to subscribe to or regularly read one or more of the cat magazines on the newsstands today. (See a list in the back of this book.) These journals will keep you on the cutting edge of "catdom," and provide you with schedules for local and national events.

When you select a show to enter, obtain an entry form from the club that is sponsoring it and submit it well in advance. Often, entry forms need to be sent in as far as two months ahead of time to be valid, because the organizers have a lot of work to do to set up the show.

Prior to entering a show, make sure the cat is appropriately registered with the sponsoring club or registry. Of course, the cat must be in excellent health, for obvious reasons. Any infectious diseases brought into a show hall containing hundreds of cats could spread like wildfire, particularly if the contagion is airborne. No female cat can be visibly pregnant. No cat can be contaminated with internal or external parasites. And no cat will be allowed to compete if it is extremely fearful or obviously aggressive to humans.

Cats that are missing a body part (including eyes, ears, legs, or tail) cannot usually compete, unless they are members of a tailless breed such as the Manx. Many of the associations also do not condone declawing and, therefore, will not permit declawed cats to compete.

Preparations for the Show

Make sure your cat is up-to-date on vaccinations. Gather the documentation for these (a certificate from your veterinarian), because you may be asked to present proof of vaccination at the show hall. Along with health certificates, assemble all other necessary paperwork, including identification (for you) and the cat's pedigree.

Here are some of the other supplies you'll need for a show:

- Grooming supplies (brushes, combs, baby powder, nail trimmers, dry shampoo, and a hair dryer for fast touch-ups)
- A fold-out table or TV tray to use as a grooming stand
- A folding chair for you to sit in
- Pet carrier
- A litter box, cat litter, and litter scoop
- Plastic bags for litter and trash disposal
- Paper towels
- Food and water dishes
- Cat food and water
- Your cat's favorite toy or two

The Benching Cage

Often, part of the entry costs includes renting an exhibition or benching cage that will be set up for you at the show hall. The entry form should disclose the particular benching requirements, that is, whether you can rent or need to bring your own cage. You will need to purchase the appropriate cage coverings and supplies to ensure your cat's comfort and privacy during the show. Some people make their own colorful curtains to cover the cage, while others simply drape it with sheets. Some shows hold a contest and award fun prizes for the best-decorated cage.

Accommodations

If you'll be staying overnight, reserve a hotel room near the show hall well in advance. Make sure the hotel allows cats in the room. Usually, the entry-form information will suggest nearby hotels that allow cats, and often a discounted rate is arranged for exhibitors. Remember to pack a litter box for the hotel room.

If you must leave your cat alone in the hotel room to go grab yourself a meal, stow the animal safely in the pet carrier, and hang the DO NOT DISTURB sign on the door. You don't want the maid to enter the room while you're gone and accidentally let your cat escape.

For safe car travel, keep your cat in a pet carrier, and strap the crate down with a seat belt. This reduces the risk of escape through an open door or window. It also will prevent the cat from being thrown around inside the vehicle in the event of an accident, thereby reducing the risk of injury.

Air Travel

If it's necessary to travel to a show by air, search for an airline that will let you take your cat in its carrier into the passenger cabin. The pet carrier must conform to airline standards and fit under the airline seat.

Some airlines will only transport animals in the cargo section, which holds special dangers. Avoid this route, if possible. Cargo compartments are generally not pressurized or temperature-controlled while the plane is on the ground. Temperatures can fluctuate rapidly, placing any animals inside at risk.

Some air freight companies specialize in shipping animals. Research these carefully before you book your cat on a flight. Talk to other cat owners who have shipped their cats by air. Then talk to your veterinarian about any health certificates that might be needed, and any other concerns you may have about your cat's comfort and safety during travel.

Rehearsing for the Big Day

Before you step into the show ring spotlight, you and your cat need to rehearse just what is to happen. Your cat is going to be taken to a strange place and subjected to all sorts of foreign smells and sounds. The room will be filled with the scent of perhaps hundreds of other cats. In addition, strangers (the judges) will be liberally handling your cat, not only to check its physical attributes but also to confirm its state of health. Neither judge nor show veterinarian wants or expects your cat to bite, scratch, or panic, so make sure your cat is well socialized and accustomed to handling from kittenhood. To practice, have a friend remove the cat from its crate, place it on a table and give it a cursory exam, including checking the ears, eyes, mouth, body, and feet.

Here are some other tips for conditioning your cat for the show ring:

- Allow friends to pick up and handle your cat whenever they visit.
- Condition your cat from kittenhood to tolerate being in a travel crate or cage.
- Get your cat used to riding in a car (safely in a pet crate) from an early age.
- A day or two before the show, bathe your cat and make sure it has no fleas. Trim the front and back claws. You might also want to brush the cat's teeth and clean its ears. (For details about bathing and grooming, see Chapter 11.)

Arriving at the Show

One of the first steps at many cat shows today is called vetting and involves an examination of your cat by a qualified veterinarian. Not all shows are vetted, but when one is, this procedure usually occurs upon your arrival. Any signs that might point to parasites or contagion are immediate grounds for disqualification and removal from the venue. If your cat passes this exam (which it most certainly will, if you have done your job properly), you will be given a card stating this. You will place this card on your cat's numbered cage in the main show hall.

Non-vetted Shows

At non-vetted shows, a cat is examined only if someone at the show voices a concern regarding a particular animal. If the cat in question is found to be suffering from some disorder or infestation, it will be disqualified. The most common objections raised by competitors are usually regarding parasites (mostly fleas) or dermatitis. Certainly, if you see any signs of illness in a competitor's cat, it is your right and responsibility to bring it to the attention of the show authorities. After all, you are there to enjoy the show, and not to expose your cat to some potentially life-threatening disease.

Settling In

Upon arrival, you and your cat will be given a card with your name, your cat's name, and your cage number printed on it. You should also receive a program listing the schedule of events, as well as the names of the judges overseeing the show. Make sure you acquire a list of the competitors at the show (available for purchase at the door). You need to know the competition!

Settle your cat into its cage and check out the show ring. The "ring" is actually just a table with a judge stationed behind it. Surrounding the table are cages in which the cats will be placed just prior to judging. Entrants' numbers are placed on the cages just before each class. When your class is announced, you will take your cat to the appropriately numbered cage. A show secretary will be present to enter your name (and your cat's), and she will also make sure that all information is correct before the actual judging begins.

No matter how careful you are regarding infection, there will always be a risk to your cat when attending a show. Some competitors politely ask spectators at shows to not touch their cats, to minimize the chance of passing infection from one cage to the next. A few even put up plastic sheets on the front of their cages so that no one is tempted to stick fingers through the cage bars.

The Judging

When it's your cat's turn to be judged, the judge will remove the cat from its cage, position it on the judging table, and proceed to thoroughly inspect it. Owners and interested spectators usually sit and watch quietly from the rows of chairs set up at each ring. After the judge finishes his inspection, he will place your cat back in the cage, and clean off his hands and the table surface with a disinfectant. (Do not be offended, as this is just a precaution to protect the cats.) The judge may make some notations in her notebook; this is normal, so don't get nervous. Enjoy yourself!

After all entries are properly examined, the judge will compare your cat against the others and determine which one most closely conforms to the ideal breed standard. When the decision is made, he will hang ribbons on the winning cages, so keep your fingers crossed!

After the Show

When the show is over, go home, feed your cat, and give it some well-deserved downtime. Keep children and other pets away for a while to allow the cat to chill out and relax undisturbed, in peace and quiet. If you have other animals, wash up well before making contact with them, again to help ensure that no contagions are passed along. For a week or so, ask nothing of your show cat. Just allow your pet to go about its business. Just offer love and appreciation when the cat begs for attention.

Cherish your cat and be thankful that you have the chance to peer through that feline window into the enigmatic heart and soul of nature and share moments of companionship. The cat is, above all else, an elegant bridge between human civilization and the mysteries of all things wild and untamed.

Appendix A: Books and Magazines

Books

Carlson, Delbert G., D.V.M., and James M. Giffin, M.D. *Cat Owner's Veterinary Handbook*. New York: Howell Book House, 1983.

Christensen, Wendy. *The Humane Society of the United States Complete Guide to Cat Care*. New York: St. Martin's Griffin, 2002.

Davis, Karen Leigh. *The Cat Handbook*. Hauppauge, NY: Barron's Educational Series, Inc., 2000.

Davis, Karen Leigh. *Fat Cat, Finicky Cat: A Pet Owner's Guide to Pet Food and Feline Nutrition*. Hauppauge, NY: Barron's Educational Series, Inc., 1997.

Davis, Karen Leigh. *Mixed-Breed Cats*. Hauppauge, NY: Barron's Educational Series, Inc., 1999.

Helgren, J. Anne. *Encyclopedia of Cat Breeds: A Complete Guide to the Domestic Cats of North America.* Hauppauge, NY: Barron's Educational Series, Inc., 1997.

Siegal, Mordecai, and Cornell University. *The Cornell Book of Cats*. New York: Villard Books, 1989.

Whiteley, H. Ellen, D.V.M. *Understanding and Training Your Cat or Kitten.* New York: Crown Trade Paperbacks, 1994.

Magazines

Cat Fancy
Subscriptions:
P.O. Box 52864
Boulder, CO 80322-2864
(800) 365-4421
Editorial offices:
P.O. Box 6040
Mission Viejo, CA 92690
(949) 855-8822
www.catfancy.com

I Love Cats
450 Seventh Ave., Suite 1701
New York, NY 10123
(212) 244-2351
www.iluvcats.com

PETS Magazine
10 Gateway Blvd., Suite 490
North York, Ontario, Canada M3C 3T4
(416) 969-5488
www.petsmagazine.ca

CATsumer Report: The Consumer Newsletter for Cat People
P.O. Box 10069
Austin, TX 78766-1069
www.prodogs.com/dmn/gooddog

Catnip: The Newsletter for Caring Cat Owners
Tufts University School of Veterinary Medicine
P.O. Box 420235
Palm Coast, FL 32142
(800) 829-0926
www.tufts.edu/vet/publications/catnip

Appendix B: Associations, Organizations, and Breed Registries

American Association of Cat Enthusiasts (AACE)
P.O. Box 213
Pine Brook, NJ 07058
(973) 335-6717
www.aaceinc.org

American Cat Association (ACA)
8101 Katherine Avenue
Panorama City, CA 91402
(818) 781-5656

American Cat Fanciers' Association (ACFA)
P.O. Box 1949
Nixa, MO 65714-1949
(417) 725-1530
www.acfacat.com

American Humane Society
P.O. Box 1266
Denver, CO 80201
(303) 695-0811
www.americanhumane.org

American Society for the Prevention of Cruelty to Animals (ASPCA)
424 East 92nd Street
New York, NY 10128
(212) 876-7700
www.aspca.org

Animal Network, Pets in General
www.petchannel.com

Animal Poison Control Center
(888) 426-4435
(800) 548-2423
www.aspca.org

Association of American Feed Control Officials
www.aafco.org

Canadian Cat Association (CCA)
289 Rutherford Road, S, #18
Brampton, Ontario
Canada L6W 3R9
(905) 459-1481
www.cca-afc.com

Cat Fanciers' Association (CFA)
1805 Atlantic Avenue
P.O. Box 1005
Manasquan, NJ 08736-0805
(732) 528-9797
www.cfa.org

Cat Fanciers' Federation (CFF)
P.O. Box 661
Gratis, OH 45330
(937) 787-9009
www.cffinc.org

The Humane Society of the United States (HSUS)
2100 L Street, NW
Washington, DC 20037
(202) 452-1100
www.hsus.org

The International Cat Association (TICA)
P.O. Box 2684
Harlingen, TX 78551
(956) 428-8046
www.tica.org

National Cat Fanciers' Association (NCFA)
10215 West Mount Morris Road
Flushing, MI 48433
(810) 659-9517
www.nationalcatfanciersassociation.com

The Traditional Cat Association, Inc. (TCA)
P.O. Box 178
Heisson, WA 98622-0178
www.traditionalcats.com

United Feline Organization (UFO)
5603 16th Street
Brandeton, FL 34207
(941) 753-8637
www.unitedfelineorganization.org

Index

A

Accidents, cleaning up. *See* Litter and litter box
Adopting out cats, 106–7
Aggression. *See* Territorial and aggressive behavior
Allergies, of cats, 187
Allergies, to cats, 43–44
Anatomy/physiology of cats, 158–63
Animal shelters, 45
  adopting from, 46, 49, 59–60
  adopting out to, 107
Antifreeze, 94
Arthritis, 193, 255

B

Beds and perches, 79–80, 100
Benefits of cats, 40–41
Big cats (non-domesticated), 16–18
Biting, 256–57
Body language, 11–12, 249
Breeders
  finding, 65–66
  good, hallmarks of, 63–65
  questions for/from, 68–70
  visiting, 67–71
Breeding purebreds, 273–83
  arranging mating, 279–80
  creating stock for, 277–79
  feline genetics and, 275–77
  selling kittens, 280–83
Breeds, 19–38. *See also* Longhaired cats; Shorthaired cats; Short-tailed cats
  achieving recognition of, 24
  coat-length genetics, 24–25
  colors, 35–38
  defined, 21
  mixed-breed (random-breed) vs. purebred, 44–46
  new, development process, 23–24
  other, with striking features, 34–35
  overview, 20–44
  purebred, 20–22, 44–46. *See also* Breeders; Breeding purebreds
  with unusual coats, 32–33
  wild-looking spotted, 33–34
Burns, 205–6

C

Cancer, 188, 255
Cat-proofing home, 86–89
Cat show(s), 274, 285–96
  after, 295–96
  classes, 288–90
  entering, 290–91
  origins of, 286
  participating in, 294–95
  preparing/rehearsing for, 291–93
  reasons for, 274, 287–88
Chemical hazards, 89–90, 93, 94, 205, 256
Chlamydia, 181
Choking, 208
Choosing cats, 55–72. *See also* Homecoming
  from breeders, 63–71
  from classified ads (private owners), 61–63
  health indicators, 60–61
  from pet shops, 71–72
  from shelters, 46, 49, 59–60
  strays, 56–59
Coats. *See also* Grooming
  characteristics of, 17–18
  colors of, 35–38, 276
  fur structure, 147–48
  as health indicator, 60, 148
  length of, genetics, 24–25
  skin and, 159
  unusual, breeds, 32–33
Colors, of cats, 35–38
Commitment, to having cats, 42–43, 44
Communication, 11–13, 249
Conditioned responses, 16
Conjunctivitis, 187
Costs, of cats, 42, 47, 48
CPR (cardiopulmonary resuscitation), 206–7

Crate training, 241

D

Death, of cat, 173–75
Deciding, for cat companion(s), 39–54. *See also* Choosing cats; Homecoming
  adult cat or kitten, 49–50
  benefits of cats, 40–41
  breed options, 44–46. *See also* Breeds
  gender, 47–48
  important considerations, 41–44
  indoor vs. outdoor debate, 50–53
  one or two cats, 46–47. *See also* Multiple cats
  pet identification and, 53–54
Declawing, 229–30
Dental care, 133–43
  common problems, 134–37
  controlling plaque, 138–39
  diet, health and, 141–42
  lost/broken teeth, 137–38
  neglecting, consequences, 138
  preventative, importance of, 134, 142–43
  products, 140
  professional cleaning, 141
  signs of problems, 137–38
  teeth overview, 134
  toothbrushing, 139–41
Diabetes, 191–92
Diarrhea, 186–87
Digestive system, 159–60
Diseases. *See* Health/illness
Dogs, new cat and, 101–4
Domestication process, 2–4

E

Ear mites, 217–18
Ears/hearing, 6–7, 11, 154–55. *See also* Hearing
Eating problems, 121–31. *See also* Food and feeding
  exercise and, 125–26
  finicky eaters, 128–29
  multi-cat households, 130–31
  obesity, 122–23, 124–25
  weight-loss diet and, 123–24
Euthanasia, 173–75
Exercise, 125–26
Eyes/vision, 5–6, 12, 187, 222

F

Feline diseases. *See* Health/illness
First aid and emergency care, 199–203
  animal attacks, 204
  burns, 205–6
  car accidents, 202–3
  choking, 208
  CPR, 206–7
  cuts and scrapes, 199–200
  falls, 202
  first aid and vital signs, 198–99, 206–7
  Hypo-hyperthermia, 208–10
  injury-induced aggression, 254–56
  insect bites, 205
  poisoning, 207–8
  puncture wounds, 201
  seizures, 211
  shock, 203
  snake bites, 204
  sprains and fractures, 200–201
  tourniquets, 201
Fleas, 215–17, 255
Food and feeding, 75–77, 109–20. *See also* Eating problems
  adult cats, 113
  bulk feeders, 76
  commercial foods, 110–11
  dental heath and, 141–42
  digestive system and, 159–60
  dishes/placement, 76–77
  kittens, 112–13
  multi-cat households, 130–31
  nutritional problems, 116–19
  older cats, 114
  reading labels, 111–12
  strategies, 114–16
  treats, 129–30
  water and, 119–20

G

Gender, of cats, 47–48
Giardia, 224
Grooming, 145–55. *See also* Coats

acclimating cat to, 148–50
bathing and, 151–53
cleaning ears, 154–55
kittens, 149
older cats, 153
removing mats, 153–54
shedding/hairballs and, 146–47, 185, 186
supplies, 81–83, 148
trimming nails, 150–51

H

Hairballs, 146–47, 185, 186
Harness and leash, 83
Health/illness. *See also* Dental care; First aid and emergency care; Parasites
aging cat care, 172–73
allergies (of cats), 187
anatomy/physiology of cats, 158–63
arthritis, 193, 255
cancer, 188, 255
Chlamydia, 181
conjunctivitis, 187
diabetes, 191–92
diarrhea, 186–87
elimination changes and, 170–71
euthanasia and, 173–75
feline calicivirus (flu), 181
feline distemper, 179–80
feline herpes virus, 180–81
feline immunodeficiency virus (FIV), 183–85
feline infectious peritonitis (FIP), 182–83
feline leukemia virus (FeLV), 181–82
heart problems, 117
incontinence, 194
indicators, of prospective pets, 60–61, 148
kidney problems, 117–18, 160–61, 189–91, 255
liver disease, 194–95
medicating cats, 171–72
nutritional problems, 116–19
obesity and, 122–23, 124–25
older cats, 193–95
rabies, 178–79, 256
ringworm, 188
sickness-induced aggression, 254–56
signs of illness, 169–71
taking temperature, 198–99
thyroid disease, 192–93, 255
urinary tract problems, 118–19, 160, 189
vomiting, 186
Hearing. *See* Ears/hearing
Heart problems, 117
Heartworms, 222–23
History, of cats, 1–4
Holiday hazards, 95–96
Homecoming, 97–107
children and, 100–101
first few days, 98–100
resident pets and, 101–4
setting routines, 104–5
stable environment and, 105–6
when it doesn't work, 106–7
Hunting habits, 10
Hypo-hyperthermia, 208–10

I

Illness. *See* Health/illness
Incontinence, 194
Indoor vs. outdoor debate, 50–53
Injuries. *See* First aid and emergency care
Insect bites, 205
Intelligence, 14

J

Jumping behavior, 239–40

K

Kidney problems, 117–18, 160–61, 189–91, 255
Kittens. *See also* Breeding purebreds; Reproduction
cats retaining qualities of, 13, 47
deciding for adult cats or, 49–50
determining sex of, 268
development of, 267–70
grooming, 149
selling (purebred), 280–88
Kneading, 12

L

Learning behaviors, 15–16
Leash and harness, 83
Leash training, 126–27

Lice, 218
Litter and litter box, 77–78
  accidents, 99
  choosing kittens and, 60
  failure to use, 232–37
  rules, 231–32
Liver disease, 194–95
Longhaired cats, 28–30, 149–50, 153–54

M
Mange mites, 218–19
Mats, removing, 153–54
Medicating cats, 171–72
Mixed-breed (random-breed) vs. purebred cats, 44–46
Multiple cats. *See also* Territorial and aggressive behavior
  bringing new cat home, 101–2
  feeding problems, 130–31
  hierarchy of, 14
  pros/cons of, 46–47
  socializing, 243
Muscles, 158

N
Name recognition, 240–41
Neutering/spaying. *See also* Reproduction
  benefits of, 47–48, 259, 261
  procedures, 260–61
  timing of, 260
Obesity, 122–23, 124–25
Older cats
  common health conditions, 193–95, 255–56
  euthanasia and, 173–75
  feeding, 114
  grooming, 153
  health care, 172–73

O
Outdoor safety, 93–94, 224
Outdoor vs. indoor debate, 50–53

P
Parasites, 213–24
  ear mites, 217–18
  fleas, 215–17, 255
  fly-related, 221–22
  heartworms, 222–23
  infections from, 214–15
  internal (worms), 219–21, 222–23, 255
  lice/mange mites, 218–19
  protozoan (coccidia), 223–24
  ticks, 217, 255
Pet carrier, 74–75
Pet identification, 53–54
Pet shops, 71–72
Plant-eating behavior, 238–39
Plants, toxic, 91–93, 256
Poisoning, 207–8
Posture, 12
Purebreds. *See* Breeds

R
Rabies, 178–79, 256
Reproduction, 161. *See also* Neutering/spaying
  birth preparation/delivery, 263–66
  breeding purebreds, 273–83
  caring for mother/kittens, 266–67, 270–71
  cycles/mating, 261–63
  feline genetics and, 275–77
  kitten development and, 267–70
  pregnancy/gestation, 263
Resources, 297–300
Respiratory system, 159
Ringworm, 188
Routines, 104–5

S
Safety issues
  cat-proofing home, 86–89
  chemical hazards, 89–90, 93, 94, 205, 256
  general guidelines, 86
  holiday hazards, 95–96
  household appliances, 90–91
  outdoors, 93–94, 224
  toxic plants, 91–93
Scratches, fever from, 179
Scratching behavior, 226–30, 246–47, 256–57
Scratching post, 78–79, 226–28
Seizures, 211
Senses, 5–9
Shedding/hairballs, 146–47, 185, 186

Shock, 203
Shorthaired cats, 25–28
Short-tailed cats, 31–32
Skeletal system, 158
Sleeping habits, 9–10
Smell, sense of, 7–8, 159
Snake bites, 204
Socialization, 241–43
Spaying. *See* Neutering/spaying
Stray cats, 56–59
Supplies, shopping list, 74. *See also* specific supplies
Systems, anatomy and physiology, 158–63

T

Tail, 11, 17
Taste, sense of, 8
Teeth. *See* Dental care
Territorial and aggressive behavior, 244–57
- aggression and temperament, 247–48
- biting/scratching, 256–57
- competitive aggression, 252–54
- fear aggression, 248–49
- marking behaviors, 233–37, 246–47
- maternal/paternal aggression, 250–51
- play aggression, 251–52
- redirected aggression, 254–57
- territorial aggression, 250

Territorial marking, 233–37
Thyroid disease, 192–93, 255
Ticks, 217, 255
Time commitment, 42–43, 44
Touch, sense of, 8–9
Toxoplasmosis, 223–24
Toys, 80–81
Training/learning behaviors, 15–16, 225–43. *See also* Litter and litter box; Territorial and aggressive behavior
- crate training, 241
- jumping behavior, 239–40
- name recognition, 240–41
- plant-eating behavior, 238–39
- scratching behavior, 226–30, 246–47, 256–57
- socialization, 241–43

Tumors, 255. *See also* Cancer

U

Urinary tract problems, 118–19, 160, 189

V

Veterinarian. *See also* Dental care; First aid and emergency care; Health/illness; Parasites
- annual checkups from, 166–69
- choosing, considerations, 163–65
- finding, 165–66

Vision. *See* Eyes/vision
Vital signs, 198–99
Vomiting, 186. *See also* Hairballs

W

Water, 76, 119–20
Whiskers, 9, 11–12
Wildcats, 2. *See also* Big cats (non-domesticated)
Wild-looking spotted breeds, 33–34
Worms, 219–21, 222–23, 255

THE EVERYTHING® SERIES!

BUSINESS & PERSONAL FINANCE

Everything® Accounting Book
Everything® Budgeting Book
Everything® Business Planning Book
Everything® Coaching and Mentoring Book
Everything® Fundraising Book
Everything® Get Out of Debt Book
Everything® Grant Writing Book
Everything® Home-Based Business Book, 2nd Ed.
Everything® Homebuying Book, 2nd Ed.
Everything® Homeselling Book, 2nd Ed.
Everything® Investing Book, 2nd Ed.
Everything® Landlording Book
Everything® Leadership Book
Everything® Managing People Book, 2nd Ed.
Everything® Negotiating Book
Everything® Online Auctions Book
Everything® Online Business Book
Everything® Personal Finance Book
Everything® Personal Finance in Your 20s and 30s Book
Everything® Project Management Book
Everything® Real Estate Investing Book
Everything® Robert's Rules Book, $7.95
Everything® Selling Book
Everything® Start Your Own Business Book, 2nd Ed.
Everything® Wills & Estate Planning Book

COOKING

Everything® Barbecue Cookbook
Everything® Bartender's Book, $9.95
Everything® Chinese Cookbook
Everything® Classic Recipes Book
Everything® Cocktail Parties and Drinks Book
Everything® College Cookbook
Everything® Cooking for Baby and Toddler Book
Everything® Cooking for Two Cookbook
Everything® Diabetes Cookbook
Everything® Easy Gourmet Cookbook
Everything® Fondue Cookbook
Everything® Fondue Party Book
Everything® Gluten-Free Cookbook
Everything® Glycemic Index Cookbook
Everything® Grilling Cookbook
Everything® Healthy Meals in Minutes Cookbook
Everything® Holiday Cookbook
Everything® Indian Cookbook
Everything® Italian Cookbook
Everything® Low-Carb Cookbook
Everything® Low-Fat High-Flavor Cookbook
Everything® Low-Salt Cookbook
Everything® Meals for a Month Cookbook
Everything® Mediterranean Cookbook
Everything® Mexican Cookbook
Everything® One-Pot Cookbook
Everything® Quick and Easy 30-Minute, 5-Ingredient Cookbook
Everything® Quick Meals Cookbook
Everything® Slow Cooker Cookbook
Everything® Slow Cooking for a Crowd Cookbook
Everything® Soup Cookbook
Everything® Tex-Mex Cookbook
Everything® Thai Cookbook
Everything® Vegetarian Cookbook
Everything® Wild Game Cookbook
Everything® Wine Book, 2nd Ed.

GAMES

Everything® 15-Minute Sudoku Book, $9.95
Everything® 30-Minute Sudoku Book, $9.95
Everything® Blackjack Strategy Book
Everything® Brain Strain Book, $9.95
Everything® Bridge Book
Everything® Card Games Book
Everything® Card Tricks Book, $9.95
Everything® Casino Gambling Book, 2nd Ed.
Everything® Chess Basics Book
Everything® Craps Strategy Book
Everything® Crossword and Puzzle Book
Everything® Crossword Challenge Book
Everything® Cryptograms Book, $9.95
Everything® Easy Crosswords Book
Everything® Easy Kakuro Book, $9.95
Everything® Games Book, 2nd Ed.
Everything® Giant Sudoku Book, $9.95
Everything® Kakuro Challenge Book, $9.95
Everything® Large-Print Crossword Challenge Book
Everything® Large-Print Crosswords Book
Everything® Lateral Thinking Puzzles Book, $9.95
Everything® Mazes Book
Everything® Pencil Puzzles Book, $9.95
Everything® Poker Strategy Book
Everything® Pool & Billiards Book
Everything® Test Your IQ Book, $9.95
Everything® Texas Hold 'Em Book, $9.95
Everything® Travel Crosswords Book, $9.95
Everything® Word Games Challenge Book
Everything® Word Search Book

HEALTH

Everything® Alzheimer's Book
Everything® Diabetes Book
Everything® Health Guide to Adult Bipolar Disorder
Everything® Health Guide to Controlling Anxiety
Everything® Health Guide to Fibromyalgia
Everything® Health Guide to Thyroid Disease
Everything® Hypnosis Book
Everything® Low Cholesterol Book
Everything® Massage Book
Everything® Menopause Book
Everything® Nutrition Book
Everything® Reflexology Book
Everything® Stress Management Book

HISTORY

Everything® American Government Book
Everything® American History Book
Everything® Civil War Book
Everything® Freemasons Book
Everything® Irish History & Heritage Book
Everything® Middle East Book

HOBBIES

Everything® Candlemaking Book
Everything® Cartooning Book
Everything® Coin Collecting Book
Everything® Drawing Book
Everything® Family Tree Book, 2nd Ed.
Everything® Knitting Book
Everything® Knots Book
Everything® Photography Book
Everything® Quilting Book
Everything® Scrapbooking Book
Everything® Sewing Book
Everything® Woodworking Book

Bolded titles are new additions to the series.
All Everything® books are priced at $12.95 or $14.95, unless otherwise stated. Prices subject to change without notice.

HOME IMPROVEMENT

Everything® Feng Shui Book
Everything® Feng Shui Decluttering Book, $9.95
Everything® Fix-It Book
Everything® Home Decorating Book
Everything® Home Storage Solutions Book
Everything® Homebuilding Book
Everything® Lawn Care Book
Everything® Organize Your Home Book

KIDS' BOOKS

All titles are $7.95

Everything® Kids' Animal Puzzle & Activity Book
Everything® Kids' Baseball Book, 4th Ed.
Everything® Kids' Bible Trivia Book
Everything® Kids' Bugs Book
Everything® Kids' Cars and Trucks Puzzle & Activity Book
Everything® Kids' Christmas Puzzle & Activity Book
Everything® Kids' Cookbook
Everything® Kids' Crazy Puzzles Book
Everything® Kids' Dinosaurs Book
Everything® Kids' First Spanish Puzzle and Activity Book
Everything® Kids' Gross Hidden Pictures Book
Everything® Kids' Gross Jokes Book
Everything® Kids' Gross Mazes Book
Everything® Kids' Gross Puzzle and Activity Book
Everything® Kids' Halloween Puzzle & Activity Book
Everything® Kids' Hidden Pictures Book
Everything® Kids' Horses Book
Everything® Kids' Joke Book
Everything® Kids' Knock Knock Book
Everything® Kids' Learning Spanish Book
Everything® Kids' Math Puzzles Book
Everything® Kids' Mazes Book
Everything® Kids' Money Book
Everything® Kids' Nature Book
Everything® Kids' Pirates Puzzle and Activity Book
Everything® Kids' Princess Puzzle and Activity Book
Everything® Kids' Puzzle Book
Everything® Kids' Riddles & Brain Teasers Book
Everything® Kids' Science Experiments Book
Everything® Kids' Sharks Book
Everything® Kids' Soccer Book
Everything® Kids' Travel Activity Book

KIDS' STORY BOOKS

Everything® Fairy Tales Book

LANGUAGE

Everything® Conversational Chinese Book with CD, $19.95
Everything® Conversational Japanese Book with CD, $19.95
Everything® French Grammar Book
Everything® French Phrase Book, $9.95
Everything® French Verb Book, $9.95
Everything® German Practice Book with CD, $19.95
Everything® Inglés Book
Everything® Learning French Book
Everything® Learning German Book
Everything® Learning Italian Book
Everything® Learning Latin Book
Everything® Learning Spanish Book
Everything® Russian Practice Book with CD, $19.95
Everything® Sign Language Book
Everything® Spanish Grammar Book
Everything® Spanish Phrase Book, $9.95
Everything® Spanish Practice Book with CD, $19.95
Everything® Spanish Verb Book, $9.95

MUSIC

Everything® Drums Book with CD, $19.95
Everything® Guitar Book
Everything® Guitar Chords Book with CD, $19.95
Everything® Home Recording Book
Everything® Music Theory Book with CD, $19.95
Everything® Reading Music Book with CD, $19.95
Everything® Rock & Blues Guitar Book (with CD), $19.95
Everything® Songwriting Book

NEW AGE

Everything® Astrology Book, 2nd Ed.
Everything® Birthday Personology Book
Everything® Dreams Book, 2nd Ed.
Everything® Love Signs Book, $9.95
Everything® Numerology Book
Everything® Paganism Book
Everything® Palmistry Book
Everything® Psychic Book
Everything® Reiki Book
Everything® Sex Signs Book, $9.95
Everything® Tarot Book, 2nd Ed.
Everything® Wicca and Witchcraft Book

PARENTING

Everything® Baby Names Book, 2nd Ed.
Everything® Baby Shower Book
Everything® Baby's First Food Book
Everything® Baby's First Year Book
Everything® Birthing Book
Everything® Breastfeeding Book
Everything® Father-to-Be Book
Everything® Father's First Year Book
Everything® Get Ready for Baby Book
Everything® Get Your Baby to Sleep Book, $9.95
Everything® Getting Pregnant Book
Everything® Guide to Raising a One-Year-Old
Everything® Guide to Raising a Two-Year-Old
Everything® Homeschooling Book
Everything® Mother's First Year Book
Everything® Parent's Guide to Children and Divorce
Everything® Parent's Guide to Children with ADD/ADHD
Everything® Parent's Guide to Children with Asperger's Syndrome
Everything® Parent's Guide to Children with Autism
Everything® Parent's Guide to Children with Bipolar Disorder
Everything® Parent's Guide to Children with Dyslexia
Everything® Parent's Guide to Positive Discipline
Everything® Parent's Guide to Raising a Successful Child
Everything® Parent's Guide to Raising Boys
Everything® Parent's Guide to Raising Siblings
Everything® Parent's Guide to Sensory Integration Disorder
Everything® Parent's Guide to Tantrums
Everything® Parent's Guide to the Overweight Child
Everything® Parent's Guide to the Strong-Willed Child
Everything® Parenting a Teenager Book
Everything® Potty Training Book, $9.95
Everything® Pregnancy Book, 2nd Ed.
Everything® Pregnancy Fitness Book
Everything® Pregnancy Nutrition Book
Everything® Pregnancy Organizer, 2nd Ed., $16.95
Everything® Toddler Activities Book
Everything® Toddler Book
Everything® Tween Book
Everything® Twins, Triplets, and More Book